COMMON
AMERICAN
PHRASES
IN
EVERYDAY CONTEXTS

ABOUT THE AUTHOR

Richard A. Spears, Ph.D., is Adjunct Associate Professor of Linguistics, Northwestern University, and a specialist in lexicography; English language structure; phonetics; language standardization and codification; English as a second language; and American culture. Dr. Spears is also Director of the Dictionary Department at National Textbook Company.

COMMON
AMERICAN
PHRASES

IN
EVERYDAY CONTEXTS

A Detailed Guide to Real-life
Conversation and Small Talk

Richard A. Spears

Printed on recyclable paper

National Textbook Company
a division of *NTC Publishing Group* • Lincolnwood, Illinois USA

1996 Printing

Contents

About This Dictionary   vi

Guide to the Use of the Dictionary   vii

Terms and Abbreviations   ix

Dictionary of Common American Phrases   1

Phrase-Finder Index   205

About This Dictionary

This dictionary is a basic collection of some 1700 everyday phrases and sentences that Americans use over and over in their greetings, good-byes, and everyday small talk. Whereas it is true that there is an infinite number of possible sentences in any language, it is also true that some of those sentences are used repeatedly from day to day. The effective use of language is not in being able to create and understand an infinite number of sentences, but to use the right sentence the right way in a given context.

This collection is not only a dictionary but also a resource for the learning of these expressions. The user is encouraged not only to use the dictionary as a reference book, but to read it from cover to cover.

In many instances the meaning of a phrase is quite clear, but the typical context for the phrase is not. Each entry expression is illustrated in a typical context, usually in the form of a short script that illustrates a typical use of the expression. In some instances, the meaning of the full expression is quite clear, but the expression typically occurs in an elliptical form that is *not* easy to understand. This dictionary cross-references the elliptical forms to the full forms.

The style of the typical entry phrase and the examples is highly colloquial. Many of the examples express joking, anger, and sarcasm. A surprising number of examples—all taken from real conversational exchanges—contain exaggerations and *non sequiturs*. In general, this is not the type of language that one would choose to write or even speak on many occasions. It is the type of language that one hears every day and needs to understand, however.

This dictionary also includes a Phrase-Finder Index that allows the user to find the full form of a phrase by looking up any word in the phrase.

Guide to the Use of the Dictionary

1. Entry heads are alphabetized according to an absolute alphabetical order that ignores all punctuation, spaces, and hyphens.

2. Entry heads appear in **boldface type**. When words or expressions that are not entries in this dictionary are cited, they appear in *italics*.

3. An entry head may have one or more alternative forms. The alternatives are printed in **boldface type** and are preceded by "AND." Alternative forms are separated by semicolons.

4. An entry head enclosed in square brackets, e.g., **[how are]**, leads to other entry heads that contain some form of the word(s) in brackets. Entry heads in square brackets do not have definitions or paraphrases.

5. Definitions and paraphrases are in roman type. Alternative or closely related definitions and paraphrases are separated by semicolons.

6. A definition or paraphrase may be followed by comments in parentheses. These comments give additional information about the expression, including cautions, comments on origins, or cross-referencing. Each numbered sense can have its own comments.

7. Many expressions have more than one major sense or meaning. These meanings are numbered with boldface numerals.

8. Sometimes a numbered sense will have an alternative form that does not belong to the other senses. In such cases the AND and the alternative form follow the numeral.

9. In some entries, comments direct the user to other entries for additional information through the use of the terms "compare to," "see," "see also," or "see under." The expressions referred to are in *slanted type*.

10. The first step in finding an expression is to try looking it up in the dictionary. Entries that consist of two or more words are entered in their normal order, such as **Act your age!** Phrases are never inverted or reordered like **age!, Act your**.

11. If you do not find the expression you want, or if you cannot decide on the exact form of the expression, look up any major word in the expression in the Phrase-Finder Index, which begins on page 205. There you will find all the multiword expressions that contain the word you have looked up. Pick out the expression you want, and look it up in the dictionary.

Terms and Abbreviations

☐ (a box) marks the beginning of an example.

AND indicates that an entry head has one or more variant forms that are the same or similar in meaning as the entry head. One or more variant forms are preceded by AND.

catch phrase describes an expression meant to catch attention because of its cleverness or aptness.

compare to means to consult the entry indicated and look for similarities to the entry head containing the "compare to" instruction.

entry head is the first word or phrase, in boldface, of an entry; the word or phrase that the definition explains.

see means to turn to the entry indicated.

see also means to consult the entry indicated for additional information or to find expressions similar in form or meaning to the entry head containing the "see also" instruction.

see under means to turn to the entry head indicated and look for the phrase you are seeking *within* the entry indicated.

A

Absolutely!   a strong affirmation.   ☐ MOTHER: *Do you want another piece of cake?* CHILD: *Absolutely!*   ☐ BOB: *Are you ready to go?* MARY: *Absolutely!*

Absolutely not!   a strong denial or refusal. (Compare to *Definitely not!*)   ☐ BOB: *Will you please slip this bottle into your pocket?* BILL: *Absolutely not!*   ☐ BOB: *Can I please have the car again tonight?* FATHER: *Absolutely not! You can't have the car every night!*

Act your age!   Behave more maturely! (A rebuke for someone who is acting childish. Often said to a child who is acting like an even younger child.)   ☐ *Johnny was squirming around and pinching his sister. His mother finally said, "Johnny, act your age!"*   ☐ CHILD: *Aw, come on! Let me see your book!* MARY: *Be quiet and act your age. Don't be such a baby.*

Adios.   *Good-bye.* (From Spanish. Used in casual or familiar conversation.)   ☐ BOB: *See you later, man.* BILL: *Yeah, man. Adios.*   ☐ BOB: *Adios, my friend.* MARY: *See you, Bob.*

Afraid not.   See *(I'm) afraid not.*

Afraid so.   See *(I'm) afraid so.*

Afternoon.   See *(Good) afternoon.*

After while(, crocodile).   Good-bye till later.; *See you later.* (The word *crocodile* is used only for the sake of the rhyme. It is the response to *See you later, alligator.*)   ☐ MARY: *See you later.* BILL: *After while, crocodile.*   ☐ JANE: *After while.* MARY: *Toodle-oo.*

After you. a polite way of encouraging someone to go ahead of one-self; a polite way of indicating that someone else should or can go first. □ *Bob stepped back and made a motion with his hand indicating that Mary should go first. "After you," smiled Bob.* □ BOB: *It's time to get in the food line. Who's going to go first?* BILL: *After you.* BOB: *Thanks.*

Again(, please). Say it one more time, please. □ *The play director said, "Again, please. And speak more clearly this time."* □ TOM: *I need some money. I'll pay you back.* BILL (pretending not to hear): *Again, please.* TOM: *I said I need some money. How many times do I have to say it?*

Age before beauty. a comical and slightly rude way of encouraging someone to go ahead of oneself; a comical, teasing, and slightly grudging way of indicating that someone else should or can go first. □ *As they approached the door, Bob laughed and said to Bill, "Age before beauty."* □ *"No, no. Please, you take the next available seat," smiled Tom. "Age before beauty, you know."*

all in all AND **all things considered; on balance** a transition indicating a summary, a generalization, or the announcement of a conclusion. □ BILL: *All in all, this was a fine evening.* ALICE: *I think so too.* □ *"Our time at the conference was well spent, all in all," thought Fred.* □ BILL: *How did it go?* ALICE: *On balance, it went quite well.* □ BOB: *Did the play turn a profit?* FRED: *I suppose that we made a nice profit, all things considered.*

Allow me. AND **Permit me.** a polite way of announcing that one is going to assist someone, unasked. (Typically said by a man assist-ing a woman by opening a door, lighting a cigarette, or providing support or aid in moving about. In *Allow me*, the stress is usually on *me*. In *Permit me*, the stress is usually on *mit*.) □ *Tom and Jane approached the door. "Allow me," said Tom, grabbing the doorknob.* □ *"Permit me," said Fred, pulling out a gold-plated lighter and lighting Jane's cigarette.*

All right. **1.** an indication of agreement or acquiescence. (Often pronounced *aright* in familiar conversation.) □ FATHER: *Do it now, before you forget.* BILL: *All right.* □ TOM: *Please remember to bring me back a pizza.* SALLY: *All right, but I get some of it.* **2.** a shout of agreement or encouragement. (Usually **All right!**) □ ALICE:

Come on, let's give Sally some encouragement. FRED: *All right, Sally! Keep it up! You can do it!* □ *"That's the way to go! All right!" shouted various members of the audience.*

All right already! AND **All righty already!** an impatient way of indicating agreement or acquiescence. (The second version is more comical than rude. Dated but still used.) □ ALICE: *All right already! Stop pushing me!* MARY: *I didn't do anything!* □ BILL: *Come on! Get over here!* BOB: *All righty already! Don't rush me!*

All systems are go. an indication that everything is ready or that things are going along as planned. (Borrowed from the jargon used during America's early space exploration.) □ BILL: *Can we leave now? Is the car gassed up and ready?* TOM: *All systems are go. Let's get going.* □ SALLY: *Are you all rested up for the track meet?* MARY: *Yes. All systems are go.*

All the best to someone. See *Give my best to someone.*

all the more reason for doing something AND **all the more reason to do something** with even better reason or cause for doing something. (Can be included in a number of grammatical constructions.) □ BILL: *I don't do well in calculus because I don't like the stuff.* FATHER: *All the more reason for working harder at it.* □ BOB: *I'm tired of painting this fence. It's so old it's rotting!* SALLY: *All the more reason to paint it.*

all things considered See *all in all.*

Aloha. **1.** Hello. (Hawaiian. Used in casual or familiar conversation or in Hawaii.) □ *"Aloha. Welcome," smiled the hostess.* □ ALICE: *Hello. Can I come in?* SUE: *Come in. Aloha and welcome.* **2.** Good-bye. (Hawaiian. Used in casual or familiar conversation or in Hawaii.) □ MARY: *It's time we were going. Aloha.* JANE: *Aloha, Mary. Come again.* □ *All the family stood by the little plane, cried and cried, and called "Aloha, aloha," long after my little plane took me away to the big island.*

Am I glad to see you! I am very glad to see you! (Not a question. There is a stress on *I* and another on *you.*) □ BILL: *Well, I finally got here!* JOHN: *Boy howdy! Am I glad to see you!* □ TOM (as Bill opens the door): *Here I am, Bill. What's wrong?* BILL: *Boy, am I glad to see you! Come on in. The hot water heater exploded.*

Am I right? Isn't that so? Right? (A way of demanding a response and stimulating further conversation.) □ JOHN: *Now, this is the kind of thing we should be doing. Am I right?* SUE: *Well, sure. I guess.* □ FRED: *You don't want to do this for the rest of your life. Am I right?* BOB: *Yeah.* FRED: *You want to make something of yourself. Am I right?* BOB: *I suppose.*

And how! an enthusiastic indication of agreement. □ MARY: *Wasn't that a great game? Didn't you like it?* SALLY: *And how!* □ BOB: *Hey, man! Don't you just love this pizza?* TOM: *And how!*

And you? AND **Yourself?** a way of redirecting a previously asked question to the asker or someone else. □ BILL: *Do you want some more cake?* MARY: *Yes, thanks. Yourself?* BILL: *I've had enough.* □ JANE: *Are you enjoying yourself?* BILL: *Oh, yes, and you?*

Anybody I know? See *Anyone I know?*

Any friend of someone('s) (is a friend of mine). I am pleased to meet a friend of someone. (A response when meeting or being introduced to a friend of a friend.) □ FRED: *Well, nice to meet you Tom. Any friend of my brother is a friend of mine.* TOM: *Thanks, Fred. Nice to meet you too.* □ JOHN: *Thank you so much for helping me.* SALLY: *You're welcome. Any friend of Sue's.*

anyhow See *anyway.*

Anyone I know? AND **Anybody I know?** a coy way of asking *who?* □ SALLY: *Where were you last night?* JANE: *I had a date.* SALLY: *Anyone I know?* □ BILL: *I've got a date for the formal next month.* HENRY: *Anybody I know?*

Anything else? See *(Will there be) anything else?*

Anything going on? See *(Is) anything going on?*

Anything new down your way? Has any interesting event happened where you live? (Rural and familiar.) □ BILL: *Anything* *new down your way?* BOB: *Nothing worth talking about.* □ MARY: *Hi, Sally. Anything new down your way?* SALLY: *No, what's new with you?* MARY: *Nothing.*

Anything you say. Yes.; I agree. □ MARY: *Will you please take this over to the cleaners?* BILL: *Sure, anything you say.* □ SALLY: *You're going to finish this before you leave tonight, aren't you?* MARY: *Anything you say.*

Anytime. **1.** an indication that one is available to be called upon, visited, or invited at any time in the future. □ MARY: *I'm so glad you invited me for tea.* JANE: *Anytime. Delighted to have you.* □ SALLY: *We really enjoyed our visit. Hope to see you again.* BILL: *Anytime. Please feel free to come back.* **2.** a polite but casual way of saying *You're welcome.* □ MARY: *Thanks for driving me home.* BOB: *Anytime.* □ SALLY: *We were grateful for your help after the fire last week.* JANE: *Anytime.* **3.** See *Any time you are ready.*

Anytime you are ready. an indication that the speaker is waiting for the person spoken to to make the appropriate move. □ MARY: *I think it's about time to go.* BILL: *Anytime you're ready.* DOCTOR: *Shall we begin the operation?* TOM: *Anytime you're ready.*

anyway AND **anyhow** "In spite of all this"; regardless. (Words such as this often use intonation to convey the connotation of the sentence that is to follow. The brief intonation pattern accompanying the word may indicate sarcasm, disagreement, caution, consolation, sternness, etc.) □ JOHN: *I just don't know what's going to happen.* MARY: *Things look very bleak.* JOHN: *Anyway, we'll all end up dead in the long run.* □ BOB: *Let's stop this silly argument.* FRED: *I agree. Anyhow, it's time to go home, so none of this argument really matters, does it?* BOB: *Not a bit.*

(Are) things getting you down? Are things bothering you? □ JANE: *Gee, Mary, you look sad. Are things getting you down?* MARY: *Yeah.* JANE: *Cheer up!* MARY: *Sure.* □ TOM: *What's the matter, Bob? Things getting you down?* BOB: *No, I'm just a little tired.*

(Are you) doing okay? AND **You doing okay?** **1.** How are you? □ MARY: *Doing okay?* BILL: *You bet! How are you?* □ BILL: *Hey, man! Are you doing okay?* TOM: *Sure thing! And you?* **2.** How are you surviving this situation or ordeal? □ MARY: *You doing okay?* BILL: *Sure.*

What about you? MARY: *I'm cool.* □ TOM: *Wow, that was some gust of wind! Are you doing okay?* MARY: *I'm still a little frightened, but alive.*

(Are you) feeling okay?   Do you feel well? (More than a greeting inquiry.) □ TOM: *Are you feeling okay?* BILL: *Oh, fair to middling.* □ MARY: *Are you feeling okay?* SUE: *I'm still a little dizzy, but it will pass.*

(Are you) going my way?   If you are traveling in the direction of my destination, could I please go with you or can I have a ride in your car? □ MARY: *Are you going my way?* SALLY: *Sure. Get in.* □ *"Going my way?" said Tom as he saw Mary get into her car.*

(Are you) leaving so soon? AND **You leaving so soon?**   a polite inquiry made to a guest who has announced a departure. (Appropriate only for the first few guests to leave. It would seem sarcastic to say this to the last guest to leave or to one who is leaving very late at night.) □ SUE: *We really must go.* SALLY: *Leaving so soon?* SUE: *Fred has to catch a plane at five in the morning.* □ JOHN (seeing Tom at the door): *You leaving so soon?* TOM: *Yes, thanks for inviting me. I really have to go.* JOHN: *Well, good night, then.*

(Are you) ready for this?   a way of presenting a piece of news or information that is expected to excite or surprise the person spoken to. □ TOM: *Boy, do I have something to tell you! Are you ready for this?* MARY: *Sure. Let me have it!* □ TOM: *Now, here's a great joke! Are you ready for this? It is so funny!* ALICE: *I can hardly wait.*

(Are you) ready to order?   Would you care to tell me what you want to order to eat? (A standard phrase used in eating establishments to find out what one wants to eat.) □ *The waitress came over and asked, "Are you ready to order?"* □ TOM: *I know what I want. What about you, Sally? Are you ready to order?* SALLY: *Don't rush me!*

(Are you) sorry you asked?   Now that you have heard (the unpleasant answer), do you regret having asked the question? (Compare to *You'll be sorry you asked.*) □ FATHER: *How are you doing in school?* BILL: *I'm flunking out. Sorry you asked?* □ MOTHER: *You've been looking a little down lately. Is there anything wrong?* BILL: *I probably have mono. Are you sorry you asked?*

(as) far as I know AND **to the best of my knowledge**   a signal of basic, but not well-informed agreement with an indication that the speaker's knowledge may not be adequate. □ TOM: *Is this brand* *of computer any good?* CLERK: *This is the very best one there is as far as I know.* □ FRED: *Are the trains on time?* CLERK: *To the best of my knowledge, all the trains are on time today.* □ BILL: *Are we just about there?* TOM: *Far as I know.* BILL: *I thought you'd been there before.* TOM: *Never.*

(as) far as I'm concerned 1. *from my point of view;* as concerns my interests. □ BOB: *Isn't this cake good?* ALICE: *Yes, indeed. This is the best cake I have ever eaten as far as I'm concerned.* □ TOM: *I think I'd better go.* BOB: *As far as I'm concerned, you all can leave now.* **2.** *Okay,* as it concerns my interests. □ ALICE: *Can I send this package on to your sister?* JOHN: *As far as I'm concerned.* □ JANE: *Do you mind if I put this coat in the closet?* JOHN: *Far as I'm concerned. It's not mine.*

as I see it AND **in my opinion; in my view** the way I think about it. □ TOM: *This matter is not as bad as some would make it out to be.* ALICE: *Yes. This whole affair has been overblown, as I see it.* □ BOB: *You're as wrong as can be.* JOHN: *In my view, you are wrong.*

as it is the way things are; the way it is now. □ *"I wish I could get a better job,"* remarked Tom. *"I'm just getting by as it is."* □ MARY: *Can we afford a new refrigerator?* FRED: *As it is, it would have to be a very small one.*

as I was saying AND **like I was saying** to repeat what I've been saying; to continue with what I was saying. (The first form is appropriate in any conversation. The second form is colloquial, informal, and familiar. In addition, this use of *like* for *as,* as in the second form, is objected to by many people.) □ BILL: *Now, Mary, this is one of the round ones that attaches to the wire here.* BOB (passing through the room): *Hello, you two! Catch you later.* BILL: *Yeah, see you around. Now, as I was saying, this goes here on this wire.* □ TOM: *I hate to interrupt, but someone's car is being broken into down on the street.* FRED: *As I was saying, these illegal practices must stop.*

as such authentic; in the way just mentioned; as one would expect. □ ALICE: *Did you have a good vacation?* JOHN: *Well, sort of. It wasn't a vacation, as such. We just went and visited Mary's parents.* ALICE: *That sounds nice.* JOHN: *Doesn't it?* □ ANDREW: *Someone said you bought a beach house.* HENRY: *Well, it's certainly not a beach house, as such. More like a duck blind, in fact.*

as we speak just now; at this very moment. (This has almost reached cliché status.) □ *"I'm sorry, sir,"* consoled the agent at the gate, *"the plane is taking off as we speak."* □ TOM: *Waiter, where is my* *steak? It's taking a long time.* WAITER: *It is being grilled as we speak, sir—just as you requested.*

as you say **1.** AND **like you say** a phrase indicating [patronizing] agreement with someone. (The *like* is used colloquially only.) □ JOHN: *Things are not going well for me today. What should I do?* BOB: *Some days are like that. As you say, it's just not going well for you, that's all.* □ JOHN: *This arrangement is not really good. There's not enough room for both of us.* MARY: *I guess you're right. It is crowded, and, like you say, there's not enough room.* **2.** (usually **As you say.**) a polite and formal way of indicating agreement or acquiescence. (Literally, I will do as you say.) □ JOHN: *Please take this to the post office.* BUTLER: *As you say, sir.* □ BUTLER: *There is a Mr. Franklin at the door.* MARY: *Thank you, James. Tell him I've gone to Egypt for the winter.* BUTLER: *As you say, madam.*

at the present time now. (Almost a cliché.) □ *"We are very sorry to report that we are unable to fill your order at the present time," stated the little note on the order form.* □ MARY: *How long will it be until we can be seated?* WAITER: *There are no tables available at the present time, madam.* MARY: *But, how long?*

aw **1.** an interjection indicating dissent. □ BILL: *Put the film in the fridge.* BOB: *Aw, that's stupid! It'll just get cold!* □ TOM: *The new cars are all unsafe.* BILL: *Aw, you don't know what you're talking about!* **2.** an interjection indicating pleading. □ TOM: *No!* FRED: *Aw, come on! Please!* □ MARY: *Get away from my door!* JOHN: *Aw, come on! Let me in!* □ FRED: *You hurt my feelings.* BOB: *Aw, I didn't mean it.*

B

Bag it! AND **Bag your face!** *Be quiet!; Shut up* and go away! (Rude and youthful slang. From *Bag your face!*) □ MARY: *Sally, you look just terrible! What happened?* SALLY: *Bag it!* MARY: *Sorry I asked!* □ BILL: *Did I ever tell you about the time I went to Germany?* SUE: *Give it a rest, Bill. Can it! Bag it!* □ SUE: *Can I borrow your car again?* MARY: *Bag your face, Sue!* SUE: *Well, I never!*

Bag your face! See the previous entry.

Beat it! *Go away!;* Get out! (Slang.) □ BILL: *Sorry I broke your radio.* BOB: *Get out of here! Beat it!* □ *"Beat it, you kids! Go play somewhere else!" yelled the storekeeper.*

Beats me. See *(It) beats me.*

Be careful. **1.** an instruction to take care in a particular situation. □ BILL: *I'm going to the beach tomorrow.* SALLY: *Be careful. Use lots of sunscreen!* □ JANE: *Well, we're off to the Amazon.* MARY: *Heavens! Be careful!* **2.** a way of saying *good-bye* while cautioning someone to take care. □ JOHN: *See you around, Fred.* FRED: *Be careful.* □ ALICE: *Well, I'm off.* JOHN: *Bye, Alice, be careful.*

Been getting by. See *(I've) been getting by.*

been keeping busy See *(I've) been keeping busy.; (Have you) been keeping busy?*

been keeping cool See *(Have you) been keeping cool?; (I've) been keeping cool.*

Been keeping myself busy. See *(I've) been keeping myself busy.*

Been keeping out of trouble.   See *(I've) been keeping out of trouble.; (Have you) been keeping out of trouble?*

been okay   See *(Have you) been okay?; (I've) been okay.*

Been under the weather.   See *(I've) been under the weather.*

Been up to no good.   See *(I've) been up to no good.*

Begging your pardon, but   See *(I) beg your pardon, but.*

Be good.   a departure response meaning *Good-bye and behave yourself.* □ JANE: *Well, we're off. Be back in a week.* MARY: *Okay, have fun. Be good.* JANE: *Do I have to?* □ TOM: *Bye. Be good.* BILL: *See ya.*

Beg pardon.   See *(I) beg your pardon.*

Beg your pardon.   See *(I) beg your pardon.*

Beg your pardon, but   See *(I) beg your pardon, but.*

Be happy to (do something).   See *(I'd be) happy to (do something).*

Behind you!   Look behind you!; There is danger behind you! □ *"Behind you!" shouted Tom just as a car raced past and nearly knocked Mary over.* □ *Alice shouted, "Behind you!" just as the pickpocket made off with Fred's wallet.*

believe it or not   an expression asserting the truth of something that the speaker has said, indicating that the statement is true whether or not the hearer believes it. □ TOM: *Well, Fred really saved the day.* SUE: *Believe it or not, I'm the one who saved the day.* □ BILL: *How good is this one?* CLERK: *This is the best one we have, believe it or not.*

Believe you me!   You really should believe me!; You'd better take my word for it! □ ALICE: *Is it hot in that room?* FRED: *It really is. Believe you me!* □ SUE: *How do you like my cake?* JOHN: *Believe you me, this is the best cake I've ever eaten!*

Be my guest.   *Help yourself.; After you.* (A polite way of indicating that one should go first, help oneself, or take the last one of something.) □ MARY: *I would just love to have some more cake, but there is only one piece left.* SALLY: *Be my guest.* MARY: *Wow! Thanks!* □ JANE: *Here's the door. Who should go in first?* BILL: *Be my guest. I'll wait out here.* JANE: *Why don't you go first?*

Be quiet! Stop talking or making noise. (Made polite with *please.*) □ BILL (entering the room): *Hey, Tom!* TOM: *Please be quiet! I'm on the phone.* □ TOM: *Hey, Bill!* BILL: *Be quiet! You're too noisy.* TOM: *Sorry.*

Be right there. See *(I'll) be right there.*

Be right with you. See *(I'll) be right with you.*

Be seeing you. See *(I'll) be seeing you.*

Best of luck (to someone). See *(The) best of luck (to someone).*

be that as it may even though that may be true. □ SUE: *I'm sorry that I am late for the test. I overslept.* RACHEL: *Be that as it may, you have missed the test and will have to petition for a make-up examination.* □ HENRY: *I lost my job, so I couldn't make the car payment on time.* RACHEL: *Be that as it may, the payment is overdue, and we'll have to take the car back.*

Better be going. See *(I'd) better be going.*

Better be off. See *(I'd) better be going.*

Better get moving. See *(I'd) better get moving; (You'd) better get moving.*

Better get on my horse. See *(I'd) better get on my horse.*

Better hit the road. See *(It's) time to hit the road.*

Better keep quiet about it. See under *(Someone had) better keep still about it.*

Better keep still about it. See under *(Someone had) better keep still about it.*

Better late than never. a catch phrase said when someone arrives late or when something happens or is done late. □ MARY: *Hi, Tom. Sorry I'm late.* BILL: *Fret not! Better late than never.* □ *When Fred showed up at the doctor's office three days after his appointment, the receptionist said, "Well, better late than never."*

better left unsaid [refers to a topic that] should not be discussed; [refers to a thought that] everyone is thinking, but would cause difficulty if talked about in public. (A typical beginning for this phrase might be *It is, That is, The details are,* or even *Some things are.* See the examples.) □ MARY: *I really don't know how to tell you this.* BOB: *Then don't. Maybe it's better left unsaid.* □ BILL: *I had a such a terrible fight with Sally last night. I can't believe what I said.* BOB: *I don't need to hear all about it. Some things are better left unsaid.*

Better luck next time. **1.** an expression that comforts someone for a minor failure. (Said with a pleasant tone of voice.) □ BILL: *That does it! I can't run any farther. I lose!* BOB: *Too bad. Better luck next time.* □ MARY: *Well, that's the end of my brand new weight-lifting career.* JANE: *Better luck next time.* **2.** an expression that ridicules someone for a failure. (Said with rudeness or sarcasm. The tone of voice distinguishes sense 2 from sense 1.) □ SALLY: *I lost out to Sue, but I think she cheated.* MARY: *Better luck next time.* □ SUE: *You thought you could get ahead of me, you twit! Better luck next time!* SALLY: *I still think you cheated.*

Better than nothing. See *(It's) better than nothing.*

Better things to do. See *(I've) (got) better things to do.*

Be with you in a minute. See under *(Someone will) be with you in a minute.*

Bingo! That's it, just what I've been waiting for! (From the game Bingo, where the word "Bingo!" is shouted by the first person to succeed in the game.) □ *Bob was looking in the button box for an old button to match the ones on his shirt. "Bingo!" he cried. "Here it is!"* □ BILL: *I've found it! Bingo!* MARY: *I guess you found your contact lens?*

Bite your tongue! an expression said to someone who has just stated an unpleasant supposition that unfortunately may be true.

☐ Mary: *I'm afraid that we've missed the plane already.* Jane: *Bite your tongue! We still have time.* ☐ Mary: *Marry him? But you're older than he is!* Sally: *Bite your tongue!*

Bottoms up. and **Down the hatch!; Here's looking at you.; Here's mud in your eye.; Here's to you.; Skoal!** an expression said as a toast when people are drinking together. (The *bottoms* refers to the bottoms of the drinking glasses.) ☐ Bill: *Bottoms up.* Tom: *Here's mud in your eye.* Bill: *Care for another?* ☐ *"Well, down the hatch," said Fred, pouring the smooth and ancient brandy slowly across his tongue.*

boy and **boy oh boy** a sentence opener expressing surprise or emphasis. (This is not a term of address and can be used with either sex, although it is quite informal. The alternate form is more informal and. more emphatic. Words such as this often use intonation to convey the connotation of the sentence that is to follow. The brief intonation pattern accompanying the word may indicate sarcasm, disagreement, caution, consolation, sternness, etc.) ☐ John: *Hi, Bill.* Bill: *Boy, am I glad to see you!* ☐ Bob: *What happened here?* Fred: *I don't know.* Bob: *Boy, this place is a mess!* ☐ *"Boy, I'm tired!" moaned Henry.* ☐ *"Boy oh boy, this cake looks good," thought Jack.*

Boy howdy! an exclamation of excited surprise. (Colloquial and folksy.) ☐ Bob: *Well, I finally got here.* Fred: *Boy howdy! Am I glad to see you!* ☐ Bill: *How do you like my horse?* Fred: *That's one fine-looking filly! Boy howdy!*

boy oh boy See *boy.*

Bravo! a cheer of praise for someone who has done something very well. ☐ *"Keep it up! Bravo!" cheered the audience.* ☐ *At the end of the tenor's aria, the members of the audience leapt to their feet and with one voice shouted, "Bravo!"*

Break a leg! a parting word of encouragement given to a performer before a performance. (It is traditionally viewed as bad luck to wish a performer good luck, so the performer is wished bad luck in hopes of causing good luck.) ☐ Bill: *The big show is tonight. I hope I don't forget my lines.* Jane: *Break a leg, Bill!* ☐ Mary: *I'm nervous about my solo.* Bob: *You'll do great. Don't worry. Break a leg!*

Break it up! Stop fighting!; Stop arguing! □ TOM: *Then I'm going to break your neck!* BILL: *I'm going to mash in your face!* BOB: *All right, you two, break it up!* □ *When the police officer saw the boys fighting, he came over and hollered, "Break it up! You want me to arrest you?"*

Bully for you! **1.** an expression that praises someone or someone's courage. (Dated, but still heard.) □ *The audience shouted, "Bravo! Bully for you!"* □ BOB: *I quit my job today.* SALLY: *Bully for you! Now what are you going to do?* BOB: *Well, I need a little loan to tide me over.* **2.** a sarcastic phrase ridiculing someone's statement or accomplishment. □ BOB: *I managed to save three dollars last week.* BILL: *Well, bully for you!* □ MARY: *I won a certificate good for a free meal!* SALLY: *Bully for you!*

Butt out! Go away and mind your own business! (Rude. Said to someone who has "butted in.") □ *Jane and Mary were talking when Bill came over and interrupted. "Butt out!" said Jane.* □ TOM: *Look, Mary, we've been going together for nearly a year.* JANE (approaching): *Hi, you guys!* TOM: *Butt out, Jane, we're talking.*

Buy you a drink? See *(Could I) buy you a drink?*

Bye. Good-bye. (Friendly and familiar.) □ TOM: *Bye.* MARY: *Take care. Bye.* □ SALLY: *See you later. Bye.* TOM: *Bye.*

Bye-bye. Good-bye. (Very familiar.) □ MARY: *Bye-bye.* ALICE: *See you later. Bye-bye.* □ TOM: *Bye-bye. Remember me to your brother.* BILL: *I will. Bye.*

by the same token a phrase indicating that the speaker is introducing parallel or contrary information. □ TOM: *I really got cheated!* BOB: *You think they've cheated you, but, by the same token, they believe that you've cheated them.* □ *"By the same token, most people really want to be told what to do," counseled Henry.*

by the skin of someone's teeth just barely. □ HENRY: *I almost didn't make it.* ANDREW: *What happened?* HENRY: *I had to flag down a taxi. I just made it by the skin of my teeth.* □ *"Well, Bob, you passed the test by the skin of your teeth," said the teacher.*

by the way AND **incidentally** **1.** a phrase indicating that the speaker is adding information. □ TOM: *Is this one any good?* CLERK: *This is the largest and, by the way, the most expensive one we have in stock.* □ BILL: *I'm a realtor. Is your house for sale?* ALICE: *My house is not for sale, and, by the way, I too am a realtor.* **2.** a phrase indicating that the speaker is casually opening a new subject. ☐ BILL: *Oh, by the way, Fred, do you still have that hammer you borrowed from me?* FRED: *I'll check. I thought I gave it back.* ☐ JANE: *By the way, don't you owe me some money?* SUE: *Who, me?*

C

Call again. Please visit this shop again sometime. (Said by shop-keepers and clerks.) □ *"Thank you,"* said the clerk, smiling, *"call again."* □ CLERK: *Is that everything?* JOHN: *Yes.* CLERK: *That's ten dollars even.* JOHN: *Here you are.* CLERK: *Thanks. Call again.*

[can] See also the entries beginning with *could*.

Can do. I can do it. (The opposite of *No can do.*) □ JANE: *Will you be able to get this finished by quitting time today?* ALICE: *Can do. Leave it to me.* □ BOB: *Can you get this pack of papers over to the lawyer's office by noon?* BILL: *Can do. I'm leaving now. Bye.*

Can I speak to someone? See *Could I speak to someone?*

Can it! *Be quiet!; Stop talking!; Drop the subject!* (Slang and fairly rude.) □ BOB: *I'm tired of this place. Let's go.* FRED: *That's enough out of you! Can it!* □ JOHN: *Hey, Tom! What are you doing, man?* TOM: *Can it! I'm studying.*

Cannot! See *(You) can't!* and all the entries beginning with *Can't.*

Can't argue with that. See *(I) can't argue with that.*

Can't beat that. See *(I) can't beat that.; (You) can't beat that.*

Can't be helped. See *(It) can't be helped.*

Can't complain. See *(I) can't complain.*

Can't fight city hall. See *(You) can't fight city hall.*

Can't get there from here. See *(You) can't get there from here.*

Can't help it. See *(I) can't help it.*

Can too. See *(I) can too.*

Can't rightly say. See *(I) can't rightly say.*

Can't say (as) I do. See *(I) can't say that I do.*

Can't say (as) I have. See *(I) can't say that I have.*

Can't say for sure. See *(I) can't say for sure.*

Can't say's I do. See *(I) can't say that I do.*

Can't say that I do. See *(I) can't say that I do.*

Can't say that I have. See *(I) can't say that I have.*

Can't take it with you. See *(You) can't take it with you.*

Can't thank you enough. See *(I) can't thank you enough.*

Can't top that. See *(I) can't beat that.; (You) can't beat that.*

Can't win them all. See *(You) can't win them all.*

Can you excuse us, please? See *Could you excuse us, please?*

Can you handle it? **1.** Are you able to deal with this problem? (May be a personal problem or a work assignment.) ☐ BILL: *This file is a mess. Can you handle it?* ☐ FATHER: *This is a difficult situation, son. Can you handle it?* BOB: *Yeah, Dad. Don't worry.* **2.** AND **Could you handle it?** Will you agree to deal with what I have described? ☐ MARY: *I need someone to work on the Jones account. Can you handle it?* JANE: *Sure.* ☐ BILL: *Someone is on the phone about the car payments. Could you handle it?* FATHER: *Yes.*

Can you hold? See *Could you hold?*

Capeesh? Do you understand? (From Italian.) ☐ TOM: *Do I have to stay here?* FRED: *That's the way it's going to be. Capeesh?* TOM: *Yeah.* ☐ MARY: *I will not tolerate any of this anymore. Capeesh?* BILL: *Sure. Gotcha!*

Care for another? See *(Would you) care for another (one)?*

Care if I join you? See *Could I join you?*

Care to? See *(would you) care to?*

Care to dance? See *(Would you) care to dance?*

Care to join us? See *(Would you) care to join us?*

Cash or credit (card)? Do you wish to pay for your purchases with cash or a credit card? □ *Mary put all her packages on the counter. Then the clerk said, "Cash or credit card?"* □ CLERK: *Is that everything?* RACHEL: *Yes. That's all.* CLERK: *Cash or credit?*

Catch me later. AND **Catch me some other time.** Please try to talk to me later. □ BILL (angry): *Tom, look at this phone bill!* TOM: *Catch me later.* □ *"Catch me some other time," hollered Mr. Franklin over his shoulder. "I've got to go to the airport."*

Catch me some other time. See the previous entry.

Catch you later. See *(I will) catch you later.*

Certainly! See *Definitely!*

Certainly not! See *Definitely not!*

Changed my mind. See *(I) changed my mind.*

Change your mind? See *(Have you) changed your mind?*

Charmed(, I'm sure). an expression said after being introduced to someone. (Almost a parody. Would not be used in most everyday situations.) □ MARY: *I want you to meet my great-aunt Sarah.* SALLY: *Charmed, I'm sure.* □ MARY: *Bill, meet Sally. Sally, this is Bill.* BILL: *My pleasure.* SALLY: *Charmed.*

Check. That is correct.; That is accounted for. □ SUE: *Is the coffee ready yet?* JOHN: *Check.* □ MARY: *Let's go over the list. Flashlight?* JOHN: *Check.* MARY: *Band-Aids?* JOHN: *Check.* MARY: *Pencils?* JOHN: *Check.* MARY: *Matches?* JOHN: *Check.* MARY: *Great!*

Check, please. AND **Could I have the bill?; Could I have the check?** Could I please have the bill for this food or drink? □ *When they both had finished their dessert and coffee, Tom said, "Check, please."* □ BILL: *That meal was really good. This is a fine place to eat.* TOM: *Waiter! Check, please.* WAITER: *Right away, sir.*

Cheerio. *Good-bye.* (Chiefly British.) □ BOB: *Bye.* TOM: *Cheerio.* □ *"Cheerio," said Mary, skipping out of the room like a schoolgirl.*

Cheer up! *Don't worry!* Try to be happy! □ TOM: *Things are really looking bad for me financially.* MARY: *Cheer up! Things'll work out for the best.* □ SUE: *Cheer up! In no time at all, things will be peachy keen.* BOB: *In no time at all, they'll be a lot worse.*

Chow. See the following entry.

Ciao. AND **Chow.** *Good-bye.* (Italian. *Chow* is not an Italian spelling.) □ JOHN: *Ciao.* MARY: *Ciao, baby.* □ *"Ciao," said Mary Francine as she swept from the room.*

Clear the way! Please get out of the way, because someone or something is coming through and needs room. □ *The movers were shouting, "Clear the way!" because they needed room to take the piano out of the house.* □ TOM: *Clear the way! Clear the way!* MARY: *Who does he think he is?* BOB: *I don't know, but I'm getting out of the way.*

Cold enough for you? See *(Is it) cold enough for you?*

Come again. **1.** Please come back again sometime. □ MARY: *I had a lovely time. Thank you for asking me.* SALLY: *You're quite welcome. Come again.* □ *"Come again," said Mrs. Martin as she let Jimmy out the door.* **2.** (usually **Come again?**) I didn't hear what you said. Please repeat it. (A little dated and folksy.) □ SALLY: *Do you want some more carrots?* MARY: *Come again?* SALLY: *Carrots. Do you want some more carrots?* □ *Uncle Henry turned his good ear toward the clerk and said, "Come again?"*

Come and get it! Dinner's ready. Come eat! (Folksy and familiar.) □ *The camp cook shouted, "Soup's on! Come and get it!"* □ TOM: *Come and get it! Time to eat!* MARY: *What is it this time? More bean soup?* TOM: *Certainly not! Lentils.*

Come back and see us. AND **Come back and see me.** Come visit us [or me] again. (Often said by a host or hostess to departing guests.) □ BILL: *Good night. Thanks for having me.* SALLY: *Oh, you're quite welcome. Come back and see us.* □ BOB: *I enjoyed my visit. Good-bye.* MARY: *It was very nice of you to pay me a visit. Come back and see me.*

Come back anytime. Please come and visit us again. You're always welcome. (Often said by a host or hostess to departing guests.) □ MARY: *So glad you could come.* BILL: *Thank you. I had a wonderful time.* MARY: *Come back anytime.* □ BOB: *Thanks for the coffee and cake. Bye.* MARY: *We're glad to have you. Please come back anytime.*

Come back when you can stay longer. Come back again sometime when your visit can be longer. (Often said by a host or hostess to departing guests.) □ JOHN: *I really must go.* SUE: *So glad you could come. Please come back when you can stay longer.* □ BILL: *Well, I hate to eat and run, but I have to get up early tomorrow.* MARY: *Well, come back when you can stay longer.*

Come in and make yourself at home. Please come into my home and make yourself comfortable. □ SUE: *Oh, hello, Tom. Come in and make yourself at home.* TOM: *Thanks. I will.* (entering) *Oh, it's nice and warm in here.* □ *"Come in and make yourself at home," invited Bob.*

Come in and sit a spell. AND **Come in and set a spell.; Come in and sit down.; Come in and take a load off your feet.** Please come in and have a seat and a visit. (Colloquial and folksy. *Set* is especially folksy.) □ *"Hi, Fred," smiled Tom. "Come in and sit a spell."* □ TOM: *I hope I'm not intruding.* BILL: *Not at all. Come in and set a spell.*

Come in and sit down. See the previous entry.

Come in and take a load off your feet. See *Come in and sit a spell.*

Come off it! Don't act so haughty!; Stop acting that way! □ TOM: *This stuff just doesn't meet my requirements.* BILL: *Come off it, Tom! This is exactly what you've always bought.* TOM: *That doesn't mean I like it.* □ MARY: *We are not amused by your childish antics.* SUE: *Come off it, Mary. Who do you think you're talking to?*

come on **1.** (Usually **Come on!**) Stop it!; Stop doing that. □ *Sally was tickling Tom, and he was laughing like mad. Finally, he sputtered, "Come on!"* □ MARY: *Are you really going to sell your new car?* SALLY: *Come on! How dumb do you think I am?* **2.** please oblige me. □ MOTHER: *Sorry. You can't go!* BILL: *Come on, let me go to the picnic!* □ *"Come on," whined Jimmy, "I want some more!"*

Come (on) in. Enter.; Come into this place. (A polite invitation to enter someone's home, office, room, etc. It is more emphatic with *on*.) □ BOB: *Hello, you guys. Come on in. We're just about to start the music.* MARY: *Great! Um! Something smells good!* TOM: *Yeah. When do we eat?* BOB: *Just hold your horses. All in good time.* □ BILL: *Come in. Nice to see you.* MARY: *I hope we're not too early.* BILL: *Not at all.*

Come right in. Come in, please, you are very welcome here. □ *"Come right in and make yourself at home!" said the host.* □ FRED (opening door): *Well, hi, Bill.* BILL: *Hello, Fred. Good to see you.* FRED: *Come right in.* BILL: *Thanks.*

Coming through(, please). Please let me pass through. (Often said by someone trying to get through a crowd of people, as in a passageway or an elevator. Compare to *Out, please.*) □ TOM: *Coming through, please.* SUE: *Give him some room. He wants to get by.* □ MARY (as the elevator stops): *Well, this is my floor. Coming through, please. I've got to get off.* JOHN: *Bye, Mary. It's been good talking to you.*

Could be better. See *(Things) could be better.*

Could be worse. See *(Things) could be worse.*

Could have fooled me. See *(You) could have fooled me.*

Could I be excused? Would you give me permission to leave?; Would you give me permission to leave the table? (Also used with *can* or *may* in place of *could*.) □ BILL: *I'm finished, Mom. Could I be excused?* MOTHER: *Yes, of course, when you use good manners like that.* □ *"Can I be excused?" said Bill, with a big grin on his face and his broccoli hidden in his napkin.*

(Could I) buy you a drink? **1.** Could I purchase a drink for you? (An offer by one person—usually in a bar—to buy a drink for another. Then the two will drink together. Also used with *can* or *may* in place of *could*.) □ *When Sally and Mary met at the agreed time in the hotel bar, Sally said to Mary, "Could I buy you a drink?"* □ *Then this strange man sat down and said, "Buy you a drink?" Well, I could have just died!* **2.** Could I make you a drink? (A slightly humorous way of offering to prepare and serve someone a drink, as in one's home. Also used with *can* or *may* in place of *could*.) □ BILL: *Come in,*

Fred. Can I buy you a drink? FRED: *Sure. What are you having?* BILL: *I've got wine and beer.* □ MARY: *Can I buy you a drink? What do you have there now?* BOB: *Oh, sure. It's just gin and tonic.* MARY: *Great! I'll be right back with it.*

Could I call you? **1.** I am too busy to talk to you now. Do you mind if I telephone you later on? (Usually in a business context. Also used with *can* in place of *could. May* is too polite here.) □ SALLY: *I can't talk to you right now. Could I call you?* TOM: *Sure, no problem.* □ BILL: *I've got to run. Sorry. Can I call you?* BOB: *No, I'm leaving town. I'll try to get in touch next week.* **2.** Do you mind if I call you and ask for another date sometime?; Do you mind if I call you sometime (in order to further our relationship)? (Usually in a romantic context. Also used with *can* or *may* in place of *could.*) □ MARY: *I had a marvelous time, Bob.* BOB: *Me too. Can I call you?* MARY: *Sure.* □ BOB: *I had a marvelous time, Mary. May I call you?* MARY: *Maybe in a week or two. I have a very busy week ahead. I'll call you, in fact.*

Could I come in? Do you mind if I enter? (Also used with *can* or *may* in place of *could.*) □ TOM (standing in the doorway): *Hello, I'm with the Internal Revenue Service. Could I come in?* MARY: *Go ahead, make my day!* □ BILL: *Hi, Tom. What are you doing here?* TOM: *Could I come in? I have to talk to you.* BILL: *Sure. Come on in.*

Could I get by, please? Would you please allow me space to pass by? (Also used with *can* or *may* in place of *could. May* is almost too polite.) □ *Poor Bill, trapped at the back of the elevator behind a huge man, kept saying, "Could I get by, please?" But nobody moved.* □ *"Can I get by, please?" Jane said, squeezing between the wall and a wheelchair.*

(Could I) get you something (to drink)? an expression offering a drink, usually an alcoholic drink. (Compare to *(Could I) buy you a drink?* Also used with *can* or *may* in place of *could.*) □ BILL: *Hi, Alice! Come on in! Can I get you something to drink?* ALICE: *Just a little soda, if you don't mind.* □ WAITER: *Get you something to drink?* JOHN: *No, thanks. I'll just order now.*

(Could I) give you a lift? Can I offer you a ride to some place? (Also used with *can* or *may* in place of *could.*) □ *Bill stopped his car at the side of the road where Tom stood. "Can I give you a lift?" asked Bill.* □ JOHN: *Well, I've got to leave.* ALICE: *Me too.* JOHN: *Give you a lift?* ALICE: *Sure. Thanks.*

Could I have a lift? AND **How about a lift?** Would you please give me a ride (in your car)? (This usually refers to a destination that is the same as the driver's or on the way to the driver's destination. Also used with *can* or *may* in place of *could*.) □ BOB: *Going north? Could I have a lift?* BILL: *Sure. Hop in.* BOB: *Thanks. That's such a long walk to the north end of campus.* □ SUE: *Can I have a lift? I'm late.* MARY: *Sure, if you're going somewhere on Maple Street.*

Could I have a word with you? See *I'd like (to have) a word with you.*

Could I have someone call you? a question asked by a telephone answerer when the person the caller is seeking is not available. (The *someone* can be a person's name or a pronoun, or even the word *someone*. Also used with *can* or *may* in place of *could*.) □ TOM: *Bill's not here now. Could I have him call you?* BOB: *Yeah. Ask him to leave a message on my machine.* TOM: *Sure.* □ *"Could I have her call you?" asked Mrs. Wilson's secretary.*

Could I have the bill? See *Check, please.*

Could I have the check? See *Check, please.*

Could I help you? Could I assist you? (Said by shopkeepers, clerks, food service workers, and telephone answerers. Also used with *can* or *may* in place of *could*.) □ *The clerk came over and said, "Could I help you?"* □ CLERK: *May I help you?* MARY: *No thanks, I'm just looking.*

Could I join you? AND **(Do you) care if I join you?; (Do you) mind if I join you?** Will you permit me to sit with you? (An inquiry seeking permission to sit at someone's table or join someone else in some activity. Also used with *can* or *may* in place of *could*.) □ *Tom came into the cafe and saw Fred and Sally sitting in a booth by the window. Coming up to them, Tom said, "Could I join you?"* □ *"Do you mind if I join you?" asked the woman. "There are no other seats."*

Could I leave a message? a phrase used on the telephone to request that a message be written down for a person who is not available to come to the telephone. (Can be said with *can* or *may*.) □ BILL: *Can I talk to Fred?* MARY: *He's not here.* BILL: *Could I leave a message?*

MARY: *Sure. What is it?* □ *"May I leave a message?" asked Mary politely.*

Could I see you again? Could we go out on another date sometime? (Also with *can* or *may*.) □ TOM: *I had a wonderful time, Mary. Can I see you again?* MARY: *Call me tomorrow, Tom. Good night.* □ *"Could I see you again?" muttered Tom, dizzy with the magic of her kiss.*

Could I see you in my office? I want to talk to you in the privacy of my office. (Typically said by the boss to an employee. Also used with *can* or *may* in place of *could*.) □ *"Mr. Franklin," said Bill's boss sort of sternly, "could I see you in my office for a minute? We need to talk about something."* □ SUE: *Could I see you in my office?* JOHN: *Sure. What's cooking?*

Could I speak to someone? AND **Can I speak to someone?; May I speak to someone?** the phrase used to request to talk to a particular person, usually on the telephone. (The *someone* stands for someone's name. Also used with *talk* in place of *speak*.) □ TOM (answering the phone): *Good morning, Acme Air Products. With whom do you wish to speak?* BILL: *Can I speak to Mr. Wilson?* TOM: *One moment.* □ SALLY: *May I speak to the manager, please?* CLERK: *Certainly, madam. I'm the manager.*

Could I take a message? the phrase used on the telephone to offer to take a message and give it to the person the caller is seeking. (Can be said with *can* or *may*.) □ BILL: *Can I talk to Fred?* MARY: *He's not here. Could I take a message?* □ *"May I take a message?" asked Mary politely.*

Could I take your order (now)? an expression used by food service personnel to determine if the customer is ready to order food. (Also used with *can* or *may* in place of *could*.) □ WAITER: *May I take your order now?* MARY: *Of course. Jane, what are you going to have?* JANE: *I'm having what you're having.* MARY: *Oh.* WAITER: *I'll be back in a minute.* □ MARY: *This is a nice place.* BILL: *Yes, it is.* WAITER: *Can I take your order?* MARY: *Yes, we're ready.*

Could I tell someone who's calling? a question asked by telephone answerers to find out politely who is asking for someone. (*Someone* is replaced by a person's name or by a pronoun. Also used with *can* or *may* in place of *could*.) □ MARY (on the phone): *Hello. Could I speak to Bill Franklin?* SALLY: *Could I tell him who's calling?* □ BILL (on the phone): *Is Tom there?* MARY: *May I tell him who's calling?* BILL: *It's Bill.* MARY: *Just a minute.*

Could I use your powder room? AND **Where is your powder room?** a polite way to ask to use the bathroom in someone's home. (Refers to powdering one's nose. Also used with *can* or *may* in place of *could*.) □ MARY: *Oh, Sally, could I use your powder room?* SALLY: *Of course. It's just off the kitchen, on the left.* □ TOM: *Nice place you've got here. Uh, where is your powder room?* BETH: *At the top of the stairs.*

Couldn't ask for more. See *(I) couldn't ask for more.*

Couldn't be better. See *(It) couldn't be better.; (I) couldn't be better.*

Couldn't be helped. See *(It) can't be helped.*

Could(n't) care less. See *(I) could(n't) care less.*

Couldn't help it. See *(I) couldn't help it.*

Could we continue this later? Could we go on with this conversation at a later time? (Also used with *can* or *may* in place of *could*.) □ BOB: *After that we both ended up going out for a pizza.* SUE: *Could we continue this later? I have some work I have to get done.* BOB: *Sure. No problem.* □ As Mary and John were discussing something private, Bob entered the room. "*Could we continue this later?*" whispered John. "*Yes, of course,*" answered Mary.

Could you excuse us, please? AND **Would you excuse us, please?; Will you excuse us, please?** We must leave. I hope you will forgive us. (A polite way of announcing a departure. Also with *can* in place of *could*.) □ BILL: *Will you excuse us, please? We really must leave now.* BOB: *Oh, sure. Nice to see you.* □ BILL: *Could you excuse us, please? We simply must rush off.* ALICE: *So sorry you have to go. Come back when you can stay longer.*

Could you handle it? See under *Can you handle it?*

Could you hold? AND **Will you hold?** Do you mind if I put your telephone call on hold? (Also used with *can* in place of *could*.) □ *"Could you hold?" asked the operator.* □ SUE: *Hello. Acme Motors. Can you hold?* BOB: *I guess.* SUE (after a while): *Hello. Thank you for holding. Can I help you?*

Could you keep a secret? I am going to tell you something that I hope you will keep a secret. (Also used with *can* in place of *could*.) □ TOM: *Could you keep a secret?* MARY: *Sure.* TOM: *Don't tell anybody, but I'm going to be a daddy.* □ SUE: *Can you keep a secret?* ALICE: *Of course.* SUE: *We're moving to Atlanta.*

Cut it out! Stop doing that!; Stop saying that! (Colloquial and familiar.) □ SUE: *Why, I think you have a crush on Mary!* TOM: *Cut it out!* □ *"Cut it out!" yelled Tommy as Billy hit him again.*

Cut the comedy! AND **Cut the funny stuff!** Stop acting silly and telling jokes!; Be serious! □ JOHN: *All right, you guys! Cut the comedy and get to work!* BILL: *Can't we ever have any fun?* JOHN: *No.* □ BILL: *Come on, Mary, let's throw Tom in the pool!* MARY: *Yeah, let's drag him over and give him a good dunking!* TOM: *Okay, you clowns, cut the funny stuff! I'll throw both of you in!* BILL: *You and what army?*

Cut the funny stuff! See the previous entry.

D

Dear me! an expression of mild dismay or regret. □ SUE: *Dear me, is this all there is?* MARY: *There's more in the kitchen.* □ *"Oh, dear me!" fretted John, "I'm late again."*

Definitely! AND **Certainly!** Yes, I agree! □ BILL: *Will you be there Saturday?* MARY: *Definitely!* □ SUE: *Would you be so kind as to carry this up the stairs?* BILL: *Certainly!*

Definitely not! AND **Certainly not!** No, without any doubt at all. (Compare to *Absolutely not!*) □ BILL: *Will you lend me some money?* BOB: *No way! Definitely not!* □ BOB: *Have you ever stolen anything?* FRED: *Certainly not!*

Delighted to have you. See *(I'm) delighted to have you (here)*.

Delighted to make your acquaintance. See *(I'm) delighted to make your acquaintance*.

did you hear? See *have you heard?*

Dig in! Please start eating your meal (heartily). □ *When we were all seated at the table, Grandfather said, "Dig in!" and we all did.* □ SUE: *Sit down, everybody.* BOB: *Wow, this stuff looks good!* ALICE: *It sure does.* SUE: *Dig in!*

Dig up! Listen carefully. (Slang.) □ JOHN: *All right, you guys! Dig up! You're going to hear this one time and one time only!* BILL: *Get quiet, you guys!* □ BILL: *Dig up! I'm only going to say this once.* BOB: *What was that?* BILL: *I said listen!*

Dinner is served. It is time to eat dinner. Please come to the table. (Formal, as if announced by a butler.) □ SUE: *Dinner is served.*

MARY (aside): *Aren't we fancy tonight?* □ *"Dinner is served," said Bob, rather formally for a barbecue.*

Does it work for you? Is this all right with you?; Do you agree? (Colloquial. Can be answered by *(It) works for me.*) □ BILL: *I'll be there at noon. Does it work for you?* BOB: *Works for me.* □ MARY: *We're having dinner at eight. Does it work for you?* JANE: *Sounds just fine.*

Doesn't bother me any. See *(It) doesn't bother me any.*

Doesn't bother me at all. See *(It) doesn't bother me any.*

Doesn't hurt to ask. See *(It) doesn't hurt to ask.*

Doesn't matter to me. See *(It) (really) doesn't matter to me.*

(Do) have some more. an invitation to take more of something, usually food or drink. □ BILL: *Wow, Mrs. Franklin, this scampi is great!* SALLY: *Thank you, Bill. Do have some more.* □ JANE: *What a lovely, light cake.* MARY: *Oh, have some more. Otherwise the boys will just wolf it down.*

Do I have to paint (you) a picture? See the following entry.

Do I have to spell it out (for you)? AND **Do I have to paint (you) a picture?** What do I have to do to make this clear enough for you to understand? (Shows impatience.) □ MARY: *I don't think I understand what you're trying to tell me, Fred.* FRED: *Do I have to spell it out for you?* MARY: *I guess so.* FRED: *We're through, Mary.* □ SALLY: *Would you please go over the part about the square root again?* MARY: *Do I have to paint you a picture? Pay attention!*

Do I make myself (perfectly) clear? Do you understand exactly what I mean? (Very stern.) □ MOTHER: *You're going to sit right here and finish that homework. Do I make myself perfectly clear?* CHILD: *Yes, ma'am.* □ SUE: *No, the answer is no! Do I make myself clear?* BILL: *Are you sure?*

doing okay See *(I'm) doing okay.*; *(Are you) doing okay?*

Don't ask. You would not like the answer you would get, so do not ask.; It is so bad, I do not wish to be reminded about it, so do not ask about it. □ JOHN: *How was your class reunion?* ALICE: *Oh, heavens! Don't ask.* □ TOM: *What was your calculus final exam like?* MARY: *Don't ask.* □ SUE: *How old were you on your last birthday?* FRED: *Don't ask.*

Don't ask me. See *How should I know?*

Don't be gone (too) long. *Good-bye.* Hurry back here. □ TOM: *I've got to go to the drugstore to get some medicine.* SUE: *Don't be gone too long.* TOM: *I'll be right back.* □ *"Don't be gone long," said Bill's uncle. "It's about time to eat."*

Don't believe I've had the pleasure. See *(I) don't believe I've had the pleasure.*

Don't believe so. See *(I) don't believe so.*

Don't be too sure. I think you are wrong, so do not sound so certain.; You may be wrong, you know. (Compare to *Don't speak too soon.*) □ BILL: *Ah, it's sure great being home and safe—secure in one's castle.* MARY: *Don't be too sure. I just heard glass breaking downstairs.* □ BILL: *I think I've finally saved up enough money to retire.* JOHN: *Don't be too sure. Inflation can ruin your savings.*

Don't bother. Please don't do it. It is not necessary, and it is too much trouble. □ MARY: *Should I put these in the box with the others?* BILL: *No, don't bother.* □ SUE: *Do you want me to save this spoonful of mashed potatoes?* JANE: *No, don't bother. It isn't worth it.* SUE: *I hate to waste it.*

Don't bother me! Go away!; *Leave me alone!* □ TOM: *Hey, Bill!* BILL: *Don't bother me! I'm busy. Can't you see?* □ *"Don't bother me! Leave me alone!" the child shouted at the dog.*

Don't bother me none. See *(It) don't bother me none.*

Don't breathe a word of this to anyone. This is a secret or secret gossip. Do not tell it to anyone. □ MARY: *Can you keep a secret?* JOHN: *Sure.* MARY: *Don't breathe a word of this to anyone, but Tom is in jail.* □ BILL: *Have you heard about Mary and her friends?* SALLY: *No. Tell me! Tell me!* BILL: *Well, they all went secretly to Mexico for the weekend. Everyone thinks they are at Mary's, except Mary's mother, who thinks they are at Sue's. Now, don't breathe a word of this to anyone.* SALLY: *Of course not! You know me!*

Don't call us, we'll call you. We will let you know if we wish to talk to you further.; We will let you know if you got the job, so don't bother calling and asking. (Often a dismissal.) □ SALLY: *Thank you for coming by for the interview. We'll let you know.* BILL: *How soon do you think Mr. Franklin will decide?* SALLY: *Don't call us, we'll call you.*

☐ *"Don't call us, we'll call you,"* said the assistant director, as if he had said it a hundred times already today, which he probably had.

Don't do anything I wouldn't do. an expression said when two friends are parting. (Familiar and colloquial.) ☐ BILL: *See you tomorrow, Tom.* TOM: *Yeah, man. Don't do anything I wouldn't do.* BILL: *What wouldn't you do?* ☐ MARY: *Where are you going, Bill?* BILL: *Oh, just around.* MARY: *Sure, you're spinning. Well, don't do anything I wouldn't do.* BILL: *Okay, but what wouldn't you do?* MARY: *Beat it, you clown!* BILL: *I'm off.*

Don't even look like something! Do not even appear to be doing something! (The *something* can be thinking about something or actually doing something.) ☐ MARY: *Are you thinking about taking that last piece of cake?* BOB: *Of course not.* MARY: *Well, don't even look like you're doing it!* ☐ JOHN: *You weren't going to try to sneak into the theater, were you?* BOB: *No.* JOHN: *Well, don't even look like it, if you know what's good for you.*

Don't even think about (doing) it. Do not do it, and do not even think about doing it. ☐ *John reached into his jacket for his wallet. The cop, thinking John was about to draw a gun, said, "Don't even think about it."* ☐ MARY: *Look at that diver! It must be forty feet down to the water.* BOB: *Don't even think about doing it yourself.*

Don't even think about it (happening). Do not even think about something like that happening. (Compare to *Don't even think about (doing) it.*) ☐ MARY: *Oh, those cars almost crashed! How horrible!* FRED: *Don't even think about it.* ☐ SALLY: *If the banks fail, we'll lose everything we have.* SUE: *Don't even think about it!*

Don't forget to write. See *Remember to write.*

Don't get up. Please, there is no need to rise to greet me or in deference to me. (Often with *please.*) ☐ *Mary approached the table to speak to Bill. Bill started to push his chair back as if to rise. Mary said, "Don't get up. I just want to say hello."* ☐ TOM (rising): *Hello, Fred. Good to see you.* FRED (standing): *Don't get up. How are you?*

Don't get your bowels in an uproar! Do not get so excited! (Slang.) ☐ BILL: *What have you done to my car? Where's the bumper? The side*

window is cracked! BOB: *Calm down! Don't get your bowels in an uproar!*
☐ FATHER: *Now, son, we need to talk a little bit about you and your pet snake. Where is it?* JOHN: *I don't know.* FATHER (outraged): *What!* JOHN: *Don't get your bowels in an uproar! It always turns up.*

Don't give it another thought. See *Think nothing of it.*

Don't give it a (second) thought. See *Think nothing of it.*

Don't give up! Do not stop trying!; Keep trying! ☐ JOHN: *Get in there and give it another try. Don't give up!* BILL: *Okay. Okay. But it's hopeless.* ☐ JANE: *I asked the boss for a raise, but he said no.* TOM: *Don't give up. Try again later.*

Don't give up the ship! Do not give up yet!; Do not yield the entire enterprise! (From a naval expression.) ☐ BILL: *I'm having a devil of a time with calculus. I think I want to drop the course.* SALLY: *Keep trying. Don't give up the ship!* ☐ BILL: *Every time we get enough money saved up to make a down payment on a house, the price of houses skyrockets. I'm about ready to stop trying.* SUE: *We'll manage. Don't give up the ship!*

Don't give up too eas(il)y! AND **Don't give up without a fight!** Do not yield so easily.; Keep struggling and you may win.; Do not give up too soon. ☐ SUE: *She says no every time I ask her for a raise.* MARY: *Well, don't give up too easily. Keep after her.* ☐ JOHN: *I know it's my discovery, not hers, but she won't admit it.* SALLY: *Don't give up without a fight.*

Don't give up without a fight. See the previous entry.

Don't hold your breath. Do not stop breathing while you are waiting for something to happen. (Meaning that it will take longer for it to happen than you can possibly hold your breath.) ☐ TOM: *The front yard is such a mess.* BOB: *Bill's supposed to rake the leaves.* TOM: *Don't hold your breath. He never does his share of the work.* ☐ SALLY: *Someone said that gasoline prices would go down.* BOB: *Oh, yeah? Don't hold your breath.*

Don't I know it! I know that very well! ☐ MARY: *Goodness gracious! It's hot today.* BOB: *Don't I know it!* ☐ SUE: *You seem to be putting on a little weight.* JOHN: *Don't I know it!*

Don't I know you from somewhere? a way of striking up a conversation with a stranger, probably at a party or other gathering. □ BILL: *Don't I know you from somewhere?* MARY: *I don't think so. Where did you go to school?* □ HENRY: *Don't I know you from somewhere?* ALICE: *No, and let's keep it that way.*

Don't let someone or something get you down. Don't let someone or something bother you. □ TOM: *I'm so mad at her I could scream!* SUE: *Don't let her get you down.* □ JOHN: *This project at work is getting to be a real mess.* JANE: *Don't let it get you down. It will be over with soon.*

Don't let the bastards wear you down. Don't let those people get the best of you. (Exercise caution with *bastard*.) □ BILL: *The place I work at is really rough. Everybody is rude and jealous of each other.* TOM: *Don't let the bastards wear you down.* □ JANE: *I have to go down to the county clerk's office and figure out what this silly bureaucratic letter means.* SUE: *You might call them on the phone. In any case, don't let the bastards wear you down.*

Don't make me laugh! Do not make such ridiculous statements; they only make me laugh. (Compare to *You make me laugh!*) □ MARY: *I'll be a millionaire by the time I'm thirty.* TOM: *Don't make me laugh!* MARY: *I will! I will!* □ MARY: *I'm trying out for cheerleader.* SUE: *You, a cheerleader? Don't make me laugh!*

Don't make me no nevermind. See *(It) don't bother me none.*

Don't make me say it again! AND **Don't make me tell you again!** I have told you once, and now I'm mad, and I'll be madder if I have to tell you again. (Typically said to a child who will not mind.) □ MOTHER: *I told you thirty minutes ago to clean up this room! Don't make me tell you again!* CHILD: *Okay. I'll do it.* □ BILL: *No, Sue, I will not buy you a beach house. Don't make me say it again!* SUE: *Are you sure?*

Don't make me tell you again! See the previous entry.

Don't mind if I do. See *(I) don't mind if I do.*

Don't mind me. Don't pay any attention to me.; Just ignore me. (Sometimes sarcastic.) □ *Bill and Jane were watching television when*

Jane's mother walked through the room, grabbing the newspaper on the way. "Don't mind me," she said. □ *Bob was sitting at the table and Mary and Bill started up this sort of quiet and personal conversation. Bob stared off into space and said, "Don't mind me." Bill and Mary didn't even notice.*

Don't push (me)! Don't put pressure on me to do something! (Also a literal meaning.) □ SUE: *You really must go to the dentist, you know.* JOHN: *Don't push me. I'll go when I'm good and ready.* □ BOB: *Come on! You can finish. Keep trying.* BILL: *Don't push me! I have to do it under my own steam!*

Don't quit trying. See *Keep (on) trying.*

Don't rush me! Don't try to hurry me! □ BILL: *Hurry up! Make up your mind!* BOB: *Don't rush me!* BILL: *I want to get out of here before midnight.* □ BILL: *The waiter wants to take your order. What do you want?* JANE: *Don't rush me! I can't make up my mind.* WAITER: *I'll come back in a minute.*

Don't say it! I don't want to hear it!; I know, so you don't have to say it. □ JOHN (joking): *What is that huge pile of stuff on your head?* BILL: *Don't say it! I know I need a haircut.* □ FRED: *And then I'll trade that car in on a bigger one, and then I'll buy a bigger house.* BOB: *Fred!* FRED: *Oh, don't say it!* BOB: *You're a dreamer, Fred.* FRED: *I had hoped you wouldn't say that.*

Don't see you much around here anymore. See *(We) don't see you much around here anymore.*

Don't speak too soon. I think you may be wrong. Don't speak before you know the facts. (Compare to *Don't be too sure.*) □ BILL: *It looks like it'll be a nice day.* MARY: *Don't speak too soon. I just felt a raindrop.* □ TOM: *It looks like we made it home without any problems.* BILL: *Don't speak too soon, there's a cop behind us in the driveway.*

Don't spend it all in one place. a catch phrase said after giving someone some money, especially a small amount of money. □ FRED: *Dad, can I have a dollar?* FATHER: *Sure. Here. Don't spend it all in one place.* □ *"Here's a quarter, kid," said Tom, flipping Fred a quarter. "Don't spend it all in one place."* □ ALICE: *Here's the five hundred dollars I owe you.* TOM: *Oh, thanks. I need this.* ALICE: *Thank you. Don't spend it all in one place.* TOM: *I have to or they'll take my car back.*

Don't stand on ceremony. Do not wait for a formal invitation.; Please be at ease and make yourself at home. (Some people read this as "Don't remain standing because of ceremony," and others read it "Don't be totally obedient to the requirements of ceremony.") □ JOHN: *Come in, Tom. Don't stand on ceremony. Get yourself a drink and something to eat and mingle with the other guests.* TOM: *Okay, but I can only stay for a few minutes.* □ *"Don't stand on ceremony, Fred,"* urged Sally. "Go around and introduce yourself to everyone."

Don't stay away so long. Please visit more often. (Said upon the arrival or departure of a guest.) □ JOHN: *Hi, Bill! Long time no see. Don't stay away so long!* BILL: *Thanks, John. Good to see you.* □ MARY: *I had a nice time. Thanks for inviting me.* SALLY: *Good to see you, Mary. Next time, don't stay away so long.*

Don't sweat it! Don't worry about it. (Slang.) □ BILL: *I think I'm flunking algebra!* BOB: *Don't sweat it! Everybody's having a rough time.* □ MARY: *Good grief! I just stepped on the cat's tail, but I guess you heard.* SUE: *Don't sweat it! The cat's got to learn to keep out of the way.*

Don't tell a soul. Please do not tell anyone this gossip. □ BILL: *Is your brother getting married?* SALLY: *Yes, but don't tell a soul. It's a secret.* □ MARY: *Can you keep a secret?* JOHN: *Sure.* MARY: *Don't tell a soul, but Tom is in jail.*

Don't tell me what to do! Do not give me orders. □ BOB: *Get over there and pick up those papers before they blow away.* SALLY: *Don't tell me what to do!* BOB: *Better hurry. One of those papers is your paycheck. But it's no skin off my nose if you don't.* □ SUE: *Next, you should get a haircut, then get some new clothes. You really need to fix yourself up.* SALLY: *Don't tell me what to do! Maybe I like me the way I am!*

Don't think so. See *I guess not.*

Don't waste my time. Do not take up my valuable time with a poor presentation.; Do not waste my time trying to get me to do something. □ BOB: *I'd like to show you our new line of industrial strength vacuum cleaners.* BILL: *Beat it! Don't waste my time.* □ *"Don't waste my time!"* said the manager when Jane made her fourth appeal for a raise.

Don't waste your breath. You will not get a positive response to what you have to say, so don't even say it.; Talking will get you nowhere. □ ALICE: *I'll go in there and try to convince her otherwise.*

FRED: *Don't waste your breath. I already tried it.* □ SALLY: *No, I won't agree! Don't waste your breath.* BILL: *Aw, come on.*

Don't waste your time. You will not get anywhere with it, so don't waste time trying. □ MARY: *Should I ask Tom if he wants to go to the convention, or is he still in a bad mood?* SALLY: *Don't waste your time.* MARY: *Bad mood, huh?* □ JANE: *I'm having trouble fixing this door-knob.* MARY: *Don't waste your time. I've ordered a new one.*

Don't work too hard. an expression said at the end of a conversation after or in place of *good-bye.* □ MARY: *Bye, Tom.* TOM: *Bye, Mary. Don't work too hard.* □ SUE: *Don't work too hard!* MARY: *I never do.*

Don't worry. Do not become anxious, everything will be all right. □ *"Don't worry, Fred," comforted Bill, "everything will be all right."* □ BILL: *I think I left the car windows open.* SUE: *Don't worry, I closed them.*

Don't worry about a thing. Everything will be taken care of. Do not be anxious. □ MARY: *This has been such an ordeal.* SUE: *I'll help. Don't worry about a thing.* □ *"Don't worry about a thing," the tax collector had said. "We'll take care of everything." Or was it "We'll take everything?"*

Don't you know? **1.** Don't you know the answer?; I don't know, I thought you did. □ MARY: *How do I get to the Morris Building? Where do I turn?* JANE: *Don't you know? I have no idea!* □ SUE: *We're supposed to either sign these contracts or rewrite them. Which is it?* JOHN: *Don't you know?* **2.** AND **Don't you see?** Do you understand?; Do you see? (Usually pronounced *doan-cha know*, often without rising question intonation. Typically, nothing more than a call for some quick response from the person being talked to.) □ JOHN: *This whole thing can be straightened out with hardly any trouble at all, don't you know?* SUE: *What makes you so sure?* JOHN: *I've had this same problem before.* □ BILL: *Why are you stopping the car?* JOHN: *We usually stop here for the night, don't you know?* BILL: *I know a better place down the road.*

Don't you know it! You can be absolutely sure about that!; You're exactly right, and I agree with you. (This is not a question.) □ ALICE: *Man, is it hot!* FRED: *Don't you know it!* □ BOB: *This is the* *best cake I have ever eaten. The cook is the best in the world!* BILL: *Don't you know it!*

(Don't you) see? See under *Don't you know?*

(Don't) you wish! Don't you wish that what you have just said were really true? □ MARY: *I'm going to get a job that lets me travel a lot.* SALLY: *Don't you wish!* □ SALLY: *Sorry you lost the chess game. It was close, but your opponent was top-notch.* BOB: *Next time, I'll do it! I'll win the next round.* SALLY: *Don't you wish!*

Do sit down. *Don't stand on ceremony.; please sit down.* (A polite phrase encouraging people to resume their seats after rising for an introduction or out of deference.) □ *Tom rose when Mary approached the table, but she said graciously, "Do sit down. I just wanted to thank you again for the lovely gift."* □ TOM: *Hello, Bill.* BILL (rising): *Hi, Tom.* TOM (standing): *Do sit down. I just wanted to say hello.*

Do tell. a response to one of a series of statements by another person. (The expression can indicate disinterest. Each word has equal stress. See also *You don't say.*) □ BILL: *The Amazon basin is about ten times the size of France.* MARY: *Do tell.* □ FRED: *Most large ships produce their own fresh water.* SUE: *Do tell. Say, Fred, has anyone ever told you how interesting you are?* FRED: *No.* SUE: *I suspected as much.*

Do we have to go through all that again? Do we have to discuss that matter again? (Compare to *Let's not go through all that again.*) □ BILL: *Now, I still have more to say about what happened last night.* SALLY: *Do we have to go through all that again?* □ SALLY: *I can't get over the way you treated me at our own dinner table.* FRED: *I was irritated at something else. I said I was sorry. Do we have to go through all that again?*

Down the hatch! See *Bottoms up.*

(Do you) care if I join you? See *Could I join you?*

Do you expect me to believe that? That is so unbelievable that you do not expect me to believe it, do you? (A bit impatient. Compare to *You can't expect me to believe that.*) □ BILL: *I'm going to quit my job and open a restaurant.* MARY: *That's silly. Do you expect me to be-*

lieve that? BILL: *I guess not.* □ MARY: *Wow! I just got selected to be an astronaut!* SALLY: *Do you expect me to believe that?* MARY: *Here's the letter! Now do you believe me?*

Do you follow? Do you understand what I am saying?; Do you understand my explanation? □ MARY: *Keep to the right past the fork in the road, then turn right at the crossroads. Do you follow?* JANE: *No. Run it by me again.* □ JOHN: *Take a large bowl and break two eggs into it and beat them. Do you follow?* SUE: *Sure.*

(Do you) get my drift? AND **(Do you) get the message?** Do you understand what I mean?; Do you understand what I am getting at? (Slang.) □ FATHER: *I want you to settle down and start studying. Get my drift?* BOB: *Sure, Pop. Whatever you say.* □ MARY: *Get out of my way and stop following me around. Get the message?* JOHN: *I guess so.*

(Do you) get the message? See the previous entry.

(Do you) get the picture? Do you understand the situation?; Do you know what this means you have to do? □ BILL: *I want to get this project wrapped up before midnight. Do you get the picture?* TOM: *I'm afraid I do.* BILL: *Well, then, get to work.* □ FRED: *I'm really tired of all this. Get the picture? I want you to straighten up and get moving. Get the picture?* BILL: *I got it.*

(Do) you hear? Do you hear and understand what I said? (Typically southern.) □ JOHN: *I want you to clean up this room this instant! Do you hear?* SUE: *Okay. I'll get right on it.* □ BOB: *Come over here, Sue. I want to show you something, you hear?* SUE: *Sure. What is it?*

(Do you) know what? AND **You know what?** an expression used to open a conversation or switch to a new topic. □ BOB: *You know what?* MARY: *No, what?* BOB: *I think this milk is spoiled.* □ BOB: *Know what?* BILL: *Tell me.* BOB: *Your hair needs cutting.* BILL: *So what?*

(Do you) know what I mean? See the following entry.

(Do you) know what I'm saying? AND **You know (what I'm saying)?; (Do you) know what I mean?; You know what I mean?** Do you understand me?; Do you agree? (The *You know?* is frowned on by many people.) □ JOHN: *This is really great* *for me and the whole group. You know?* SUE: *Yes, I know.* □ SUE: *This is, like, really great! Do you know what I'm saying?* MARY: *Yeah, I've been there. It's great.*

(Do) you mean to say something? AND **(Do) you mean to tell me something?** Are you really saying something? (A way of giving someone an opportunity to alter a comment. The *something* represents a quote or a paraphrase.) □ MARY: *I'm leaving tomorrow.* SALLY: *Do you mean to say you're leaving school for good?* MARY: *Yes.* □ BOB: *Do you mean to tell me that this is all you've accomplished in two weeks?* BILL: *I guess so.* BOB: *I expected more.*

(Do) you mean to tell me something? See the previous entry.

Do you mind? **1.** You are intruding on my space!; You are offending me! (Impatient or incensed. Essentially, "Do you mind stopping what you are doing?") □ *The lady behind her in line kept pushing against her every time the line moved. Finally, Sue turned and said sternly, "Do you mind?"* □ *All through the first part of the movie, two people in the row behind John kept up a running conversation. Finally, as the din grew loud enough to cause a number of people to go "shhh," John rose and turned, leaned over into their faces, and shouted, "Do you mind?"* **2.** Do you object to what I am poised to do? □ *Mary had her hand on the lovely silver cake knife that would carry the very last piece of cake to her plate. She looked at Tom, who stood next to her, eyeing the cake. "Do you mind?" she asked coyly.* □ *"Do you mind?" asked John as he raced by Sally through the door.*

(do you) mind if? a polite way of seeking someone's permission or agreement. (See examples.) □ MARY: *Do you mind if I sit here?* JANE: *No, help yourself.* □ TOM: *Mind if I smoke?* BILL: *I certainly do.* TOM: *Then I'll go outside.*

(Do you) mind if I join you? See *Could I join you?*

Do you read me? **1.** an expression used by someone communicating by radio, asking if the hearer understands the transmission clearly. □ CONTROLLER: *This is Aurora Center, do you read me?* PILOT: *Yes, I read you loud and clear.* □ CONTROLLER: *Left two degrees. Do you read me?* PILOT: *Roger.* **2.** Do you understand what I am telling you? (Used in general conversation, not in radio communication.) □ MARY: *I want you to pull yourself together and go out and get a job. Do you read me?* BILL: *Sure. Anything you say.* □ MOTHER: *Get this place picked up immediately. Do you read me?* CHILD: *Yes, ma'am.*

(Do you) want to know something? AND **(You want to) know something?** an expression used to open a conversation or switch to a new topic. □ JOHN: *Want to know something?* SUE: *What?* JOHN: *Your hem is torn.* □ BILL: *Hey, Tom! Know something?* TOM: *What is it?* BILL: *It's really hot today.* TOM: *Don't I know it!*

(Do you) want to make something of it? AND **You want to make something of it?** Do you want to start a fight about it? (Rude and contentious.) □ TOM: *You're really bugging me. It's not fair to pick on me all the time.* BILL: *You want to make something of it?* □ BOB: *Please be quiet. You're making too much noise.* FRED: *Do you want to make something of it?* BOB: *Just be quiet.*

(Do) you want to step outside? an expression inviting someone to go out of doors to settle an argument by fighting. □ JOHN: *Drop dead!* BOB: *All right, I've had enough out of you. You want to step outside?* □ BILL: *So you're mad at me! What else is new? You've been building up to this for a long time.* BOB: *Do you want to step outside and settle this once and for all?* BILL: *Why not?*

Drive safely. an expression used to advise a departing person to be careful while driving. □ MARY: *Good-bye, Sally. Drive safely.* SALLY: *Good-bye. I will.* □ *"Drive safely!" everyone shouted as we left on our trip.*

Drop by for a drink (sometime). AND **Drop by sometime.; Drop over sometime.** a casual invitation for someone to pay a visit. (This probably is not meant literally. It leaves an opening for invitations from either party.) □ BOB: *Good to see you, Mary. Drop by for a drink sometime.* MARY: *Love to. Bye.* □ *"Drop by sometime, stranger," said Bill to his old friend, Sally.*

Drop by sometime. See the previous entry.

Drop in sometime. Visit my home or office sometime when you are nearby. □ BOB: *Bye, Bill, nice seeing you.* BILL: *Hey, drop in sometime.* BOB: *Okay.* BILL: *Great! Bye.* □ *"Drop in sometime," said Bob to his uncle.*

Drop it! See *Drop the subject!*

Drop me a line. Communicate with me by telephone or mail and tell me your news. □ JOHN: *If you get into our area, drop me a line.* FRED: *I sure will, John.* JOHN: *Bye.* □ MARY: *I'm going to Cleveland for a few days.* SUE: *Drop me a line when you get there.* MARY: *I will. Bye.*

Drop me a note. Communicate with me by mail, and let me know what is going on with you. □ MARY: *I'm off for Brazil. Good-bye.* SALLY: *Have a good time. Drop me a note.* □ *"Drop me a note from France," said Bill, waving good-bye.*

Drop over sometime. See *Drop by for a drink (sometime).*

Drop the subject! AND **Drop it!** Do not discuss it further! □ BILL: *Yes, you're gaining a little weight. I thought you were on a diet.* SALLY: *That's enough! Drop the subject!* □ BILL: *That house looks expensive. What do you think it's worth?* MARY: *That's my aunt's house. Just what did you want to know about it?* BILL: *Oh, drop it! Sorry I asked.*

E

Easy does it. **1.** Move slowly and carefully. □ BILL (holding one end of a large crate): *It's really tight in this doorway.* BOB (holding the other end): *Easy does it. Take your time.* □ NURSE (holding Sue's arm): *Easy does it. These first few steps are the hardest.* SUE: *I didn't know I was so weak.* **2.** Calm down.; Don't lose your temper. □ JOHN: *I'm so mad I could scream.* BOB: *Easy does it, John. No need to get so worked up.* JOHN: *I'm still mad!* □ SUE (frantic): *Where is my camera? My passport is gone too!* FRED: *Easy does it, Sue. I think you have someone else's purse.*

Enjoy! I hope you enjoy what you are going to do.; I hope you enjoy what I have served you to eat.; I hope you enjoy life in general. □ *"Here's your coffee, dear," said Fred. "Enjoy!"* □ SUE: *What a beautiful day! Good-bye.* TOM: *Good-bye. Enjoy!*

Enjoy your meal. an expression used by food service personnel after the food has been served. □ *The waiter set the plates on the table, smiled, and said, "Enjoy your meal."* □ WAITER: *Here's your dinner.* JANE: *Oh, this lobster looks lovely!* TOM: *My steak looks just perfect.* WAITER: *Enjoy your meal.*

Enough is enough! That is enough! I won't stand for any more! □ SUE: *That color of lipstick is all wrong for you, Sally.* SALLY: *Enough is enough! Sue, get lost!* SUE: *I was just trying to help.* □ BOB: *Enough is enough! I'm leaving!* BILL: *What on earth did I do?* BOB: *Good-bye.*

Enough (of this) foolishness! See *(That's) enough (of this) foolishness!*

Evening. See *(Good) evening.*

Everything okay? See *(Is) everything okay?*

Everything's going to be all right. AND **Everything will be all right.** Do not worry, everything will be okay. (A number of other expressions can be substituted for *all right*, such as *okay, just fine, great*, etc.) □ *"Don't worry, Fred,"* comforted Bill. *"Everything will be all right."* □ MARY: *I just don't know if I can go on!* BOB: *Now, now. Everything will be just fine.*

Everything will work out (all right). See *Things will work out (all right).*

Everything will work out for the best. See *Things will work out (all right).*

Excellent! Great!; Fine! □ BOB: *What's happening?* FRED: *Hi! I'm getting a new car.* BOB: *Excellent!* □ BOB: *All the players are here and ready to go.* SUE: *Excellent!* BOB: *When do we start the game?*

Excuse me. AND **Excuse, please.; Pardon (me).; 'Scuse (me); 'Scuse, please.** (*'Scuse* is colloquial, and the apostrophe is not always used.) **1.** an expression asking forgiveness for some minor social violation, such as belching or bumping into someone. □ JOHN: *Ouch!* BOB: *Excuse me. I didn't see you there.* □ MARY: *Oh! Ow!* SUE: *Pardon me. I didn't mean to bump into you.* □ TOM: *Ouch!* MARY: *Oh, dear! What happened?* TOM: *You stepped on my toe.* MARY: *Excuse me. I'm sorry.* **2.** Please let me through.; Please let me by. □ TOM: *Excuse me. I need to get past.* BOB: *Oh, sorry. I didn't know I was in the way.* □ MARY: *Pardon me.* SUE: *What?* MARY: *Pardon me. I want to get past you.*

Excuse me? AND **Pardon (me)?; 'Scuse me?** What do you mean by that last remark?; *I beg your pardon?* (Shows amazement at someone's rudeness.) □ MARY: *Your policies seem quite inflexible to me.* BILL: *Excuse me?* □ BOB: *These silly people are getting on my nerves.* MARY: *Pardon me?*

Excuse, please. See *Excuse me.*

F

Fair to middling. a response to a greeting inquiry into the state of one's health. (Colloquial and folksy.) □ JOHN: *How are you doing?* BOB: *Oh, fair to middling, I guess. And you?* JOHN: *Things could be worse.* □ BILL: *How are you feeling?* JANE: *Oh, fair to middling, thanks.* BILL: *Still a little under the weather, huh?* JANE: *Just a little.*

Fancy meeting you here! I am very surprised to meet you here! (A catch phrase.) □ TOM: *Hi, Sue! Fancy meeting you here!* SUE: *Hi, Tom. I was thinking the same thing about you.* □ *"Fancy meeting you here," said Mr. Franklin when he bumped into Mrs. Franklin at the race-track.*

Fancy that! AND **Imagine that!** I am very surprised to hear that.; That is hard to imagine or believe. □ MARY: *My father was elected president of the board.* SALLY: *Fancy that!* □ SUE: *This computer is ten times faster than the one we had before.* JANE: *Imagine that! Is it easy to operate?* SUE: *Of course not.*

far as I know See *(as) far as I know.*

far as I'm concerned See *(as) far as I'm concerned.*

Farewell. *Good-bye.* □ MARY: *See you later, Bill.* BILL: *Farewell, my dear.* MARY: *Take care.* □ BOB: *Have a good trip.* SUE: *Farewell, Bob.* BOB: *Don't do anything I wouldn't do.*

Feeling okay. See *(Are you) feeling okay?; (I'm) feeling okay.*

Fill in the blanks.   You can figure out the rest.; You can draw a conclusion from that. □ MARY: *What happened at Fred's house last night?* BILL: *There was a big fight, then the neighbors called the police.* MARY: *Then what happened?* BILL: *Fill in the blanks. What do you think?* □ JOHN: *They had been lost for two days, then the wolves came, and the rest is history.* JANE: *Yes, I think I can fill in the blanks.*

Fine by me.   See *(That's) fine with me.*

Fine with me.   See *(That's) fine with me.*

first of all   first, and perhaps, most important. □ *"First of all, let me say how happy I am to be here,"* said Fred, beginning his speech. □ HENRY: *How much is all this going to cost, Doctor?* DOCTOR: *First of all, do you have any insurance?*

for all intents and purposes   seeming as if; looking as if. □ *Tom stood there, looking, for all intents and purposes, as if he were going to strangle Sally, but, being the gentleman that he is, he just glowered.* □ MARY: *Is this finished now?* JOHN: *For all intents and purposes, yes.*

For crying in a bucket!   See the following entry.

For crying out loud! AND **For crying in a bucket!**   an exclamation of shock, anger, or surprise. □ FRED: *For crying out loud! Answer the telephone!* BOB: *But it's always for you!* □ JOHN: *Good grief! What am I going to do? This is the end!* SUE: *For crying in a bucket! What's wrong?*

Forget (about) it!   1. *Drop the subject!; Never mind!;* Don't bother me with it. □ JANE: *Then, there's this matter of the unpaid bills.* BILL: *Forget it!* □ SALLY: *What's this I hear about you and Tom?* SUE: *Forget about it!* 2. *Nothing.* □ SUE: *What did you say?* MARY: *Forget it!* □ TOM: *Now I'm ready to go.* SUE: *Excuse me?* TOM: *Oh, nothing. Just forget it.* 3. *You're welcome.; It was nothing.* □ JOHN: *Thank you so much for helping me!* BILL: *Oh, forget it!* □ BOB: *We're all very grateful to you for coming into work today.* MARY: *Forget about it! No problem!*

For Pete('s) sake(s)!   See the following entry.

For pity('s) sake(s)! AND **For Pete('s) sake(s)!** a mild exclamation of surprise or shock. (The extra *(s)* is colloquial.) □ FRED: *For pity's sake. What on earth is this?* ALICE: *It's just a kitten.* □ JOHN: *Good grief! What am I going to do? This is the end!* SUE: *What is it now, for Pete's sake?*

For shame! That is shameful! □ SUE: *Did you hear that Tom was in jail?* FRED: *For shame! What did he do?* SUE: *Nobody knows.* □ MARY: *I've decided not to go to the conference.* JOHN: *For shame! Who will represent us?*

For sure. Yes.; *Certainly.* (Colloquial.) □ SALLY: *Are you ready to go?* BOB: *For sure.* SALLY: *Then, let's go.* □ JANE: *Are you coming with us?* JOHN: *For sure. I wouldn't miss this for the world.*

for what it's worth a phrase added to a piece of information. □ MARY: *What do you think about it, Fred?* FRED: *Well, let me tell you something, for what it's worth.* □ JOHN: *For what it's worth, you're doing great!* SUE: *Thanks! It's worth a lot!*

for your information a phrase that introduces or follows a piece of information. (Can be spoken with considerable impatience.) □ MARY: *What is this one?* SUE: *For your information, it is exactly the same as the one you just asked about.* □ BOB: *How long do I have to wait here?* BILL: *For your information, we will be here until the bus driver feels that it is safe to travel.*

'Fraid not. See *(I'm) afraid not.*

'Fraid so. See *(I'm) afraid so.*

frankly See *(speaking) (quite) frankly.*

frankly speaking See *(speaking) (quite) frankly.*

Fret not! *Don't worry!;* Do not fret about it! □ MARY: *Oh, look at the clock! I'm going to be late for my appointment!* BOB: *Fret not! I'll drive you.* □ *"Fret not!" said Sally. "We're almost there!"*

from my perspective AND **from where I stand; from my point of view; the way I see it** a phrase used to introduce one's own opinion. □ MARY: *What do you think of all this?* TOM: *From my perspective, it is just terrible.* □ BOB: *From my point of view, this looks like a very good deal.* BILL: *That's good for you. I stand to lose money on it.* □ ALICE: *From where I stand, it appears that you're going to have to pay a lot of money to get this matter settled.* SUE: *I'll pay anything. I just want to get all this behind me.*

from my point of view See the previous entry.

from where I stand See *from my perspective.*

G

Gangway! *Clear the way!;* Get out of the way! □ *"Gangway!" cried Fred. "Here comes the band!"* □ TOM: *Please move so we can get by.* BOB: *You'll never get anywhere with that. Gangway! Gangway! Gangway!*

gee an exclamation expressing disappointment, disagreement, surprise, or other emotions. (Words such as this often use intonation to convey the connotation of the sentence that is to follow. The brief intonation pattern accompanying the word may indicate sarcasm, disagreement, caution, consolation, sternness, etc.) □ *"Gee, why not?" whined Billy.* □ BILL: *Gee, I really want to go.* JANE: *Well then, go ahead and go!* □ JOHN: *Gee, Tom, I'm sort of surprised.* TOM: *You shouldn't be.* □ ALICE: *Gee, I thought you were gone.* BOB: *No, I'm still here.*

Get back to me (on this). Report back to me. (Often a deadline is added.) □ TOM: *Here's a contract for you to go over. Get back to me on this by Monday morning.* MARY: *Sure thing, Tom.* □ ALICE: *When you have this thing figured out, get back to me, and we'll talk.* TOM: *Righto.*

Get lost! *Go away!;* Stop bothering me! □ BILL: *I'm still real mad at you.* TOM: *Bill! Bill! I'm sorry about it. Let's talk.* BILL: *Get lost!* □ *Fred kicked his foot at the dog behind him and said, "Get lost, you worthless mutt!"*

Get my drift? See *(Do you) get my drift?*

Get off my back! Stop harassing me!; Leave me alone about this matter! (Slang.) □ TOM: *You'd better get your paper written.* BILL: *I'll do it when I'm good and ready. Get off my back!* □ ALICE: *I'm tired of your constant criticism! Get off my back!* JANE: *I was just trying to help.*

Get off my tail! **1.** Stop following me!; Stop following me so closely! (Slang.) □ *There was a car following too close, and Tom shouted into the rearview mirror, "Get off my tail!"* □ TOM: *Look, Bill. Don't you have something else to do? Quit following me around! Get off my tail!* BILL: *Can I help it if we both go the same places?* **2.** Get off my back! □ TOM: *You'd better get your laundry done.* BILL: *I'll do it when I'm good and ready. Get off my tail!* □ BILL: *Get off my tail! I don't need a watchdog!* JANE: *You do too.*

Get out of here! *Go away!*; Leave this place! □ JOHN: *I've heard enough of this! Get out of here!* BILL: *I'm going! I'm going!* □ BILL: *Where have you been? You smell like a sewer! Get out of here!* FRED: *I can't imagine what you smell.*

Get out of my face! Go away and stop bothering me!; Get yourself away from me! □ ALICE: *Beat it! Get out of my face! Go away and stop bothering me!* FRED: *What on earth did I do?* □ BILL: *You really think I'll buy something that has been copied?* BOB: *I want you to give my proposal some thought.* BILL: *Get out of my face! I'll never buy something that's stolen!*

Get the lead out! AND **Shake the lead out!** *Hurry up!* (Slang. As if slowed down by lead in one's pockets or somewhere else.) □ *"Move it, you guys!" hollered the coach. "Shake the lead out!"* □ BOB: *Get the lead out, you loafer!* BILL: *Don't rush me!*

Get the message? See *(Do you) get my drift?*

Get the picture? See *(Do you) get the picture?*

Get your nose out of my business. See *Mind your own business.*

Get you something (to drink)? See *(Could I) get you something (to drink)?*

Give it a rest! Stop talking so much. Give your mouth a rest. (Familiar or rude. Compare to *Give me a rest!*) □ MARY: *So, I really think we need to discuss things more and go over all our differences in detail. You never seem to want to talk. You just sit there, staring straight ahead.* BILL: *Okay, I've heard enough. Give it a rest!* MARY: *Oh, am I disturbing you?* □ TOM: *Now, I would also like to say something else.* ALICE: *Give it a rest, Tom. We're tired of listening to you.*

Give it up! Stop trying. You are wasting your time. (Informal.) □ BOB: *Today was too much! I just can't do calculus!* BILL: *Give it up! Get*

out of that course and get into something less cruel. BOB: *I think I will.* □
TOM: *I'm just not a very good singer, I guess.* SUE: *It's no good, Tom. Give
it up!* TOM: *Don't you think I'm doing better, though?* SUE: *Give it up,
Tom!*

Give me a break! **1.** Please *give me a chance!*; Please give me another chance! □ BOB: *I know I can do it. Let me try again.* MARY:
Well, I don't know. BOB: *Give me a break!* MARY: *Well, okay.* □ *"Give
me a break!" cried Mary to the assistant director. "I know I can handle the
part."* **2.** I have had enough! Drop this matter!; Stop bothering
me! □ TOM: *Now I'm going to sing a song about the hill people in my
country.* MARY: *Give me a break! Sing something I know!* □ *"Give me a
break!" shouted Bob. "Go away and stop bother me!"*

Give me a call. AND **Give me a ring.** Please call me (later) on the
telephone. □ MARY: *See you later, Fred.* FRED: *Give me a call if you
get a chance.* □ *"When you're in town again, Sue, give me a call," said
John.* □ BOB: *When should we talk about this again?* BILL: *Next week
is soon enough. Give me a ring.*

Give me a chance! **1.** Please give me an opportunity to do something! □ MARY: *I just know I can do it. Oh, please give me a chance!*
SUE: *All right. Just one more chance.* □ BOB: *Do you think you can do
it?* JANE: *Oh, I know I can. Just give me a chance!* **2.** Please give me a
fair chance and enough time to complete the task. □ ALICE:
Come on! I need more time. Give me a chance! JANE: *Would another ten
minutes help?* □ BOB: *You missed that one!* BILL: *You moved it! There
was no way I could hit it. Give me a chance! Hold it still!*

Give me a rest! Stop being such a pest!; Stop bothering me with
this problem! (Compare to *Give it a rest!*) □ *"Go away and stop
bothering me!" moaned Bob. "Give me a rest!"* □ BOB: *I need an answer
to this right away!* BILL: *I just gave you an answer!* BOB: *That was something different. This is a new question.* BILL: *Give me a rest! Can't it wait?*

Give me a ring. See *Give me a call.*

Give me five! AND **Give me (some) skin!; Skin me!; Slip me five!;
Slip me some skin!** Shake my hand!; Slap my hand in greeting!
(Slang.) □ *"Yo, Tom! Give me five!" shouted Henry, raising his hand.*
□ BOB: *Hey, man! Skin me!* BILL: *How you doing, Bob?*

Give me (some) skin! See the previous entry.

Give my best to someone. AND **All the best to someone.** Please convey my good wishes to a particular person. (The *someone* can be a person's name or a pronoun. See also *Say hello to someone (for me).*) □ ALICE: *Good-bye, Fred. Give my best to your mother.* FRED: *Sure, Alice. Good-bye.* □ TOM: *See you, Bob.* BOB: *Give my best to Jane.* TOM: *I sure will. Bye.* □ BILL: *Bye, Rachel. All the best to your family.* RACHEL: *Thanks. Bye.*

Give you a lift? See *(Could I) give you a lift?*

Glad to hear it. See *(I'm) glad to hear it.*

Glad to meet you. See *(I'm) (very) glad to meet you.*

Glad you could come. See *(I'm) glad you could come.*

Glad you could drop by. See *(I'm) glad you could drop by.*

Glad you could stop by. See *(I'm) glad you could drop by.*

Glory be! an exclamation expressing surprise or shock. (A bit old-fashioned.) □ MARY: *Glory be! Is that what I think it is?* SUE: *Well, it's a kitten, if that's what you thought.* □ SALLY: *First a car just missed hitting her, then she fell down on the ice.* MARY: *Glory be!*

Go ahead. Please do it.; You have my permission and encouragement to do it. □ ALICE: *I'm leaving.* JOHN: *Go ahead. See if I care.* □ JANE: *Can I put this one in the refrigerator?* JANE: *Sure. Go ahead.*

(Go ahead,) make my day! **1.** Just try to do me harm or disobey me. I will enjoy punishing you. (From a phrase said in a movie where the person saying the phrase is holding a gun on a villain and would really like the villain to do something that would justify firing the gun. Now a cliché. Compare to *Keep it up!*) □ *The crook reached into his jacket for his wallet. The cop, thinking the crook was about to draw a gun, said, "Go ahead, make my day!"* □ *As Bill pulled back his clenched fist to strike Tom, who is much bigger and stronger than Bill, Tom said, "Make my day!"* **2.** Go ahead, ruin my day!; Go ahead, give me the bad news. (A sarcastic version of sense 1.) □

TOM (standing in the doorway): *Hello, I'm with the Internal Revenue Service. Could I come in?* MARY: *Go ahead, make my day!* □ SALLY: *I've got some bad news for you.* JOHN: *Go ahead, make my day!*

Go away! Leave me!; Get away from me! □ MARY: *You're such a pest, Sue. Go away!* SUE: *I was just trying to help.* □ *"Go away!" yelled the child at the bee.*

Go chase yourself! AND **Go climb a tree!; Go fly a kite!; Go jump in the lake!** Go away and stop bothering me! □ BOB: *Get out of here! You're driving me crazy! Go chase yourself!* BILL: *What did I do to you?* BOB: *You're just in the way. Go!* □ BILL: *Dad, can I have ten bucks?* FATHER: *Go climb a tree!* □ FRED: *Stop pestering me. Go jump in the lake!* JOHN: *What did I do?* □ BOB: *Well, Bill, don't you owe me some money?* BILL: *Go fly a kite!*

Go climb a tree! See the previous entry.

God forbid! a phrase expressing the desire that God would forbid the situation that the speaker has just mentioned from ever happening. □ TOM: *It looks like taxes are going up again.* BOB: *God forbid!* □ BOB: *Bill was in a car wreck. I hope he wasn't hurt!* SUE: *God forbid!*

God only knows! Only God knows.; No one knows but God. □ TOM: *How long is all this going to take?* ALICE: *God only knows!* □ BOB: *Where are we going to find one hundred thousand dollars?* MARY: *God only knows!*

God willing. an expression indicating that there is a high certainty that something will happen, so high that only God could prevent it. □ JOHN: *Please try to be on time.* ALICE: *I'll be there on time, God willing.* □ BOB: *Will I see you after your vacation?* MARY: *Of course, God willing.*

Go fly a kite! See *Go chase yourself!*

Go for it! *Go ahead!* Give it a good try! □ SALLY: *I'm going to try out for the basketball team. Do you think I'm tall enough?* BOB: *Sure you are! Go for it!* □ BOB: *Mary can't quit now! She's almost at the finish line!* BILL: *Go for it, Mary!* ALICE: *Come on, Mary!*

Going my way? See *(Are you) going my way?*

Go jump in the lake! See *Go chase yourself!*

Golly! an expression of surprise or interest. □ ALICE: *Golly, is it real?* MARY: *Of course it's real!* □ JANE: *Look at the size of that fish!* SUE: *Golly!*

(Good) afternoon. **1.** the appropriate greeting for use between noon and supper time. □ SALLY: *How are you today?* JANE: *Good afternoon. How are you?* SALLY: *Fine, thank you.* □ BOB: *Afternoon. Nice to see you.* BILL: *Good afternoon. How are you?* BOB: *Fine, thanks.* **2.** an expression used on departure or for dismissal between noon and supper time. (Meaning "I wish you a good afternoon.") □ SALLY: *See you later, Bill.* BILL: *Afternoon. See you later.* □ MARY: *Nice to see you.* TOM: *Good afternoon. Take care.*

Good-bye. the standard thing to say when departing. □ SALLY: *It's time to go. Good-bye.* MARY: *Good-bye. See you later.* □ JOHN: *We had a wonderful time. Good-bye.* MARY: *Good-bye, come again.*

good-bye and good riddance a phrase marking the departure of someone or something unwanted. □ FRED: *Supposing I was to just walk out of here, just like that?* MARY: *I'd say good-bye and good riddance.* □ *As the garbage truck drove away, carrying the drab old chair that Mary hated so much, she said, "Good-bye and good riddance."*

Good-bye for now. AND **(Good-bye) until next time.; Till next time.; Till we meet again.; Until we meet again.** Good-bye, I'll see you soon.; Good-bye, I'll see you next time. (Often said by the host at the end of a radio or television program.) □ ALICE: *See you later. Good-bye for now.* JOHN: *Bye, Alice.* □ MARY: *See you later.* BOB: *Good-bye for now.* □ *The host of the talk show always closed by saying, "Good-bye until next time. This is Wally Ott, signing off."*

(Good-bye) until next time. See the previous entry.

(Good-bye) until then. AND **(Good-bye) till then.; (Good-bye) till later.; (Good-bye) until later.** Good-bye until sometime in the future. □ SALLY: *See you tomorrow. Good-bye until then.* SUE: *Sure thing. See you.* □ MARY: *See you later.* BOB: *Until later.* □ *The an-*

nouncer always ended by saying, "Be with us again next week at this time. Good-bye until then."

Good enough.   That's good.; That's adequate.   □ BILL: *Well, now. How's that?* BOB: *Good enough.*   □ BOB: *I'll be there about noon.* BOB: *Good enough. I'll see you then.*

(Good) evening.   **1.** the appropriate greeting for use between supper time and the time of taking leave for the night or by midnight. (Compare to *Good night.*)   □ BOB: *Good evening, Mary. How are you?* MARY: *Evening, Bob. Nice to see you.*   □ *"Good evening," said each of the guests as they passed by Mr. and Mrs. Franklin.* **2.** the appropriate phrase used for leave-taking between supper time and before the time of final leave-taking to go to bed.   □ MARY: *Let's call it a day. See you tomorrow, Bill.* BILL: *Yes, it's been a long and productive day. Good evening, Mary.*   □ BOB: *Nice seeing you, Mr. Wilson.* MR. WILSON: *Good evening, Bob.*

Good for you!   a complimentary expression of encouragement for something that someone has done.   □ SUE: *I just got a raise.* BILL: *Good for you!*   □ JANE: *I really told him what I thought of his rotten behavior.* SUE: *Good for you! He needs it.*

Good grief!   an exclamation of surprise, shock, or amazement.   □ ALICE: *Good grief! I'm late!* MARY: *That clock's fast. You're probably okay on time.*   □ BILL: *There are seven newborn kittens under the sofa!* JANE: *Good grief!*

(Good) heavens!   an exclamation of surprise, shock, or amazement. (See also *(My) heavens!*)   □ JOHN: *Good heavens! A diamond ring!* BILL: *I bet it's not real.*   □ JANE: *Ouch!* JOHN: *Good heavens! What happened?* JANE: *I just stubbed my toe.*

Good job!   See *Nice going!*

Good luck!   **1.** a wish of good fortune to someone.   □ MARY: *I have my recital tonight.* JANE: *I know you'll do well. Good luck!*   □ SALLY: *I hear you're leaving for your new job tomorrow morning.* BOB: *That's right.* SALLY: *Well, good luck!* **2.** You will certainly need luck, but it probably will not work. (Sarcastic.)   □ BILL: *I'm going to try to get this tax bill lowered.* SUE: *Good luck!*   □ BILL: *I'm sure I can get this cheaper at another store.* CLERK: *Good luck!*

(Good) morning. the standard greeting phrase used any time between midnight and noon. □ BOB: *Good morning.* BILL: *Good morning, Bob. You sure get up early!*

Goodness! See *(My) goodness (gracious)!*

(Good) night. **1.** the appropriate departure phrase for leave taking after dark. (This assumes that the speakers will not see one another until morning at the earliest. *Night* alone is familiar.) □ JOHN: *Bye, Alice.* ALICE: *Night. See you tomorrow.* □ BILL: *Good night, Mary.* MARY: *Night, Bill.* **2.** the appropriate phrase for wishing someone a good night's sleep. □ FATHER: *Good night Bill.* BILL: *Night, Pop.* □ FATHER: *Good night.* MOTHER: *Good night.* **3.** a mild exclamation. □ JANE: *Good night! It's dark! What time is it?* MARY: *It's two AM.* JANE: *In that case, good morning.* □ *"Good night!" cried Fred. "Look at this mess!"*

Good talking to you. See *(It's been) good talking to you.*

Good to be here. See *(It's) good to be here.*

Good to have you here. See *(It's) good to have you here.*

Good to hear your voice. See *(It's) good to hear your voice.*

Good to see you (again). See *(It's) good to see you (again).*

Good to talk to you. See *(It's been) good talking to you.*

Go on. **1.** That's silly!; You don't mean that! (Usually **Go on!**) □ JOHN: *Go on! You're making that up!* BILL: *I am not. It's the truth!* □ BILL: *Gee, that looks like a snake there in the path.* BOB: *Go on! That isn't a snake. No snake is that big.* **2.** Please continue. □ ALICE: *I guess I should stop here.* TOM: *No. Don't stop talking. I'm very interested. Go on.* □ BILL: *Don't turn here. Go on. It's the next corner.* BILL: *Thanks. I didn't think that was where we should turn.*

Got better things to do. See *(I've) (got) better things to do.*

Gotcha! **1.** I understand what you said or what you want. □ JOHN: *I want this done now! Understand?* ALICE: *Gotcha!* □ BILL:

Now, this kind of thing can't continue. We must do anything to prevent it happening again. Do you understand what I'm saying to you? BOB: *Got-cha!* **2.** I've caught you at your little game. □ *Mary was standing by the hall table, going through mail very slowly. Fred came through and saw her. "Gotcha!" said Fred to an embarrassed Mary.* □ BILL: *My flight was nearly six hours late.* BOB: *Gotcha! I just heard you tell Mary it was three hours late.*

Got me beat. See *(It) beats me.*

Got me stumped. See *(You've) got me stumped.*

Got to be shoving off. See *(I) have to shove off.*

Got to fly. See *(I've) got to fly.*

Got to get moving. See *(I've) got to get moving.*

Got to go. See *(I've) got to go.*

Got to go home and get my beauty sleep. See *(I've) got to go home and get my beauty sleep.*

Got to hit the road. See *(It's) time to hit the road.*

Got to run. See *(I've) got to run.*

Got to shove off. See *(I) have to shove off.*

Got to split. See *(I've) got to split.*

Got to take off. See *(I've) got to take off.*

Great! That is wonderful!; I am pleased to hear it. □ JANE: *I'm getting a new job.* BILL: *Great!* □ MARY: *I'm done now.* SALLY: *Great! We can leave right away.*

Great Scott! an exclamation of shock or surprise. □ *"Great Scott! You bought a truck!" shrieked Mary.* □ FRED: *The water heater just exploded!* BILL: *Great Scott! What do we do now?* FRED: *Looks like cold showers for a while.*

Greetings. Hello. □ SALLY: *Greetings, my friend.* BOB: *Hello, Sally.* □ MARY: *Hi, Tom.* TOM: *Greetings, Mary. How are things?* MARY: *Just great, thanks. What about you?* TOM: *I'm cool.*

Greetings and felicitations! AND **Greetings and salutations!** Hello and good wishes. (A bit stilted.) □ *"Greetings and felicitations! Welcome to our talent show!" said the master of ceremonies.* □ BILL: *Greetings and salutations, Bob!* BOB: *Come off it, Bill. Can't you just say "Hi" or something?*

Greetings and salutations! See the previous entry.

Guess what! a way of starting a conversation; a way of forcing someone into a conversation. □ ALICE: *Guess what!* BOB: *I don't know. What?* ALICE: *I'm going to Europe this summer.* BOB: *That's very nice.* □ JOHN: *Guess what!* JANE: *What?* JOHN: *Mary is going to have a baby.* JANE: *Oh, that's great!*

H

Had a nice time. See *(I) had a nice time.*

Hang in there. Be patient, things will work out. □ BOB: *Everything is in such a mess. I can't seem to get things done right.* JANE: *Hang in there, Bob. Things will work out.* □ MARY: *Sometimes I just don't think I can go on.* SUE: *Hang in there, Mary. Things will work out.*

Hang on (a minute). AND **Hang on a moment.; Hang on a second.** Please wait a minute. □ MARY: *Hang on a minute.* TOM: *What do you want?* MARY: *I want to ask you something.* □ JANE (entering the room): *Oh, Bill.* BILL (covering the telephone receiver): *Hang on a second. I'm on the phone.*

Hang on a moment. See the previous entry.

Hang on a second. See *Hang on (a minute).*

Happy to (do something) See *(I'd be) happy to (do something).*

Hasn't been easy. See *(It) hasn't been easy.*

Hate to eat and run. See *(I) hate to eat and run.*

Have a ball! Enjoy yourself! (Informal.) □ BILL: *Well, we're off to the party.* JANE: *Okay. Have a ball!* □ *"Have a ball!" said Mary as her roommate went out the door.*

Have a go at it. Give it a try.; Try your hand at it. □ ALICE: *Wow! This is fun!* BOB: *Can I have a go at it?* □ TOM: *I am having a good time painting this fence. It takes a lot of skill.* HENRY: *It does look challenging.* TOM: *Here, have a go at it.* HENRY: *Thanks!*

Have a good day. See *Have a nice day.*

Have a good one. See *Have a nice day.*

Have a good time. Enjoy yourself in what you are about to do. □
BILL: *I'm leaving for the party now.* FATHER: *Have a good time.* □
SUE: *Tonight is the formal dance at the Palmer House, and I'm going.*
MARY: *Have a good time. I'm watching television right here.*

Have a good trip. AND **Have a nice trip.** Have a pleasant journey.
(Compare to *Have a safe trip.* This phrase avoids references to
safety.) □ *As Sue stepped onto the plane, someone in a uniform said,*
"Have a nice trip." □ *"Have a good trip," said Bill, waving his*
good-byes.

Have a heart! Please be kind and compassionate. □ TEACHER:
Things are looking bad for your grade in this class, Bill. BILL: *Gee, have a*
heart! I work hard. □ *"Have a heart, officer. I wasn't going all that*
fast," pleaded Alice.

Have a nice day. AND **Have a good day.; Have a good one.** an expression said when parting or saying good-bye. (This is now quite
hackneyed, and many people do not like to hear it.) □ CLERK:
Thank you. TOM: *Thank you.* CLERK: *Have a nice day.* □ BOB: *See*
you, man! JOHN: *Bye, Bob. Have a good one!*

Have a nice flight. Please enjoy your flight. (Said when wishing
someone well on an airplane trip. Often said by airline personnel
to their passengers.) □ CLERK: *Here's your ticket, sir. Have a nice*
flight. FRED: *Thanks.* □ *As Mary boarded the plane, almost everyone*
said, "Have a nice flight."

Have a nice trip. See *Have a good trip.*

Have a safe journey. See the following entry.

Have a safe trip. AND **Have a safe journey.** I hope that your journey is safe.; Be careful and assure that your journey is safe. □
BILL: *Well, we're off for London.* SALLY: *Have a safe trip.* □ BILL:
You're driving all the way to San Francisco? BOB: *Yes, indeed.* BILL: *Well,*
have a safe trip.

Have at it. Start doing it.; Start eating it. □ JOHN: *Here's your ham-*
burger. Have at it. JANE: *Thanks. Where's the mustard?* □ JOHN: *Did you*
notice? The driveway needs sweeping. JANE: *Here's the broom. Have at it.*

Have fun. Have a good time.; Have an enjoyable time. □ BILL: *I'm leaving for the picnic now.* MOTHER: *Have fun.* □ BILL: *Good-bye.* BOB: *Good-bye, Bill.* FRED: *Bye, Bill. Have fun.*

Have it your way. It will be done your way.; You will get your way. (Usually shows irritation on the part of the speaker.) □ TOM: *I would like to do this room in blue.* SUE: *I prefer yellow. I really do.* TOM: *Okay. Have it your way.* □ JANE: *Let's get a pie. Apple would be good.* BOB: *No, if we are going to buy a whole pie, I want a cherry pie, not apple.* JANE: *Oh, have it your way!*

Haven't got all day. See *(I) haven't got all day.*

Haven't I seen you somewhere before? AND **Haven't we met before?** a polite way of trying to meet someone. □ BOB: *Hi. Haven't I seen you somewhere before?* MARY: *I hardly think so.* □ BILL (moving toward Jane): *Haven't we met before?* JANE (moving away from Bill): *No way!*

Haven't seen you in a long time. See *(I) haven't seen you in a long time.*

Haven't seen you in a month of Sundays. See *(I) haven't seen you in a month of Sundays.*

Haven't we met before? See *Haven't I seen you somewhere before?*

Have some more. See *(Do) have some more.*

Have to be moving along. See *(I) have to be moving along.*

Have to go now. See *(I) have to go now.*

Have to move along. See *(I) have to be moving along.*

Have to run along. See *(I) have to run along.*

Have to shove off. See *(I) have to shove off.*

(Have you) been keeping busy? AND **(Have you been) keeping busy?; You been keeping busy?** a vague greeting inquiry ask-

59

ing about how someone has been occupied. □ TOM: *Been keeping busy?* BILL: *Yeah. Too busy.* □ SUE: *Hi, Fred. Have you been keeping busy?* FRED: *Not really. Just doing what I have to.*

(Have you) been keeping cool? AND **(Have you been) keeping cool?; You been keeping cool?** an inquiry about how someone is surviving very hot weather. □ TOM: *What do you think of this hot weather? Been keeping cool?* SUE: *No, I like this weather just as it is.* □ MARY: *Keeping cool?* BILL: *Yup. Run the air-conditioning all the time.*

(Have you) been keeping out of trouble? AND **(Have you been) keeping out of trouble?; You been keeping out of trouble?** a vague greeting inquiry asking one what one has been doing. □ BOB: *Hi, Mary. Have you been keeping out of trouble?* MARY: *Yeah. And you?* BOB: *Oh, I'm getting by.* □ TOM: *Hey, man! Been keeping out of trouble?* BOB: *Hell, no! What are you up to?* TOM: *Nothing.*

(Have you) been okay? AND **You been okay?** a vague greeting inquiry asking if one has been well. □ TOM: *Hey, man. How you doing?* BOB: *I'm okay. You been okay?* TOM: *Sure. See you!* □ MARY: *I heard you were sick.* SALLY: *Yes, but I'm better. Have you been okay?* MARY: *Oh, sure. Healthy as an ox.*

(Have you) changed your mind? AND **You changed your mind?** Have you decided to alter your decision? □ SALLY: *As of last week, they said you are leaving. Changed your mind?* BILL: *No. I'm leaving for sure.* □ TOM: *Well, have you changed your mind?* SALLY: *Absolutely not!*

have you heard? AND **did you hear?** a question used to introduce a piece of news or gossip. □ SALLY: *Hi, Mary.* MARY: *Hi. Have you heard about Tom and Sue?* SALLY: *No, what happened?* MARY: *I'll let one of them tell you.* SALLY: *Oh, come on! Tell me!* □ BOB: *Hi, Tom. What's new?* TOM: *Did you hear that they're raising taxes again?* BOB: *That's not new.*

Have you met someone? a question asked when introducing someone to someone else. (The question need not be answered. The *someone* is usually a person's name.) □ TOM: *Hello, Mary. Have you met Fred?* MARY: *Hello, Fred. Glad to meet you.* FRED: *Glad to meet you, Mary.* □ TOM: *Hey, Mary! Good to see you. Have you met Fred?*

MARY: *No, I don't believe I have. Hello, Fred. Glad to meet you.* FRED: *Hello, Mary.*

Having a wonderful time; wish you were here. See *(I'm) having a wonderful time; wish you were here.*

Having quite a time. See *(I'm) having quite a time.*

Having the time of my life. See *(I'm) having the time of my life.*

Heads up! Look around! There is danger! □ *The load the crane was lifting swung over near the foreman. "Heads up!" shouted one of the workers, and the foreman just missed getting bonked on the head.* □ *Boxes were falling everywhere as the boat rolled back and forth in the storm. "Heads up!" called a sailor, and a big case of marmalade just missed my left shoulder.*

Heavens! See *(Good) heavens!; (My) heavens!*

Hello. the standard, general word of greeting and the standard way to answer a telephone. (The answer to a telephone call is usually spoken with rising question intonation and written with a question mark.) □ TOM: *Hello.* SUE: *Hello, how are you?* TOM: *Fine. How are you?* □ JANE: *Hello.* ALICE: *What's up, Jane?* JANE: *Nothing much.* □ RACHEL: *Hello?* TOM: *Is Andrew there?* RACHEL: *Just a minute.* (calling loudly) *Andrew! It's for you!*

Hell's bells (and buckets of blood)! an exclamation of anger or surprise. □ ALICE: *Your pants are torn in back.* JOHN: *Oh, hell's bells! What will happen next?* □ BILL: *Congratulations, you just flunked calculus.* JANE: *Hell's bells and buckets of blood! What do I do now?*

Hell with that! See *(To) hell with that!*

Help yourself. Please take what you want without asking permission. □ SALLY: *Can I have one of these doughnuts?* BILL: *Help yourself.* □ *Mother led the little troop of my friends to the kitchen table, which was covered with cups of juice and plates of cookies. "Help yourself," she said.*

Here! Stop that!; No more of that! □ BOB: *You say that again and I'll bash you one.* BILL: *You and what army?* FATHER: *Here! That's enough!* □ *"Here! Stop that fighting, you two," shouted the school principal.*

Here's looking at you. See *Bottoms up.*

Here's mud in your eye. See *Bottoms up.*

Here's to you.   See *Bottoms up.*

Here we go again.   We are going to experience the same thing again.; We are going to hear about or discuss the same thing again. ☐ JOHN: *Now, I would like to discuss your behavior in class yesterday.* BILL (to himself): *Here we go again.* ☐ FRED: *We must continue our discussion of the Wilson project.* SUE: *Here we go again.* FRED: *What's that?* SUE: *Nothing.*

hey   **1.** a word used to get someone's attention; a sentence opener that catches someone's attention. (Informal. Words such as this often use intonation to convey the connotation of the sentence that is to follow. The brief intonation pattern accompanying the word may indicate sarcasm, disagreement, caution, consolation, sternness, etc. See also *say.* Often **Hey!**) ☐ BILL: *Hey, Tom. Over here. I'm over here by the tree.* TOM: *Hi, Bill. What's up?* ☐ TOM: *Hey, who are you?* MARY: *Who do you think, Tom?* ☐ *"Hey, let's go for a ride!" cried little Billy.* ☐ BOB: *Hey, stop that!* ALICE: *Gee! What did I do?* ☐ *"Hey, look out!" warned Henry.* ☐ FRED: *Hey, come over here.* BOB: *What do you want?* ☐ FRED: *Hey, come here, Bob!* BOB: *What's up?* **2.** Hello! (A Southern U.S. greeting.) ☐ MARY: *Hey, Bill.* BILL: *Hey, Mary. What's up?* ☐ JANE: *Hey!* MARY: *Hey!* JANE: *You okay?* MARY: *Wonderful!*

Hi!   Hello! (Very common.) ☐ *"Hi! What's cooking?" asked Tom.* ☐ BILL: *Hi, Tom. How are you?* TOM: *Fine. How are you doing?* ☐ FRED: *Hi, old buddy. Give me some skin.* TOM: *Good to see you, man.*

Hiya!   Hello! (Very informal. From *Hi to you.*) ☐ HENRY: *Hiya, chum. What are you doing?* BILL: *Nothing.* ☐ JOHN: *Hey, man! How's by you?* BOB: *Hiya! Nothing much.*

Hold everything!   Stop everything!; Everyone, stop! ☐ *"Hold everything!" cried Mary. "There's a squirrel loose in the kitchen!"* ☐ BILL: *Hold everything! Let's try this part again.* BOB: *But we've already rehearsed it four times.*

Hold it!   Stop right there. ☐ TOM: *Hold it!* MARY: *What's wrong?* TOM: *You almost stepped on my contact lens.* ☐ BILL: *Hold it!* BOB: *What is it?* BILL: *Sorry. For a minute, that stick looked like a snake.*

Hold on (a minute)! AND **Hold on for a minute!**   Stop right there!; Wait a minute! (*Minute* can be replaced by *moment, second,* or other time periods.) ☐ BOB: *Hold on, Tom.* TOM: *What?* BOB: *I want to* *talk to you.* □ *"Hold on!" hollered Tom. "You're running off with my shopping cart!"*

Hold, please. See *Hold the wire(, please).*

Hold the line(, please). See the following entry,

Hold the wire(, please). AND **Hold, please.; Hold the line(, please).; Please hold.** Please wait on the telephone and do not hang up. (A phrase in use before telephone "hold" circuitry was in wide use.) □ BILL: *Hold the wire, please.* (turning to Tom) *Tom, the phone's for you.* TOM: *Be right there.* □ RACHEL: *Do you wish to speak to Mr. Jones or Mr. Franklin?* HENRY: *Jones.* RACHEL: *Thank you. Hold the line, please.* □ SUE: *Good afternoon, Acme Motors, hold please.* (click) BILL (hanging up): *That makes me so mad!*

Hold your horses! Slow down! Don't be so eager! □ MARY: *Come on, Sally, let's get going!* SALLY: *Oh, hold your horses! Don't be in such a rush!* □ *"Hold your horses!" said Fred to the herd of small boys trying to get into the station wagon.*

Hold your tongue! You have said enough!; You have said enough rude things. □ BILL: *You're seeing Tom a lot, aren't you? You must be in love.* JANE: *Hold your tongue, Bill Franklin!* □ *After listening to the tirade against him for nearly four minutes, Tom cried out, "Hold your tongue!"*

hopefully it is to be hoped that. (Many people object to this usage.) □ HENRY: *Hopefully, this plane will get in on time so I can make my connection.* RACHEL: *I hope so, too.* □ RACHEL: *Hopefully, all the problems are solved.* HENRY: *Don't be too sure.*

Hope not. See *(I) hope not.*

Hope so. See *(I) hope so.*

Hope to see you again (sometime). See *(I) hope to see you again (sometime).*

Hop to it! Get started right now! □ BILL: *I have to get these things stacked up before I go home.* BOB: *Then hop to it! You won't get it done* *standing around here talking.* □ *"Hurry up! Hop to it!" urged Bill. "We've got to get this done!"*

Horsefeathers! Nonsense! □ FRED: *I'm too old to walk that far.* SUE: *Horsefeathers!* □ *"Horsefeathers!" said Jane. "You're totally wrong!"*

Hot diggety (dog)! AND **Hot dog!; Hot ziggety!** an expression of excitement and delight. (These expressions have no meaning and no relationship to dogs.) □ RACHEL: *I got an A! Hot diggety dog!* HENRY: *Good for you!* □ BILL: *Look, here's the check! We're rich!* JANE: *Hot dog!* BILL: *What'll we spend it on?* JANE: *How about saving it?* □ TOM: *You won first place!* MARY: *Hot ziggety!*

Hot dog! See the previous entry.

Hot enough for you? See *(Is it) hot enough for you?*

Hot ziggety! See *Hot diggety (dog)!*

How about a lift? See *Could I have a lift?*

How about you? What do you think?; What is your choice?; *What about you?* □ BOB: *How are you, Bill?* BILL: *I'm okay. How about you?* BOB: *Fine, fine. Let's do lunch sometime.* □ WAITER: *Can I take your order?* BILL: *I'll have the chef's salad and iced tea.* WAITER (turning to Sue): *How about you?* SUE: *I'll have the same.*

[how are] See also the entries beginning with *How're*.

How (are) you doing? a standard greeting inquiry. (The entry without *are* is informal and usually pronounced "How ya doin'?") □ JANE: *How are you doing?* MARY: *I'm okay. What about you?* JANE: *Likewise.* □ SALLY: *Sue, this is my little brother, Bill.* SUE: *How are you, Bill?* BILL: *Okay. How you doing?*

How (are) you feeling? an inquiry into the state of someone's health. □ SALLY: *How are you feeling?* BILL: *Oh, better, thanks.* SALLY: *That's good.* □ BILL: *Hey, Jane! You been sick?* JANE: *Yeah.* BILL: *How you feeling?* JANE: *Not very well.*

How are you getting on? How are you managing?; How are you doing? □ JANE: *Well, Mary, how are you getting on?* MARY: *Things couldn't be better.* □ SUE: *Hey, John! How are you getting on? What's it like with all the kids out of the house?* JOHN: *Things are great, Sue!*

How can I help you? See *How may I help you?*

How can I serve you? See *How may I help you?*

How come? How did that come about?; Why? □ SALLY: *I have to go to the doctor.* MARY: *How come?* SALLY: *I'm sick, silly.* □ JOHN: *I have to leave now.* BILL: *How come?* JOHN: *I just have to, that's all.* □ HENRY: *How come you always put your right shoe on first?* RACHEL: *Do I have to have a reason for something like that?*

How could you (do something)? How could you bring yourself to do a thing like that? (No answer is expected.) □ *Looking first at the broken lamp and then at the cat, Mary shouted, "How could you do that?"* □ TOM: *Then I punched him in the nose.* RACHEL: *Oh, how could you?*

How-de-do. AND **Howdy(-do).** a greeting inquiry meaning *How do you do.*; a response to the greeting inquiry *How-de-do.* (These forms never have rising question intonation, but the first instance of either one calls for a response. Familiar and folksy.) □ BILL: *Well, here's my old pal, Tom. How-de-do Tom.* TOM: *How-de-do. How you been?* □ SALLY: *How do you do, Mr. Johnson.* TOM: *Howdy, ma'am.* SALLY: *Charmed, I'm sure.*

How do you do. a standard greeting inquiry and response. (This expression never has rising question intonation, but the first instance of its use calls for a response. Sometimes the response does, in fact, explain how one is.) □ SALLY: *Hello. How do you do.* BOB: *How do you do.* □ MARY: *How do you do. So glad to meet you, Tom.* TOM: *Thank you. How are you?* MARY: *Just fine. Your brother tells me you like camping.* TOM: *Yes. Are you a camper?* MARY: *Sort of.*

How do you know? **1.** How did you get that information? (A straightforward question. The stress in on *know*.) □ BILL: *The train is about to pull into the station.* SUE: *How do you know?* BILL: *I hear it.* □ FRED: *I have to apologize for the coffee. It probably isn't very good.* JANE: *How do you know?* FRED: *Well, I made it.* **2.** What makes you think you are correct? Why do you think you have enough information to make this judgment? (Contentious. The heaviest stress is on *you*.) □ BILL: *This is the best recording made all year.* BOB: *How do you know?* BILL: *Well, I guess it's just my opinion.* □ TOM: *Having a baby can be quite an ordeal.* MARY: *How do you know?* TOM: *I read a lot.*

How do you like school? a phrase used to start a conversation with a school-age person. □ BOB: *Well, Billy, how do you like school?*

BILL: *I hate it.* BOB: *Too bad.* ☐ MARY: *How do you like school?* BOB: *It's okay. Almost everything else is better, though.*

How do you like that? **1.** Do you like that?; Is that to your liking? ☐ TOM: *There's a bigger one over there. How do you like that?* BILL: *It's better, but not quite what I want.* ☐ CLERK: *Here's one without pleats. How do you like that?* FRED: *That's perfect!* **2.** an expression said when administering punishment. ☐ *"How do you like that?" growled Tom as he punched John in the stomach.* ☐ BILL (being spanked): *Ouch! Ow! No!* MOTHER (spanking): *How do you like that?* BILL: *Not much.* MOTHER: *It hurts me more than it hurts you.* **3.** an expression said to show surprise at someone's bad or strange behavior or at some surprising event. ☐ TOM (shouting at Sue): *Can it! Go away!* SUE (looking at Mary, aghast): *Well, how do you like that!* MARY: *Let's get out of here!* ☐ FRED: *How do you like that?* SUE: *What's the matter?* FRED: *My wallet's gone.*

How do you like this weather? a greeting inquiry. (A direct answer is expected.) ☐ HENRY: *Hi, Bill. How do you like this weather?* BILL: *Lovely weather for ducks. Not too good for me, though.* ☐ ALICE: *Gee, it's hot! How do you like this weather?* RACHEL: *You can have it!*

How dumb do you think I am? Your question is insulting. I am not stupid. (Shows agitation. An answer is not expected or desired.) ☐ MARY: *Are you really going to sell your new car?* SALLY: *Come on! How dumb do you think I am?* ☐ TOM: *Do you think you could sneak into that theater without paying?* BOB: *Good grief! How dumb do you think I am?*

Howdy(-do)? See *How-de-do?*

How goes it (with you)? How are things going with you? ☐ TOM: *How goes it?* JANE: *Great! How goes it with you?* TOM: *Couldn't be better.* ☐ SALLY: *Greetings, Sue. How goes it?* SUE: *Okay, I guess. And you?* SALLY: *The same.*

How (have) you been? one of the standard greeting inquiries. (See also *How you is?*) ☐ BOB: *Hi, Fred! How have you been?* FRED: *Great! What about you?* BOB: *Fine.* ☐ BOB: *How you been?* SUE: *Okay, I guess. You okay?* BOB: *Yup.*

[how is] See the entries beginning with *how's.*

How many times do I have to tell you? a phrase admonishing someone who has forgotten instructions. ☐ MOTHER: *How many* *times do I have to tell you? Do your homework!* BILL: *Mom! I hate school!* □ MARY: *Clean this place up! How many times do I have to tell you?* BILL: *I'll do it! I'll do it!*

How may I help you? AND **How can I help you?; How can I serve you?; May I help you?; What can I do for you?**   In what way can I serve you? (Usually said by shopkeepers and food service personnel. The first question is the most polite, and the last is the least polite.) □ WAITER: *How can I help you?* SUE: *I'm not ready to order yet.* □ CLERK: *May I help you?* JANE: *I'm looking for a gift for my aunt.*

How're things going?   one of the standard greeting inquiries. □ BOB: *Hi, Fred! How're things going?* FRED: *Could be better. How's by you?* □ BILL: *How are things going?* MARY: *Fine, but I need to talk to you.*

How're things (with you)?   a greeting inquiry. □ SALLY: *How are you?* BILL: *Fine. How are things?* □ BILL: *How are things going?* MARY: *Fine. How are things with you?*

How's business?   a question asked in a conversation about the state of someone's business or job. □ TOM: *Hello, Sally. How's business?* SALLY: *Okay, I suppose.* □ BOB: *Good to see you, Fred.* FRED: *Hello, Bob. How's business?* BOB: *Just okay.*

How's by you?   a greeting inquiry. (Informal.) □ FRED: *Hey, man! How's by you?* JOHN: *Groovy, Fred. Tsup?* □ BOB: *Hello. What's cooking?* BILL: *Nothing. How's by you?*

How's every little thing?   *How are things with you?* (Informal and familiar.) □ BILL: *Hello, Tom.* TOM: *Hi, Bill. How's every little thing?* BILL: *Couldn't be better.* □ BILL: *Hi, Mary. How's every little thing?* MARY: *Things are fine. How are you?* BILL: *Fine, thanks.*

How should I know? AND **Don't ask me.**   I do not know. Why should I be expected to know? (Shows impatience or rudeness.) □ BILL: *Why is the orca called the killer whale?* MARY: *How should I know?* □ SALLY: *Where did I leave my glasses?* TOM: *Don't ask me.*

How's it going?   one of the standard informal greeting inquiries. □ SUE: *How's it going?* BILL: *Just great! How are you?* SUE: *Fine, thanks.* □ MARY: *How are you, Sue?* SUE: *Things just couldn't be better! I'm gloriously in love!* MARY: *Anybody I know?*

How's (it) with you?   A greeting inquiry. (Slang.) □ TOM: *Hey, man. How's with you?* BOB: *Great! And you?* TOM: *Okay.* □ BILL: *How's with you, old buddy?* JOHN: *Can't complain. And you?* BILL: *Couldn't be better.*

How's my boy? AND **How's the boy?**   How are you? (Male to male and familiar. The speaker may outrank the person addressed.) □ BOB: *How's my boy?* BILL: *Hi, Tom. How are you?* □ FRED: *Hello, old buddy. How's the boy?* BOB: *Hi, there! What's cooking?* FRED: *Nothing much.*

How's that again?   Please say that again.; I did not hear it all. □ SUE: *Would you like some coffee?* MARY: *How's that again?* SUE: *I said, would you like some coffee?* □ TOM: *The car door is frozen closed.* BOB: *How's that again?* TOM: *The car door is frozen closed.*

How's the boy?   See *How's my boy?*

How's the family? AND **How's your family?**   an expression that carries the greeting inquiries beyond the speakers present. □ BOB: *Hello, Fred. How are you?* FRED: *Fine, thanks.* BOB: *How's the family?* FRED: *Great! How's yours?* BOB: *Couldn't be better.* □ *"How's the family?" asked Bill, greeting his boss.*

How's the wife?   a phrase inquiring about one's wife. (Usually male to male.) □ TOM: *Hi, Fred, how are you?* FRED: *Good. And you?* TOM: *Great! How's the wife?* FRED: *Okay, and yours?* TOM: *Couldn't be better.* □ BILL: *Hi, Bill. How's the wife?* BOB: *Doing fine. How's every little thing?* BILL: *Great!*

How's the world (been) treating you?   How are things going for you? □ SUE: *Hello there, Bob. How's the world treating you?* BOB: *I can't complain. How are you?* SUE: *Doing just fine, thanks.* □ MARY: *Morning, Bill.* BILL: *Good morning, Mary. How's the world been treating you?* MARY: *Okay, I guess.*

How's tricks?   a greeting inquiry. (Slang.) □ BOB: *Fred! How's tricks?* FRED: *How are you doing, Bob?* BOB: *Doing great!* □ BILL: *What's up? How's tricks?* BOB: *I can't complain. How are things going for you?* BILL: *Can't complain.*

How's with you?   See *How's (it) with you?*

How's your family?   See *How's the family?*

How time flies.   See *(My,) how time flies.*

How will I know you? See the following entry.

How will I recognize you? AND **How will I know you?** a question asked by one of two people who have agreed to meet for the first time in a large busy place. □ TOM: *Okay, I'll meet you at the west door of the station.* MARY: *Fine. How will I recognize you?* TOM: *I'll be wearing dark glasses.* □ BILL: *I'll meet you at six. How will I recognize you?* MARY: *I'll be carrying a brown umbrella.*

How you be? See *How you is?*

How you been? See *How (have) you been?*

How you doing? See *How (are) you doing?*

How you feeling? See *How (are) you feeling?*

How you is? AND **How you be?; How you was?** *How are you?* (Usually a jocular version of *How are you?*) □ BOB: *Hey, man! How you is?* JOHN: *Great!* □ FRED: *How you was?* JOHN: *Okay. Yourself?* FRED: *I'm cool, man.*

How you was? See the previous entry.

Hurry on! Keep going! Move faster! □ TOM: *Get going! Hurry on!* SUE: *I'm hurrying as fast as I can.* □ MARY: *Hurry on!* CHILD: *I can't go any faster!*

Hurry up! *Come on*, move faster. □ SUE: *Hurry up! We're late!* BILL: *I'm hurrying.* □ BOB: *We're about to miss the bus!* SUE: *Well, then, hurry up!*

I

[I am]   See the entries beginning with *I'm*.

(I) beg your pardon.   1. AND **Beg pardon.**   a phrase said to excuse oneself for interrupting or committing some very minor social offense. □ *As Sue brushed by the old man, she turned and said, "Beg pardon."* □ JANE: *Ouch! That's my toe you stepped on!* SUE: *I beg your pardon. I'm so sorry.* **2.** a phrase that indicates the speaker's need to pass by another person. □ *The hallway was filled with people. Bob said, "I beg your pardon," and then he said it again and again.* □ FRED: *Beg pardon. Need to get by.* SUE: *I'm sorry.* **3.** an exclamation that shows, as politely as possible, one's indignation at something that someone has said. (In a way, this signals the offender of the magnitude of the offense and invites a revision of the original offending statement.) □ BILL: *I think you've really made a poor choice this time.* MARY: *I beg your pardon!* BILL: *I mean, you normally do better.* MARY: *Well, I never!* □ SUE: *Your spaghetti sauce is too sweet.* SALLY: *I beg your pardon!* SUE: *Maybe not.*

(I) beg your pardon, but AND **Begging your pardon, but**   Please excuse me, but. (A very polite and formal way of interrupting, bringing something to someone's attention, or asking a question of a stranger.) □ RACHEL: *Beg your pardon, but I think your right front tire is a little low.* HENRY: *Well, I guess it is. Thank you.* □ JOHN: *Begging your pardon, ma'am, but weren't we on the same cruise ship in Alaska last July?* RACHEL: *Couldn't have been me.*

I believe so.   See *I guess (so)*.

I believe we've met.   a phrase indicating that one has already met a person to whom one is being introduced. □ JOHN: *Alice, have you* *met Fred?* ALICE: *Oh, yes, I believe we've met. How are you, Fred?* FRED: *Hello, Alice. Good to see you again.* □ ALICE: *Tom, this is my cousin, Mary.* TOM: *I believe we've met. Nice to see you again, Mary.* MARY: *Hello, Tom. Good to see you again.*

I can accept that.   I accept your evaluation as valid.   □   BOB: *Now, you'll probably like doing the other job much better. It doesn't call for you to do the things you don't do well.* TOM: *I can accept that.*   □   SUE: *On your evaluation this time, I noted that you need to work on telephone manners a little bit.* BILL: *I can accept that.*

I can live with that.   That is something I can get used to.; That is all right *as far as I'm concerned.*   □   SUE: *I want to do this room in green.* BILL: *I can live with that.*   □   CLERK: *This one will cost twelve dollars more.* BOB: *I can live with that. I'll take it.*

I can't accept that.   I do not believe what you said.; I reject what you said.   □   SUE: *The mechanic says we need a whole new engine.* JOHN: *What? I can't accept that!*   □   TOM: *You're now going to work on the night shift. You don't seem to be able to get along with some of the people on the day shift.* BOB: *I can't accept that. It's them, not me.*

(I) can't argue with that.   I agree with what you said.; It sounds like a good idea.   □   TOM: *This sure is good cake.* BOB: *Can't argue with that.*   □   SUE: *What do you say we go for a swim?* FRED: *I can't argue with that.*

(I) can't beat that. AND **(I) can't top that.**   I cannot do better than that.; I cannot exceed that.   □   HENRY: *That was really great. I can't beat that.* RACHEL: *Yes, that was really good.*   □   *"What a great joke! I can't top that," said Kate, still laughing.*

I can't believe (that)!   That is unbelievable!   □   TOM: *What a terrible earthquake! All the houses collapsed, one by one.* JANE: *I can't believe that!*   □   BILL: *This lake is nearly two hundred feet deep.* SUE: *I can't believe that!* BILL: *Take my word for it.*

(I) can't complain. AND **(I have) nothing to complain about.**   a response to a greeting inquiry asking how one is or how things are going for one.   □   SUE: *How are things going?* MARY: *I can't complain.*   □   MARY: *Hi, Fred! How are you doing?* FRED: *Nothing to complain about.*

I can't get over something!   I am just so amazed! (The *something* can be a fact or a pronoun, such as *that* or *it*. Also with *just,* as in the examples.) ☐ *"I just can't get over the way everybody pitched in and helped," said Alice.* ☐ BOB: *The very idea, Sue and Tom doing something like that!* BILL: *I can't get over it!*

(I) can't help it. There is nothing I can do to help the situation.; That is the way it is; there is nothing I can do. (Often in answer to a criticism.) ☐ MARY: *Your hair is a mess.* SUE: *It's windy. I can't help it.* ☐ FRED: *I wish you'd quit coughing all the time.* SALLY: *I can't help it. I wish I could too.*

(I) can too. You are wrong, I can.; Don't say I can't, because I can! (The response to *(You) can't!*) ☐ SUE: *I'm going to the party.* MOTHER: *You can't.* SUE: *I can too.* MOTHER: *Cannot!* SUE: *Can too!* ☐ *"Can too!" protested Fred. "I can, if you can!"*

(I) can't rightly say. I do not know with any certainty. (Colloquial and a little folksy.) ☐ FRED: *When do you think we'll get there?* BILL: *Can't rightly say.* ☐ BOB: *Okay, how does this look to you?* BILL: *I can't rightly say. I've never seen anything like it before.*

(I) can't say (as) I do. See *(I) can't say that I do.*

(I) can't say for sure. I do not know with any certainty. ☐ TOM: *When will the next train come through?* JANE: *I can't say for sure.* ☐ BOB: *How can the driver hit so many potholes?* BILL: *Can't say for sure. I know he doesn't see too well, though.*

(I) can't say's I do. See the following entry.

(I) can't say that I do. AND **(I) can't say's I do.; (I) can't say (as) I do.** a vague response to a question about whether one remembers, knows about, likes, etc., something or someone. (A polite way of saying no. Colloquial and folksy. The *say as* and *say's* are not standard English.) ☐ JANE: *You remember Fred, don't you?* JOHN: *Can't say as I do.* ☐ BOB: *This is a fine looking car. Do you like it?* BILL: *I can't say I do.*

(I) can't say that I have. AND **(I) can't say's I have.; (I) can't say (as) I have.** a vague response to a question about whether one has ever done something or been somewhere. (A polite way of saying no. Colloquial and folksy.) ☐ BILL: *Have you ever been to a real* *opera?* BOB: *I can't say as I have.* □ MARY: *Well, have you thought about going with me to Fairbanks?* FRED: *I can't say I have, actually.*

(I) can't thank you enough. a polite expression of gratitude. □ BILL: *Here's the book I promised you.* SUE: *Oh, good. I can't thank you enough.* □ TOM: *Well, here we are.* BILL: *Well, Tom. I can't thank you enough. I really appreciate the ride.*

(I) can't top that. See under *Can't beat that.*

I can't understand (it). See *I don't understand (it).*

(I) changed my mind. I have reversed my previous decision or statement. □ TOM: *I thought you were going to Atlanta today.* BILL: *I changed my mind. I'm leaving tomorrow.* □ MARY: *I thought that this room was going to be done in red.* SUE: *I changed my mind.*

(I) could be better. See *(Things) could be better.*

(I) could be worse. See *(Things) could be worse.*

(I) couldn't ask for more. Everything is fine, and there is no more that I could want. □ BILL: *Are you happy?* SUE: *Oh, Bill. I couldn't ask for more.* □ WAITER: *Is everything all right?* BILL: *Oh, yes, indeed. Couldn't ask for more.*

I couldn't ask you to do that. That is a very kind offer, but I would not ask you to do it. (This is not a refusal of the offer.) □ SALLY: *Look, if you want, I'll drive you to the airport.* MARY: *Oh, Sally. I couldn't ask you to do that.* □ BILL: *I'll lend you enough money to get you through the week.* SALLY: *I couldn't ask you to do that.*

(I) couldn't be better. I am fine. □ JOHN: *How are you?* JANE: *Couldn't be better.* □ BILL: *I hope you're completely well now.* MARY: *I couldn't be better.*

(I) could(n't) care less. It doesn't matter to me. (The *less* bears the heaviest stress in both versions. Both versions are idiomatic. Despite the apparent contradiction, either reading of this—both the affirmative and negative—usually has the same meaning. The exception would be in a sentence where the *could* bears the heaviest stress: *I COULD care less [, but I don't.].*) □ TOM: *It's raining in! The carpet will get wet!* MARY: *I couldn't care less.* □ BILL: *I'm going to go in there and tell him off!* JOHN: *I could care less.*

(I) couldn't help it. There was no way I could prevent it.; I was unable to prevent something from happening.; I was unable to control myself. □ SALLY: *You let the paint dry with brush marks in it.* MARY: *I couldn't help it. The telephone rang.* □ FRED: *You got fingerprints all over the window.* MARY: *Sorry. Couldn't help it.*

(I'd be) happy to (do something). AND **Be happy to (do something).** I would do it with pleasure. (The *something* is replaced with a description of an activity.) □ JOHN: *I tried to get the book you wanted, but they didn't have it. Shall I try another store?* MARY: *No, never mind.* JOHN: *I'd be happy to give it a try.* □ ALICE: *Would you fix this, please?* JOHN: *Be happy to.*

(I'd) better be going. AND **(I'd) better be off.** an expression announcing the need to depart. □ BOB: *Better be going. Got to get home.* BILL: *Well, if you must, you must. Bye.* □ FRED: *It's midnight. I'd better be off.* HENRY: *Okay. Bye, Fred.* □ HENRY: *Better be off. It's starting to snow.* JOHN: *Yes, it looks bad out.*

(I'd) better be off. See the previous entry.

(I'd) better get moving. an expression announcing the need to depart. □ JANE: *It's nearly dark. Better get moving.* MARY: *Okay. See you later.* □ BOB: *I'm off. Good night.* BILL: *Look at the time! I'd better get moving too.*

(I'd) better get on my horse. an expression indicating that it is time that one departed. (Casual and folksy.) □ JOHN: *It's getting late. Better get on my horse.* RACHEL: *Have a safe trip. See you tomorrow.* □ *"I'd better get on my horse. The sun'll be down in an hour,"* said Sue, sounding like a cowboy.

(I'd) better hit the road. See *(It's) time to hit the road.*

I didn't catch the name. AND **I didn't catch your name.** I don't remember your name.; I didn't hear your name when we were introduced. □ BILL: *How do you like this weather?* BOB: *It's not too* *good. By the way, I didn't catch your name. I'm Bob Wilson.* BILL: *I'm Bill Franklin.* BOB: *Nice to meet you, Bill.* □ BOB: *Sorry, I didn't catch the name.* BILL: *It's Bill, Bill Franklin. And you?* BOB: *I'm Bob Wilson.*

I didn't catch your name. See the previous entry.

I didn't get that. See *I didn't (quite) catch that (last) remark.*

I didn't hear you. See the following entry.

I didn't (quite) catch that (last) remark. AND **I didn't get that.; I didn't hear you.** I didn't hear what you said, so would you please repeat it. □ JOHN: *What did you say? I didn't quite catch that last remark.* JANE: *I said it's really a hot day.* □ BILL: *Have a nice time, if you can.* SALLY: *I didn't get that.* BILL: *Have a nice time! Enjoy!*

I'd like (for) you to meet someone. an expression used to introduce someone to someone else. (The *someone* can be a person's name, the name of a relationship, or the word *someone*.) □ TOM: *Sue, I'd like you to meet my brother, Bill.* SUE: *Hi, Bill. How are you?* BILL: *Great! How are you?* □ BOB: *Hello, Fred. I'd like for you to meet Bill.* FRED: *Hello, Bill. I'm glad to meet you.* BILL: *Hello, Fred. My pleasure.*

I'd like (to have) a word with you. AND **Could I have a word with you?** I need to speak to you briefly in private. (The alternate entry is also used with *can* or *may* in place of *could*.) □ BOB: *Can I have a word with you?* SALLY: *Sure. I'll be with you in a minute.* □ SALLY: *Tom?* TOM: *Yes.* SALLY: *I'd like to have a word with you.* TOM: *Okay. What's it about?*

I'd like to speak to someone, please. the standard way of requesting to speak with a specific person on the telephone or in an office. □ SUE (answering the phone): *Hello?* BILL: *Hello, this is Bill Franklin. I'd like to speak to Mary Gray.* SUE: *I'll see if she's in.* □ *"I'd like to speak to Tom," said the voice at the other end of the line.*

I (do) declare! I am surprised to hear that! (Old-fashioned.) □ MARY: *I'm the new president of my sorority!* GRANDMOTHER: *I declare! That's very nice.* □ *A plane had landed right in the middle of the cornfield. The old farmer shook his head in disbelief. "I do declare!" he said over and over as he walked toward the plane.*

I don't believe it! an expression of amazement and disbelief. □ BOB: *Tom was just elected president of the trade association!* MARY: *I don't believe it!* □ BOB: *They're going to build a Disney World in Moscow.* SALLY: *I don't believe it!*

(I) don't believe I've had the pleasure. an expression meaning *I haven't met you yet.* □ TOM: *I'm Tom Thomas. I don't believe I've had the pleasure.* BILL: *Hello. I'm Bill Franklin.* TOM: *Nice to meet you, Bill.* BILL: *Likewise.* □ BOB: *Looks like rain.* FRED: *Sure does. Oh, I don't believe I've had the pleasure.* BOB: *I'm Bob, Bob Jones.* FRED: *My name is Fred Wilson. Glad to meet you.*

(I) don't believe so. See *I guess not.*

I don't believe this! This is very strange!; I do not believe that this is happening. □ *"I don't believe this!" muttered Sally as all the doors in the house slammed at the same time.* □ SALLY: *You're expected to get here early and make my coffee every morning.* JOHN: *I don't believe this.*

I don't care. It doesn't matter to me. □ MARY: *Can I take these papers away?* TOM: *I don't care. Do what you want.* □ BILL: *Should this room be white or yellow?* SALLY: *I don't care.*

I don't have time to breathe. See the following entry.

I don't have time to catch my breath. AND **I don't have time to breathe.** I am very busy.; I have been very busy. □ HENRY: *I'm so busy these days. I don't have time to catch my breath.* RACHEL: *Oh, I know what you mean.* □ SUE: *Would you mind finishing this for me?* BILL: *Sorry, Sue. I'm busy. I don't have time to breathe.*

I don't know. a common expression of ignorance. □ FATHER: *Why can't you do better in school?* BILL: *I don't know.* □ BILL: *Well, what are we going to do now?* SUE: *I don't know.*

I don't mean maybe! I am very serious about my demand or order. □ BOB: *Do I have to do this?* SUE: *Do it now, and I don't mean maybe!* □ FATHER: *Get this place cleaned up! And I don't mean maybe!* JOHN: *All right! I'll do it!*

(I) don't mind if I do. Yes, I would like to. □ SALLY: *Have some more coffee?* BOB: *Don't mind if I do.* □ JANE: *Here are some lovely roses. Would you like to take a few blossoms with you?* JOHN: *I don't mind if I do.*

(I) don't think so. See *I guess not.*

I don't understand (it). AND **I can't understand (it).** I am confused and bewildered (by what has happened). □ BILL: *Everyone is leaving the party.* MARY: *I don't understand. It's still so early.* □ BOB: *The very idea, Sue and Tom doing something like that!* ALICE: *It's very strange. I can't understand it.*

I don't want to alarm you, but AND **I don't want to upset you, but** an expression used to introduce bad or shocking news or gossip. □ BILL: *I don't want to alarm you, but I see someone prowling around your car.* MARY: *Oh, goodness! I'll call the police!* □ BOB: *I don't want to upset you, but I have some bad news.* TOM: *Let me have it.*

I don't want to sound like a busybody, but an expression used to introduce an opinion or suggestion. □ BOB: *I don't want to sound like a busybody, but didn't you intend to have your house painted?* BILL: *Well, I guess I did.* □ BOB: *I don't want to sound like a busybody, but some of your neighbors wonder if you could stop parking your car on your lawn.* SALLY: *I'll thank you to mind your own business!*

I don't want to upset you, but See *I don't want to alarm you, but.*

I don't want to wear out my welcome. a phrase said by a guest who doesn't want to be a burden to the host or hostess or to visit too often. □ MARY: *Good night, Tom. You must come back again soon.* TOM: *Thank you. I'd love to. I don't want to wear out my welcome, though.* □ BOB: *We had a fine time. Glad you could come to our little gathering. Hope you can come again next week.* FRED: *I don't want to wear out my welcome, but I'd like to come again.* BOB: *Good. See you next week. Bye.* FRED: *Bye.*

I don't wonder. See *I'm not surprised.*

I doubt it. I do not think so. □ TOM: *Think it will rain today?* SUE: *I doubt it.* □ SALLY: *Think you'll go to New York?* MARY: *I doubt it.*

I doubt that. I do not believe that something is so. □ BOB: *I'll be there exactly on time.* SUE: *I doubt that.* □ JOHN: *Fred says he can't come to work because he's sick.* JANE: *I doubt that.*

I expect. See *I guess.*

I expect not. See *I guess not.*

I expect (so). See *I guess (so).*

if I've told you once, I've told you a thousand times an expression that introduces a scolding, usually to a child. □ MOTHER: *If I've told you once, I've told you a thousand times, don't leave your clothes in a pile on the floor!* BILL: *Sorry.* □ *"If I've told you once, I've told you a thousand times, keep out of my study!" yelled Bob.*

if I were you an expression introducing a piece of advice. □ JOHN: *If I were you, I'd get rid of that old car.* ALICE: *Gee, I was just getting to like it.* □ HENRY: *I'd keep my thoughts to myself, if I were you.* BOB: *I guess I should be careful about what I say.*

If that don't beat all! AND **That beats everything!** That surpasses everything!; That is amazing!; *That takes the cake!* (The grammar error, *that don't* is built into this catch phrase.) □ TOM: *The mayor is kicking the baseball team out of the city.* BILL: *If that don't beat all!* □ JOHN: *Now, here's a funny thing. South America used to be attached to Africa.* FRED: *That beats everything!* JOHN: *Yeah.*

If there's anything you need, don't hesitate to ask. a polite phrase offering help in finding something or by providing something. (Often said by a host or by someone helping someone settle into something.) □ MARY: *This looks very nice. I'll be quite comfortable here.* JANE: *If there's anything you need, don't hesitate to ask.* □ *"If there is anything you need, don't hesitate to ask," said the room clerk.*

if you don't mind **1.** (Usually **If you don't mind!**) an expression that rebukes someone for some minor social violation. □ *When Bill accidently sat on Mary's purse, which she had placed in the seat next to her, she said, somewhat angrily, "If you don't mind!"* □ BILL (pushing his way in front of Mary in the checkout line): *Excuse me.* MARY: *If you don't mind! I was here first!* BILL: *I'm in a hurry.* MARY: *So am I!* **2.** a polite way of introducing a request. □ BILL: *If you don't mind, could you move a little to the left?* SALLY: *No problem.* (moving) *Is that all right?* BILL: *Yeah. Great! Thanks!* □ JANE: *If you don't mind, could I have your broccoli?* JOHN: *Help yourself.* **3.** a vague phrase answering yes to a question that asks whether one should do something. (See examples.) □ TOM: *Do you want me to take these dirty dishes away?* MARY: *If you don't mind.* □ BILL: *Shall I close the door?* SALLY: *If you don't mind.*

If you don't see what you want, please ask (for it). AND **If you don't see what you want, just ask (for it).** a polite expression intended to help people get what they want. ☐ CLERK: *May I help you?* SUE: *I'm just looking.* CLERK: *If you don't see what you want, please ask.* ☐ CLERK: *I hope you enjoy your stay at our resort. If you don't see what you want, just ask for it.* SALLY: *Great! Thanks.*

if you know what's good for you if you know what will work to your benefit; if you know what will keep you out of trouble. ☐ MARY: *I see that Mary has put a big dent in her car.* SUE: *You'll keep quiet about that if you know what's good for you.* ☐ SALLY: *My boss told me I had better improve my spelling.* BILL: *If you know what's good for you, you'd better do it too.*

if you must All right, if you have to. ☐ SALLY: *It's late. I have to move along.* MARY: *If you must. Good-bye. See you tomorrow.* ☐ ALICE: *I'm taking these things with me.* JANE: *If you must, all right. They can stay here, though.*

if you please AND **if you would(, please)** **1.** a polite phrase indicating assent to a suggestion. ☐ BILL: *Shall I unload the car?* JANE: *If you please.* ☐ SUE: *Do you want me to take you to the station?* BOB: *If you would, please.* **2.** a polite phrase introducing or following a request. ☐ JOHN: *If you please, the driveway needs sweeping.* JANE: *Here's the broom. Have at it.* ☐ JANE: *Take these down to the basement, if you would, please.* JOHN: *Can't think of anything I'd rather do, sweetie.*

if you would(, please) See the previous entry.

I guess AND **I expect; I suppose; I suspect** **1.** a phrase that introduces a supposition. (Frequently, in speech, *suppose* is reduced to *'spose*, and *expect* and *suspect* are reduced to *'spect*. The apostrophe is not always used.) ☐ BOB: *I guess it's going to rain.* BILL: *Oh, I don't know. Maybe so, maybe not.* ☐ ALICE: *I expect you'll be wanting to leave pretty soon.* JOHN: *Why? It's early yet.* **2.** a vague way of answering yes. ☐ JOHN: *You want some more coffee?* JANE: *I 'spose.* ☐ ALICE: *Ready to go?* JOHN: *I 'spect.*

I guess not. AND **(I) don't think so.; I expect not.; I suppose not.; I suspect not.; I think not.** a vague statement of negation. (More polite or gentle than no. Frequently, in speech, *suppose* is reduced to *'spose*, and *expect* and *suspect* are reduced to *'spect*. The apostrophe is not always used.) □ BILL: *It's almost too late to go to the movie. Shall we try anyway?* MARY: *I guess not.* □ TOM: *Will it rain?* MARY: *I 'spect not.*

I guess (so). AND **I believe so.; I expect (so).; I suppose (so).; I suspect (so).; I think so.** a vague expression of assent. (Frequently, in speech, *suppose* is reduced to *'spose*, and *expect* and *suspect* are reduced to *'spect*. The apostrophe is not always used.) □ TOM: *Will it rain today?* BOB: *I suppose so.* □ SUE: *Happy?* BILL: *I 'spect.* SUE: *You don't sound happy.* BILL: *I guess not.*

I had a lovely time. AND **We had a lovely time.** a polite expression of thanks to the host or hostess. □ FRED: *Good-bye. I had a lovely time.* BILL: *Nice to have you. Do come again.* □ JANE: *We had a lovely time.* MARY: *Thank you and thanks for coming.*

(I) had a nice time. the standard "good-bye and thank you" said to a host or hostess by a departing guest. □ JOHN: *Thank you. I had a nice time.* SALLY: *Don't stay away so long next time. Bye.* □ MARY: *Had a nice time. Bye. Got to run.* SUE: *Bye. Drive safely.*

(I) hate to eat and run. an apology made by someone who must leave a social event soon after eating. □ BILL: *Well, I hate to eat and run, but it's getting late.* SUE: *Oh, you don't have to leave, do you?* BILL: *I think I really must.* □ MARY: *Oh, my goodness! I hate to eat and run, but I have to catch an early plane tomorrow.* BOB: *Do you have to go?* MARY: *Afraid so.*

[I have] See also the entries beginning with *I've*.

(I have) no problem with that. That is okay with me. (See also *No problem*.) □ BOB: *Is it okay if I sign us up for the party?* SALLY: *I have no problem with that.* □ BILL: *It looks as though we will have to come back later. They're not open yet. Is that all right?* JANE: *No problem with that. When do they open?*

(I have) nothing to complain about. See *(I) can't complain*.

(I) haven't got all day. Please hurry. I'm in a hurry. □ RACHEL: *Make it snappy! I haven't got all day.* ALICE: *Just take it easy. There's no* *rush.* □ HENRY: *I haven't got all day. When are you going to finish with my car?* BOB: *As soon as I can.*

(I) haven't seen you in a long time. an expression said as part of the greeting series. □ MARY: *Hi, Fred! Haven't seen you in a long time.* FRED: *Yeah. Long time no see.* □ TOM: *Well, John. Is that you? I haven't seen you in a long time.* JOHN: *Good to see you, Tom!*

(I) haven't seen you in a month of Sundays. I haven't seen you in a long time. (Colloquial and folksy.) □ TOM: *Hi, Bill. Haven't seen you in a month of Sundays!* BILL: *Hi, Tom. Long time no see.* □ BOB: *Well, Fred! Come right in! Haven't seen you in a month of Sundays!* FRED: *Good to see you, Uncle Bob.*

(I) have to be moving along. AND **(I) have to move along.** It is time for me to leave. □ BILL: *Bye, now. Have to be moving along.* SALLY: *See you later.* □ RACHEL: *I have to be moving along. See you later.* ANDREW: *Bye, now.* □ SALLY: *It's late. I have to move along.* MARY: *If you must. Good-bye. See you tomorrow.*

(I) have to go now. an expression announcing the need to leave. □ FRED: *Bye, have to go now.* MARY: *See you later. Take it easy.* □ SUE: *Would you help me with this box?* JOHN: *Sorry. I have to go now.*

(I) have to move along. See *(I) have to be moving along.*

(I) have to push off. See *(I) have to shove off.*

(I) have to run along. an expression announcing the need to leave. □ JANE: *It's late. I have to run along.* TOM: *Okay, Jane. Bye. Take care.* □ JOHN: *Leaving so soon?* SALLY: *Yes, I have to run along.*

(I) have to shove off. AND **(I've) got to be shoving off.; (I've) got to shove off.; (I) have to push off.; (It's) time to shove off.** a phrase announcing one's need to depart. □ JOHN: *Look at the time! I have to shove off!* JANE: *Bye, John.* □ JANE: *Time to shove off. I have to feed the cats.* JOHN: *Bye, Jane.* □ FRED: *I have to push off. Bye.* JANE: *See you around. Bye.*

I have to wash a few things out. an excuse for not going out or for going home early. (Of course, it can be used literally.) □ JANE:

Time to shove off. I have to wash a few things out. JOHN: *Bye, Jane.* ☐
BILL: *I have to wash out a few things.* BOB: *Why don't you use a machine?*
BILL: *Oh, I'll see you later.*

I hear what you're saying. AND **I hear you.** **1.** I know exactly what
you mean! ☐ JOHN: *The prices in this place are a bit steep.* JANE:
Man, I hear you! ☐ BILL: *I think it's about time for a small revolution!*
ANDREW: *I hear what you're saying.* **2.** an expression indicating that
the speaker has been heard, but implying that there is no agreement. ☐ TOM: *Time has come to do something about that ailing dog of
yours.* MARY: *I hear what you're saying.* ☐ JANE: *It would be a good
idea to have the house painted.* JOHN: *I hear what you're saying.*

I hear you. See the previous entry.

(I) hope not. a phrase expressing the desire and wish that something is not so. ☐ JOHN: *It looks like it's going to rain.* JANE: *Hope
not.* ☐ JOHN: *The Wilsons said they might come over this evening.*
JANE: *I hope not. I've got things to do.*

(I) hope so. a phrase expressing the desire and wish that something
is so. ☐ BILL: *Is this the right house?* BOB: *Hope so.* ☐ JOHN: *Will
you be coming to dinner Friday?* SUE: *Yes, I hope so.*

(I) hope to see you again (sometime). an expression said when
taking leave of a person one has just met. ☐ BILL: *Nice to meet
you, Tom.* TOM: *Bye, Bill. Nice to meet you. Hope to see you again sometime.* ☐ BILL: *Good talking to you. See you around.* BOB: *Yes, I hope to
see you again. Good-bye.*

(I) just want(ed) to a sentence opener that eases into a statement or
question. (Can be followed by words like *say, ask, tell you, be,* and
come.) ☐ RACHEL: *I just wanted to say that we all loved your letter.
Thank you so much.* ANDREW: *Thanks. Glad you liked it.* ☐ RACHEL:
I just wanted to tell you how sorry I am about your sister. ALICE: *Thanks. I
appreciate it.* ☐ ANDREW: *Just wanted to come by for a minute and say
hello.* TOM: *Well, hello. Glad you dropped by.*

I kid you not. I am not kidding you.; I am not trying to fool you.
☐ BILL: *Whose car is this?* SALLY: *It's mine. It really is. I kid you not.*
☐ *"I kid you not," said Tom, glowing. "I outran the whole lot of them."*

I know (just) what you mean.   I know exactly what you are talking about, and I feel the same way about it.   □   JOHN: *These final exams are just terrible.* BOB: *I know just what you mean.* JOHN: *Why do we have to go through this?*   □   MARY: *What a pain! I hate annual inventories.* JOHN: *I know what you mean. It's really boring.*

(I'll) be right there.   I'm coming.   □   BILL: *Tom! Come here.* TOM: *Be right there.*   □   MOTHER: *Can you come down here a minute?* CHILD: *I'll be right there, Mom.*

(I'll) be right with you.   Please be patient, I will attend to you soon. (Often said by someone attending a sales counter or by an office receptionist.)   □   MARY: *Oh, Miss?* CLERK: *I'll be right with you.*   □   BOB: *Sally, can you come here for a minute?* SALLY: *Be right with you.*

(I'll) be seeing you.   Good-bye, I will see you sometime in the (near) future.   □   BOB: *Bye. Be seeing you.* SALLY: *Yeah. See you later.*   □   JOHN: *Have a good time on your vacation. I'll be seeing you.* SALLY: *See you next week. Bye.*

I('ll) bet   **1.** I'm pretty sure that something is so or that something will happen.   □   BOB: *I bet you miss your plane.* RACHEL: *No, I won't.*   □   SUE: *I'll bet it rains today.* ALICE: *No way! There's not a cloud in the sky.*   **2.** I agree. (Often sarcastic.)   □   TOM: *They're probably going to raise taxes again next year.* HENRY: *I bet.*   □   FRED: *If we do that again, we'll really be in trouble.* ANDREW: *I'll bet.*

I'll bite.   Okay, I will answer your question.; Okay, I will listen to your joke or play your little guessing game.   □   BOB: *Guess what is in this box.* BILL: *I'll bite.* BOB: *A new toaster!*   □   JOHN: *Did you hear the joke about the used car salesman?* JANE: *No, I'll bite.*

I'll call back later.   a standard phrase indicating that a telephone caller will call again at a later time.   □   SALLY: *Is Bill there?* MARY (speaking into the telephone): *Sorry, he's not here right now.* SALLY: *I'll call back later.*   □   JOHN (speaking into the telephone): *Hello. Is Fred there?* JANE: *No. Can I take a message?* JOHN: *No, thanks. I'll call back later.*

(I'll) catch you later.   I will talk to you later.   □   MARY: *Got to fly. See you around.* SALLY: *Bye. Catch you later.*   □   JOHN: *I have to go to class now.* BILL: *Okay, catch you later.*

I'll drink to that!   I agree with that totally, and I salute it with a drink. (The phrase is used even when no drinking is involved.)   □

JOHN: *Hey, Tom! You did a great job!* MARY: *I'll drink to that!* TOM: *Thanks!* □ JANE: *I think I'll take everybody out to dinner.* SALLY: *I'll drink to that!*

I'll get back to you (on that). AND **Let me get back to you (on that).** I will report back later with my decision. (More likely said by a boss to an employee than vice versa.) □ BOB: *I have a question about the Wilson project.* MARY: *I have to go to a meeting now. I'll get back to you on that.* BOB: *It's sort of urgent.* MARY: *It can wait. It will wait.* □ SUE: *Shall I close the Wilson account?* JANE: *Let me get back to you on that.*

I'll get right on it. I will begin work on that immediately. □ BOB: *Please do this report immediately.* FRED: *I'll get right on it.* □ JANE: *Please call Tom and ask him to rethink this proposal.* JOHN: *I'll get right on it.*

I'll have the same. AND **The same for me.** I would like the same thing that the last person chose. □ WAITRESS: *What would you like?* TOM: *Hamburger, fries, and coffee.* JANE: *I'll have the same.* □ JOHN: *For dessert, I'll have strawberry ice cream.* BILL: *I'll have the same.*

I'll have to beg off. a polite expression used to turn down an informal invitation. □ ANDREW: *Thank you for inviting me, but I'll have to beg off. I have a conflict.* HENRY: *I'm sorry to hear that. Maybe some other time.* □ BILL: *Do you think you can come to the party?* BOB: *I'll have to beg off. I have another engagement.* BILL: *Maybe some other time.*

I'll look you up when I'm in town. I will try to visit you the next time I am in town. □ BILL: *I hope to see you again sometime.* MARY: *I'll look you up when I'm in town.* □ ANDREW: *Good-bye, Fred. It's been nice talking to you. I'll look you up when I'm in town.* FRED: *See you around, dude.*

I'll put a stop to that. I'll see that the undesirable activity is stopped. □ FRED: *There are two boys fighting in the hall.* BOB: *I'll put a stop to that.* □ SUE: *The sales force is ignoring almost every customer in the older neighborhoods.* MARY: *I'll put a stop to that!*

(I'll) see you in a little while. a phrase indicating that the speaker will see the person spoken to within a few hours at the most. □

JOHN: *I'll see you in a little while.* JANE: *Okay. Bye till later.* ☐ SALLY: *I have to get dressed for tonight.* FRED: *I'll pick you up about nine. See you in a little while.* SALLY: *See you.*

I'll see you later. AND **(See you) later.** Good-bye until I see you again. ☐ JOHN: *Good-bye, Sally. I'll see you later.* SALLY: *Until later, then.* ☐ BOB: *Time to go. Later.* MARY: *Later.*

(I'll) see you next year. a good-bye expression said toward the end of one year. ☐ BOB: *Happy New Year!* SUE: *You, too! See you next year.* ☐ JOHN: *Bye. See you tomorrow.* MARY: *It's New Year's Eve. See you next year!* JOHN: *Right! I'll see you next year!*

(I'll) see you (real) soon. *Good-bye.* I will meet you again soon. ☐ BILL: *Bye, Sue. See you.* SUE: *See you real soon, Bill.* ☐ JOHN: *Bye, you two.* SALLY: *See you soon.* JANE: *See you, John.*

(I'll) see you then. I will see you at the time we've just agreed upon. ☐ JOHN: *Can we meet at noon?* BILL: *Sure. See you then. Bye.* JOHN: *Bye.* ☐ JOHN: *I'll pick you up just after midnight.* SALLY: *See you then.*

(I'll) see you tomorrow. I will see you when we meet again tomorrow. (Typically said to someone whose daily schedule is the same as one's own.) ☐ BOB: *Bye, Jane.* JANE: *Good night, Bob. See you tomorrow.* ☐ SUE: *See you tomorrow.* JANE: *Until tomorrow. Bye.*

(I'll) talk to you soon. I will talk to you on the telephone again soon. ☐ SALLY: *Bye now. Talk to you soon.* JOHN: *Bye now.* ☐ BILL: *Nice talking to you. Bye.* MARY: *Talk to you soon. Bye.*

I'll thank you to keep your opinions to yourself. I do not care about your opinion of this matter. ☐ JANE: *This place is sort of drab.* JOHN: *I'll thank you to keep your opinions to yourself.* ☐ BILL: *Your whole family is sort of long-legged.* JOHN: *I'll thank you to keep your opinions to yourself.*

I'll thank you to mind your own business. a polite version of *Mind your own business.* (Shows a little anger.) ☐ TOM: *How much did this cost?* JANE: *I'll thank you to mind your own business.* ☐ BOB: *Is your house in your name or your brother's?* JOHN: *I'll thank you to mind your own business.*

(I'll) try to catch you later. See the following entry.

(I'll) try to catch you some other time. AND **(I'll) try to catch you later.; I'll try to see you later.** We do not have time to talk now, so *I'll try to see you later.* (An expression said when it is inconvenient for one or both parties to meet or converse.) □ BILL: *I need to get your signature on this contract.* SUE: *I really don't have a second to spare right now.* BILL: *Okay, I'll try to catch you some other time.* SUE: *Later this afternoon would be fine.* □ BILL: *I'm sorry for the interruptions, Tom. Things are very busy right now.* TOM: *I'll try to see you later.*

I'll try to see you later. See the previous entry.

(I) love it! It is just wonderful. (Colloquial. This is just a common, idiomatic variant of *I love it.*) □ MARY: *What do you think of this car?* BILL: *Love it! It's really cool!* □ BOB: *What a joke, Tom!* JANE: *Yes, love it!* TOM: *Gee, thanks.*

(I'm) afraid not. AND **'Fraid not.** I believe, regrettably, that the answer is no. (The apostrophe is not always used.) □ RACHEL: *Can I expect any help with this problem?* HENRY: *I'm afraid not.* □ ANDREW: *Will you be there when I get there?* BILL: *Afraid not.*

(I'm) afraid so. AND **'Fraid so.** I believe, regrettably, that the answer is yes. (The apostrophe is not always used.) □ ALICE: *Do you have to go?* JOHN: *Afraid so.* □ RACHEL: *Can I expect some difficulty with Mr. Franklin?* BOB: *I'm afraid so.*

Imagine that! See *Fancy that!*

I'm all ears. See *I'm listening.*

I'm busy. Do not bother me now.; I cannot attend to your needs now. □ BOB: *Can I talk to you?* BILL: *I'm busy.* BOB: *It's important.* BILL: *Sorry, I'm busy!* □ FRED: *Can you help me with this?* BILL: *I'm busy. Can it wait a minute?* FRED: *Sure. No rush.*

I'm cool. I'm fine. (Slang.) □ BOB: *How you been?* FRED: *I'm cool, man. Yourself?* BOB: *The same.* □ FATHER: *How are you, son?* BILL: *I'm cool, Dad.* FATHER (misunderstanding): *I'll turn up the heat.*

(I'm) delighted to have you (here). AND **(We're) delighted to have you (here).** You're welcome here any time.; *Glad you could come.* (See also *(It's) good to have you here.*) □ BILL: *Thank you for inviting me for dinner, Mr. Franklin.* BILL: *I'm delighted to have you.*

□ *"We're delighted to see you," said Tom's grandparents. "It's so nice to have you here for a visit."*

(I'm) delighted to make your acquaintance. I am very glad to meet you. □ TOM: *My name is Tom. I work in the advertising department.* MARY: *I'm Mary. I work in accounting. Delighted to make your acquaintance.* TOM: *Yeah. Good to meet you.* □ FRED: *Sue, this is Bob. He'll be working with us on the Wilson project.* SUE: *I'm delighted to make your acquaintance, Bob.* BOB: *My pleasure.*

(I'm) doing okay. 1. I'm just fine. □ BOB: *How you doing?* BILL: *Doing okay. And you?* BOB: *Things could be worse.* □ MARY: *How are things going?* SUE: *I'm doing fine, thanks. And you?* MARY: *Doing okay.* 2. I'm doing as well as can be expected.; I'm feeling better. □ MARY: *How are you feeling?* SUE: *I'm doing okay—as well as can be expected.* □ TOM: *I hope you're feeling better.* SALLY: *I'm doing okay, thanks.*

I'm easy (to please). I accept that. I am not particular. □ TOM: *Hey, man! Do you care if we get a sausage pizza rather than mushroom?* BOB: *Fine with me. I'm easy.* □ MARY: *How do you like this music?* BOB: *It's great, but I'm easy to please.*

(I'm) feeling okay. I am doing well.; I am feeling well. □ ALICE: *How are you feeling?* JANE: *I'm feeling okay.* □ JOHN: *How are things going?* FRED: *Feeling okay.*

(I'm) glad to hear it. a phrase expressing pleasure at what the speaker has just said. □ SALLY: *We have a new car, finally.* MARY: *I'm glad to hear it.* □ TOM: *Is your sister feeling better?* BILL: *Oh, yes, thanks.* TOM: *Glad to hear it.*

I'm glad to meet you. See *(I'm) (very) glad to meet you.*

(I'm) glad you could come. AND **(We're) glad you could come.** a phrase said by the host or hostess [or both] to a guest. □ TOM: *Thank you so much for having me.* SALLY: *We're glad you could come.* JOHN: *Yes, we are. Bye.* □ BILL: *Bye.* SALLY: *Bye, Bill. Glad you could come.*

(I'm) glad you could drop by. AND **(We're) glad you could drop by.; (I'm) glad you could stop by.; (We're) glad you could stop by.** a phrase said by the host or hostess (or both) to a guest who has appeared suddenly or has come for only a short visit. □ TOM: *Good-bye. Had a nice time.* MARY: *Thank you for coming, Tom.*

Glad you could drop by. □ TOM: *Thank you so much for having me.* SALLY: *We're glad you could drop by.*

(I'm) glad you could stop by. See the previous entry.

I'm gone. an expression said just before leaving. (Slang. See also *I'm out of here.*) □ BOB: *Well, that's all. I'm gone.* BILL: *See ya!* □ JANE: *I'm gone. See you guys.* JOHN: *See you, Jane.* FRED: *Bye, Jane.*

(I'm) having a wonderful time; wish you were here. a catch phrase that is thought to be written onto postcards by people who are away on vacation. □ *John wrote on all his cards, "Having a wonderful time; wish you were here." And he really meant it too.* □ *"I'm having a wonderful time; wish you were here," said Tom, speaking on the phone to Mary, suddenly feeling very insincere.*

I'm having quite a time **1.** I am having a very enjoyable time. □ JOHN: *Having fun?* JANE: *Oh, yes. I'm having quite a time.* □ BOB: *Do you like the seashore?* SALLY: *Yes, I'm having quite a time.* **2.** I am having a very difficult time. □ DOCTOR: *Well, what seems to be the problem?* MARY: *I'm having quite a time. It's my back.* DOCTOR: *Let's take a look at it.* □ FATHER: *How's school?* BILL: *Pretty tough. I'm having quite a time. Calculus is killing me.*

(I'm) having the time of my life. I am having the best time ever. □ BILL: *Are you having a good time, Mary?* MARY: *Don't worry about me. I'm having the time of my life.* □ MARY: *What do you think about this theme park?* BILL: *Having the time of my life. I don't want to leave.*

(I'm) just getting by. an expression indicating that one is just surviving financially or otherwise. □ BOB: *How you doing, Tom?* TOM: *Just getting by, Bob.* □ *"I wish I could get a better job," remarked Tom. "I'm just getting by as it is."*

I'm just looking. See *I'm only looking.*

(I'm just) minding my own business. an answer to a greeting inquiry asking what one is doing. (This answer also can carry the implication "Since I am minding my own business, why aren't you minding your own business?" □ TOM: *Hey, man, what are you doing?* BILL: *Minding my own business. See you around.* □ SUE:

Hi, Mary. What have you been doing? MARY: *I'm just minding my own business and trying to keep out of trouble.*

(I'm) (just) plugging along.   I am doing satisfactorily.; I am just managing to function.   □ BILL: *How are things going?* BOB: *I'm just plugging along.*   □ SUE: *How are you doing, Fred?* FRED: *Just plugging along, thanks. And you?* SUE: *About the same.*

(I'm) (just) thinking out loud.   I'm saying things that might better remain as private thoughts. (A way of characterizing or introducing one's opinions or thoughts. Also past tense.)   □ SUE: *What are you saying, anyway? Sounds like you're scolding someone.* BOB: *Oh, sorry. I was just thinking out loud.*   □ BOB: *Now, this goes over here.* BILL: *You want me to move that?* BOB: *Oh, no. Just thinking out loud.*

I'm like you   an expression introducing a statement of a similarity that the speaker shares with the person spoken to.   □ MARY: *And what do you think about this pair?* JANE: *I'm like you, I like the ones with lower heels.*   □ *"I'm like you," confided Fred. "I think everyone ought to pay the same amount."*

I'm listening. AND **I'm all ears.**   You have my attention, so you should talk.   □ BOB: *Look, old pal. I want to talk to you about something.* TOM: *I'm listening.*   □ BILL: *I guess I owe you an apology.* JANE: *I'm all ears.*

I'm not finished with you.   I still have more to say to you.   □ *Bill started to turn away when he thought the scolding was finished. "I'm not finished with you," bellowed his father.*   □ *When the angry teacher paused briefly to catch his breath, Bob turned as if to go. "I'm not finished with you," screamed the teacher, filled anew with breath and invective.*

I'm not kidding.   I am telling the truth.; I am not trying to fool you.   □ MARY: *Those guys are all suspects in the robbery.* SUE: *No! They can't be!* MARY: *I'm not kidding!*   □ JOHN (gesturing): *The fish I caught was this big!* JANE: *I don't believe it!* JOHN: *I'm not kidding!*

I'm not surprised. AND **I don't wonder.**   It is not surprising.; It should not surprise anyone.   □ MARY: *All this talk about war has my cousin very worried.* SUE: *No doubt. At his age, I don't wonder.*   □ JOHN: *All of the better-looking ones sold out right away.* JANE: *I'm not surprised.*

I'm off. an expression said by someone who is just leaving. (Slang.) □ BOB: *Time to go. I'm off.* MARY: *Bye.* □ SUE: *Well, it's been. Good-bye. Got to go.* MARY: *I'm off too. Bye.*

I'm only looking. AND **I'm just looking.** I am not a buyer, I am only examining your merchandise. (A phrase said to a shopkeeper or clerk who asks *May I help you?*) □ CLERK: *May I help you?* MARY: *No, thanks. I'm only looking.* □ CLERK: *May I help you?* JANE: *I'm just looking, thank you.*

I'm out of here. I am going to leave immediately. (Slang. The *out of* is usually pronounced *outta*.) □ JOHN: *I'm out of here.* JANE: *Bye.* □ SALLY: *Getting late. I'm out of here.* SUE: *Me too. Let's go.*

(I'm) pleased to meet you. an expression said when introduced to someone. □ TOM: *I'm Tom Thomas.* BILL: *Pleased to meet you. I'm Bill Franklin.* □ JOHN: *Have you met Sally Hill?* BILL: *I don't believe I've had the pleasure. I'm pleased to meet you, Sally.* SALLY: *My pleasure, Bill.*

I'm (really) fed up (with someone or something). I have had enough of someone or something. Something must be done. □ TOM: *This place is really dull.* JOHN: *Yeah. I'm fed up with it. I'm out of here!* □ SALLY: *Can't you do anything right?* BILL: *I'm really fed up with you! You're always picking on me!*

(I'm) sorry. the phrase used for a simple apology. □ BILL: *Oh! You stepped on my toe!* BOB: *I'm sorry.* □ JOHN: *You made me miss my bus!* SUE: *Sorry.*

(I'm) sorry to hear that. an expression of consolation. □ JOHN: *My cat died last week.* JANE: *I'm sorry to hear that.* □ BILL: *I'm afraid I won't be able to continue here as head teller.* MARY: *Sorry to hear that.*

(I'm) sorry you asked (that). I regret that you asked about something I wanted to forget. □ TOM: *What on earth is this hole in your suit jacket?* BILL: *I'm sorry you asked. I was feeding a squirrel and it bit through my pocket where the food was.* □ SALLY: *Why is there only canned soup in the cupboard?* JOHN: *Sorry you asked that. We're broke. We have no money for food.* SALLY: *Want some soup?*

I'm speechless. I am so surprised that I cannot think of anything to say. □ MARY: *Fred and I were married last week.* SALLY: *I'm speechless.* □ TOM: *The mayor just died!* JANE: *What? I'm speechless!*

I must be off. an expression announcing the speaker's intention of leaving. □ BILL: *It's late. I must be off.* BOB: *Me, too. I'm out of here.* □ SUE: *I must be off.* JOHN: *The game's not over yet.* SUE: *I've seen enough.*

I must say good night. an expression announcing the speaker's intention of leaving for the night. □ JANE: *It's late. I must say good night.* BOB: *Can I see you again?* JANE: *Call me. Good night, Bob.* BOB: *Good night, Jane.* □ SUE: *I must say good night.* MARY: *Good night, then. See you tomorrow.*

(I'm) (very) glad to meet you. a polite expression said to a person to whom one has just been introduced. □ MARY: *I'd like you to meet my brother, Tom.* BILL: *I'm very glad to meet you, Tom.* □ JANE: *Hi! I'm Jane.* BOB: *Glad to meet you. I'm Bob.*

I'm with you. I agree with you.; I will join with you in doing what you suggest. (With a stress on both *I* and *you*.) □ SALLY: *I think this old bridge is sort of dangerous.* JANE: *I'm with you. Let's go back another way.* □ BOB: *This place is horrible.* BILL: *I'm with you. Want to go somewhere else?*

in any case a phrase that introduces or follows a conclusion. □ JANE: *In any case, I want you to do this.* JOHN: *All right. I'll do it.* □ MARY: *This one may or may not work out.* SUE: *In any case, I can do it if necessary.*

incidentally See *by the way.*

in due time after the appropriate amount of time has expired; in a while. □ MARY: *When do you think the plane will arrive?* BILL: *In due time, my dear, in due time.* □ JOHN: *All these things will straighten out in due time.* JANE: *I just can't wait that long.*

I need it yesterday. an answer to the question "When do you need this?" (Indicates that the need is urgent.) □ BOB: *When do you need that urgent survey?* BILL: *I need it yesterday.* □ MARY: *Where's the Wilson contract?* SUE: *Do you need it now?* MARY: *I need it yesterday! Where is it?*

I never! See *(Well,) I never!*

(I) never heard of such a thing. an expression of amazement and disbelief. (Compare to *Well, I never!*) □ BILL: *The company sent out a representative to our very house to examine the new sofa and see what the problem was with the wobbly leg.* JANE: *I've never heard of such a thing! That's very unusual.* □ BILL: *The tax office is now open on Sunday!* SUE: *Never heard of such a thing!*

(I) never thought I'd see you here! I am surprised to see you here. □ TOM: *Hi, Sue! I never thought I'd see you here!* SUE: *Hi, Tom. I was thinking the same thing about you.* □ BILL: *Well, Tom Thomas. I never thought I'd see you here!* TOM: *Likewise. I didn't know you liked opera.*

in my humble opinion a phrase introducing the speaker's opinion. □ *"In my humble opinion," began Fred, arrogantly, "I have achieved what no one else ever could."* □ BOB: *What are we going to do about the poor condition of the house next door?* BILL: *In my humble opinion, we will mind our own business.*

in my opinion See *as I see it.*

in my view See *as I see it.*

in other words a phrase introducing a restatement of what has just been said. □ HENRY: *Sure I want to do it, but how much do I get paid?* ANDREW: *In other words, you're just doing it for the money.* □ BILL: *Well, I suppose I really should prepare my entourage for departure.* BOB: *In other words, you're leaving?* BILL: *One could say that, I suppose.* BOB: *Why didn't one?*

in the first place originally; basically; for openers. (This can run through **in the second place, in the third place**, but not much higher.) □ BILL: *What did I do?* BOB: *In the first place, you had no business being there at all. In the second place, you were acting rude.* □ BILL: *Why on earth did you do it in the first place?* SUE: *I don't know.*

in the interest of saving time I can hurry things along. □ MARY: *In the interest of saving time, I'd like to save questions for the end of my talk.* BILL: *But I have an important question now!* □ *"In the interest of saving time," said Jane, "I'll give you the first three answers."*

in the main basically; generally. □ MARY: *Everything looks all right—in the main.* SALLY: *What details need attention?* MARY: *Just a few things here and there. Like on page 27.* □ JOHN: *Are you all ready?* SUE: *I think we're ready, in the main.* JOHN: *Then, we shall go.*

in this day and age now; in these modern times. □ BILL: *Ted flunked out of school.* MOTHER: *Imagine that! Especially in this day and age.* □ BILL: *Taxes keep going up and up.* BOB: *What do you expect in this day and age?*

in view of due to; because of. □ *"In view of the bad weather,"* began Tom, *"the trip has been canceled.* □ ANDREW: *Can we hurry? We'll be late.* MARY: *In view of your attitude about going in the first place, I'm surprised you even care.*

I owe you one. Thank you, now I owe you a favor. □ BOB: *I put the extra copy of the book on your desk.* SUE: *Thanks, I owe you one.* □ BILL: *Let me pay for it.* BOB: *Thanks a lot, I owe you one.*

I promise you! I am telling you the truth! (Compare to *Trust me!*) □ JOHN: *Things will work out, I promise you!* JANE: *Okay, but when?* □ SUE: *I'll be there exactly when I said.* BOB: *Are you sure?* SUE: *I promise you, I'm telling the truth!*

(I) read you loud and clear. **1.** a response used by someone communicating by radio stating that the hearer understands the transmission clearly. (See also *Do you read me?*) □ CONTROLLER: *This is Aurora Center, do you read me?* PILOT: *Yes, I read you loud and clear.* □ CONTROLLER: *Left two degrees. Do you read me?* PILOT: *Roger. Read you loud and clear.* **2.** I understand what you are telling me. (Used in general conversation, not in radio communication.) □ BOB: *Okay. Now, do you understand exactly what I said?* MARY: *I read you loud and clear.* □ MOTHER: *I don't want to have to tell you again. Do you understand?* BILL: *I read you loud and clear.*

(I) really must go. an expression announcing or repeating one's intention to depart. □ BOB: *It's getting late. I really must go.* JANE: *Good night, then. See you tomorrow.* □ SALLY: *I really must go.* JOHN: *Do you really have to? It's early yet.*

(Is) anything going on? Is there anything exciting or interesting happening here? □ ANDREW: *Hey, Man! Anything going on?* HENRY: *No. This place is dull as can be.* □ BOB: *Come in, Tom.* TOM: *Is anything going on?* BOB: *No. You've come on a very ordinary day.*

(Is) everything okay? How are you?; How are things? □ JOHN: *Hi, Mary. Is everything okay?* MARY: *Sure. What about you?* JOHN: *I'm okay.* □ WAITER: *Is everything okay?* BILL: *Yes, it's fine.*

(Is it) cold enough for you? a greeting inquiry made during very cold weather. □ BOB: *Hi, Bill! Is it cold enough for you?* BILL: *It's unbelievable!* □ JOHN: *Glad to see you. Is it cold enough for you?* BILL: *Oh, yes! This is awful!*

(Is it) hot enough for you? a greeting inquiry made during very hot weather. □ BOB: *Hi, Bill! Is it hot enough for you?* BILL: *Yup.* □ JOHN: *Nice to see you here! Is it hot enough for you?* BILL: *Good grief, yes! This is awful!*

I 'spect See under *I guess; I guess (so).; I guess not.*

I spoke out of turn. I said the wrong thing.; I should not have said what I did. (An apology.) □ BILL: *You said I was the one who did it.* MARY: *I'm sorry. I spoke out of turn. I was mistaken.* □ BILL: *I seem to have said the wrong thing.* BOB: *You certainly did.* BILL: *I spoke out of turn, and I'm sorry.*

I spoke too soon. **1.** I am wrong.; I spoke before I knew the facts. □ BILL: *I know I said I would, but I spoke too soon.* SUE: *I thought so.* □ JOHN: *You said that everything would be all right.* JANE: *I spoke too soon. That was before I learned that you had been arrested.* **2.** What I had said was just now contradicted. □ BOB: *It's beginning to brighten up. I guess it won't rain after all.* JOHN: *I'm glad to hear that.* BOB: *Whoops! I spoke too soon. I just felt a raindrop on my cheek.* □ BILL: *Thank heavens! Here's John now.* BOB: *No, that's Fred.* BILL: *I spoke too soon. He sure looked like John.*

I 'spose See *I guess.*

I 'spose not See *I guess not.*

I 'spose (so) See *I guess (so).*

Is someone there? a way of requesting to talk to someone in particular over the telephone. (This is not just a request to find out where *someone* is. The *someone* is usually a person's name.) □ TOM: *Hello?* MARY: *Hello. Is Bill there?* TOM: *No. Can I take a message?* □ TOM: *Hello?* MARY: *Hello. Is Tom there?* TOM: *Speaking.*

Is that everything? See *(Will there be) anything else?*

Is that so? AND **Is that right?** **1.** Is what you said correct? (With rising question intonation.) □ HENRY: *These are the ones we need.* ANDREW: *Is that right? They don't look so good to me.* □ FRED: *Tom is the one who came in late.* RACHEL: *Is that so? It looked like Bill to me.* **2.** That is what you say, but I do not believe you. (No rising question intonation. Slightly rude.) □ MARY: *You are making a mess of this.* ALICE: *Is that so? And I suppose that you're perfect?* □ BOB: *I found your performance to be weak in a number of places.* HENRY: *Is that right? Why don't you tell me about those weaknesses.*

Is there anything else? See *(Will there be) anything else?*

Is there some place I can wash up? See *Where can I wash up?*

(Is) this (seat) taken? an inquiry made by a person in a theater, auditorium, etc., asking someone already seated whether an adjacent seat is available or already taken. □ *Finally, Bill came to a row where there was an empty seat. Bill leaned over to the person sitting beside the empty seat and whispered, "Is this seat taken?"* □ FRED: *'Scuse me. This taken?* ALICE: *No. Help yourself.*

I suppose See *I guess.*

I suppose not. See *I guess not.*

I suppose (so). See *I guess (so).*

I suspect See *I guess.*

I suspect not. See *I guess not.*

I suspect (so). See *I guess (so).*

(It) beats me. AND **(It's) got me beat.; You got me beat.** I do not know the answer.; I cannot figure it out.; The question has me stumped. (The stress is on *me*.) □ BILL: *When are we supposed to go over to Tom's?* JOE: *Beats me.* □ SALLY: *What's the largest river in the world?* BOB: *You got me beat.*

It blows my mind! It really amazes and shocks me. (Slang.) □ BILL: *Did you hear about Tom's winning the lottery?* SUE: *Yes, it blows my* *mind!* □ JOHN: *Look at all that paper! What a waste of trees!* JANE: *It blows my mind!*

(It) can't be helped. Nothing can be done to help the situation.; It isn't anyone's fault. (Also in the past tense, **It couldn't be helped.**) □ JOHN: *The accident has blocked traffic in two directions.* JANE: *It can't be helped. They have to get the people out of the cars and send them to the hospital.* □ BILL: *My goodness, the lawn looks dead!* SUE: *It can't be helped. There's no rain and water is rationed.* □ JOHN: *I'm sorry I broke your figurine.* SUE: *It couldn't be helped.* JOHN: *I'll replace it.* SUE: *That would be nice.* □ BILL: *I'm sorry I'm late. I hope it didn't mess things up.* BOB: *It can't be helped.*

(It) couldn't be better. AND **(Things) couldn't be better.** Everything is fine. □ JOHN: *How are things going?* JANE: *Couldn't be better.* □ BILL: *I hope everything is okay with your new job.* MARY: *Things couldn't be better.*

(It) couldn't be helped. See under *(It) can't be helped.*

(It) doesn't bother me any. AND **(It) doesn't bother me at all.** It does not trouble me at all.; I have no objection. (Compare to *(It) don't bother me none.* Not very polite or cordial. See *(It) won't bother me any.* for the future tense of this expression.) □ JOHN: *Do you mind if I sit here?* JANE: *Doesn't bother me any.* □ SALLY (smoking a cigarette): *Do you mind if I smoke?* BILL: *It doesn't bother me any.*

(It) doesn't bother me at all. See the previous entry.

(It) doesn't hurt to ask. AND **(It) never hurts to ask.** a phrase said when one asks a question, even when the answer is known to be no. □ JOHN: *Can I take some of these papers home with me?* JANE: *No, you can't. You know that.* JOHN: *Well, it doesn't hurt to ask.* □ SUE: *Can I have two of these?* SALLY: *Certainly not!* SUE: *Well, it never hurts to ask.* SALLY: *Well, it just may!*

It doesn't quite suit me. See *This doesn't quite suit me.*

(It) don't bother me none. AND **(It) don't make me no nevermind.** It does not affect me one way or the other.; *It doesn't bother me*

any. (Familiar and ungrammatical. Sometimes used for effect.)
□ JOHN: *Mind if I sit here?* BOB: *It don't bother me none.* □ MARY:
Can I smoke? BILL: *Don't bother me none.*

(It) don't make me no nevermind. See the previous entry.

(It) hasn't been easy. AND **Things haven't been easy.** Things have
been difficult, but I have survived. □ BILL: *I'm so sorry about all
your troubles. I hope things are all right now.* BOB: *It hasn't been easy, but
things are okay now.* □ JOHN: *How are you getting on after your dog
died?* BILL: *Things haven't been easy.*

I think not. See *I guess not.*

I think so. See *I guess (so).*

[it is] See also the entries beginning with *it's.*

It isn't worth it. **1.** Its value does not justify the action you propose.
□ MARY: *Should I write a letter in support of your request?* SUE: *No,
don't bother. It isn't worth it.* □ JOHN: *Do you suppose we should report
that man to the police?* JANE: *No, it isn't worth it.* **2.** Its importance
does not justify the concern you are showing. □ TOM: *I'm so
sorry about your roses all dying.* MARY: *Not to worry. It isn't worth it. They
were sort of sickly anyway.* □ JOHN: *Should I have this coat cleaned? The
stain isn't coming out.* SUE: *It isn't worth it. I only wear it when I shovel
snow anyway.*

It isn't worth the trouble. *Don't bother. It isn't worth it.* □ TOM:
Shall I wrap all this stuff back up? MARY: *No. It's not worth the trouble.
Just stuff it in a paper bag.* □ JANE: *Do you want me to try to save this
little bit of cake?* JOHN: *Oh, no! It's not worth the trouble. I'll just eat it.*

(It) just goes to show (you) (something). That incident or story
has an important moral or message. □ TOM: *The tax people finally
caught up with Henry.* SALLY: *See! It just goes to show.* □ *Indignant over
the treatment she received at the grocery and angry at the youthful clerk, Sally
muttered, "Young people. They expect too much. It just goes to show you how
society has broken down."*

(It) makes me no difference. See *(It) makes no difference to me.*

(It) makes me no nevermind. See the following entry.

(It) makes no difference to me. AND **(It) makes me no difference.; (It) makes me no nevermind.; (It) don't make me no nevermind.** I really do not care, one way or the other. (The first one is standard, the others are colloquial.) □ BILL: *Mind if I sit here?* TOM: *Makes no difference to me.* □ BILL: *What would you say if I ate the last piece of cake?* BOB: *Don't make me no nevermind.*

(It) never hurts to ask. See *(It) doesn't hurt to ask.*

(It) (really) doesn't matter to me. I do not care. □ ANDREW: *What shall I do? What shall I do?* ALICE: *Do whatever you like. Jump off a bridge. Go live in the jungle. It really doesn't matter to me.* □ TOM: *I'm leaving you. Mary and I have decided that we're in love.* SUE: *So, go ahead. It doesn't matter to me. I don't care what you do.*

It's all someone needs. See *That's all someone needs.*

It's been. a phrase said on leaving a party or other gathering. (Slang or familiar colloquial. A shortening of *It's been lovely* or some similar expression.) □ MARY: *Well, it's been. We really have to go, though.* ANDREW: *So glad you could come over. Bye.* □ FRED: *Bye, you guys. See you.* SALLY: *It's been. Really it has. Toodle-oo.*

(It's been) good talking to you. AND **(It's) been good to talk to you.; (It's been) nice talking to you.** a polite phrase said upon departure, at the end of a conversation. □ MARY (as the elevator stops): *Well, this is my floor. I've got to get off.* JOHN: *Bye, Mary. It's been good talking to you.* □ JOHN: *It's been good talking to you, Fred. See you around.* FRED: *Yeah. See you.*

(It's been) good to talk to you. See the previous entry.

(It's been) nice talking to you. See *(It's been) good talking to you.*

(It's) better than nothing. Having something that is not satisfactory is better than having nothing at all. □ JOHN: *How do you like your dinner?* JANE: *It's better than nothing.* JOHN: *That bad, huh?* □ JOHN: *Did you see your room? How do you like it?* JANE: *Well, I guess it's better than nothing.*

It's for you.   This telephone call is for you.   □ HENRY: *Hello?* FRED: *Hello. Is Bill there?* HENRY: *Hey, Bill! It's for you.* BILL: *Thanks. Hello?*   □ *"It's for you," said Mary, handing the telephone receiver to Sally.*

(It's) good to be here. AND **(It's) nice to be here.**   I feel welcome in this place.; It is good to be here.   □ JOHN: *I'm so glad you could come.* JANE: *Thank you. It's good to be here.*   □ ALICE: *Welcome to our house!* JOHN: *Thank you, it's nice to be here.*

(It's) good to have you here. AND **(It's) nice to have you here.**   Welcome to this place.; It is good that you are here.   □ JOHN: *It's good to have you here.* JANE: *Thank you for asking me.*   □ ALICE: *Oh, I'm so glad I came!* FRED: *Nice to have you here.*

(It's) good to hear your voice.   a polite phrase said upon beginning or ending a telephone conversation.   □ BOB: *Hello?* BILL: *Hello, it's Bill.* BOB: *Hello, Bill. It's good to hear your voice.*   □ BILL: *Hello, Tom. This is Bill.* TOM: *Hi, Bill. It's good to hear your voice. What's cooking?*

(It's) good to see you (again).   a polite phrase said when greeting someone whom one has met before.   □ BILL: *Hi, Bob. Remember me? I met you last week at the Wilsons'.* BOB: *Oh, hello, Bill. Good to see you again.*   □ FRED: *Hi. Good to see you again!* BOB: *Nice to see you, Fred.*

(It's) got me beat.   See *(It) beats me.*

(It's) just what you need.   See *That's all someone needs.*

It's nice to be here.   See *(It's) good to be here.*

It's nice to have you here.   See *(It's) good to have you here.*

(It's) nice to meet you.   an expression said just after being introduced to someone.   □ TOM: *Sue, this is my sister, Mary.* SUE: *It's nice to meet you, Mary.* MARY: *How are you, Sue?*   □ BOB: *I'm Bob. Nice to see you here.* JANE: *Nice to meet you, Bob.*

(It's) nice to see you.   **1.** an expression said when greeting or saying good-bye to someone.   □ MARY: *Hi, Bill. It's nice to see you.* BILL:

Nice to see you, Mary. How are things? □ JOHN: *Come on in, Jane. Nice to see you.* JANE: *Thanks, and thank you for inviting me.*

(It's) none of your business! It is nothing that you need to know. It is none of your concern. (Not very polite.) □ ALICE: *How much does a little diamond like that cost?* MARY: *None of your business!* □ JOHN: *Do you want to go out with me Friday night?* MARY: *Sorry, I don't think so.* JOHN: *Well, what are you doing then?* MARY: *None of your business?*

(It's) not half bad. Not as bad as one might have thought. □ MARY: *How do you like this play?* JANE: *Not half bad.* □ JANE: *Well, how do you like college?* FRED: *It's not half bad.*

(It's) no trouble. Do not worry, this is not a problem. □ MARY: *Do you mind carrying all this up to my apartment?* TOM: *It's no trouble.* □ BOB: *Would it be possible for you to get this back to me today?* BILL: *Sure. No trouble.*

(It's) not supposed to. AND **(Someone's) not supposed to.** a phrase indicating that someone or something is not meant to do something. (Often with a person's name or a pronoun as a subject. See the examples.) □ FRED: *This little piece keeps falling off.* CLERK: *It's not supposed to.* □ BILL: *Tom just called from Detroit and says he's coming back tomorrow.* MARY: *That's funny. He's not supposed to.*

It's on me. I will pay this bill. (Usually a bill for a meal or drinks. Compare to *This one's on me.*) □ *As the waiter set down the glasses, Fred said, "It's on me," and grabbed the check.* □ JOHN: *Check, please.* BILL: *No, it's on me this time.*

(It's) out of the question. It cannot be done.; No! (A polite but very firm "No!") □ JANE: *I think we should buy a watchdog.* JOHN: *Out of the question.* □ JOHN: *Can we go to the mountains for a vacation this year?* JANE: *It's out of the question.*

(It's) time for a change. an expression announcing a decision to make a change. □ BILL: *Are you really going to take a new job?* MARY: *Yes, it's time for a change.* □ JANE: *Are you going to Florida for your vacation?* FRED: *No. It's time for a change. We're going skiing.*

(It's) time to go. It is now time to leave. (Usually said by guests, but can be said by an adult to children who are guests.) □ JANE: *Look at the clock! Time to go!* JOHN: *Yup! I'm out of here too.* □

MOTHER: *It's four o'clock. The party's over. Time to go.* BILL: *I had a good time. Thank you.*

(It's) time to hit the road. AND **(I'd) better hit the road.; (I've) got to hit the road.** a phrase indicating that it is time that one departed. (See *(I) have to shove off* for other possible variations.) □ HENRY: *Look at the clock. It's past midnight. It's time to hit the road.* ANDREW: *Yeah. We got to go.* SUE: *Okay, good night.* □ BILL: *I've got to hit the road. I have a long day tomorrow.* MARY: *Okay, good night.* BILL: *Bye, Mary.*

(It's) time to move along. See *(It's) time to run.*

(It's) time to push along. See *(It's) time to run.*

(It's) time to push off. See the following entry.

(It's) time to run. AND **(It's) time to move along.; (It's) time to push along.; (It's) time to push off.; (It's) time to split.** an announcement of one's desire or need to depart. (See *(I) have to shove off* for an illustration of other possible variations.) □ ANDREW: *Time to push off. I've got to get home.* HENRY: *See you, dude.* □ JOHN: *It's time to split. I've got to go.* SUE: *Okay. See you tomorrow.*

(It's) time to shove off. See *(I) have to shove off.*

(It's) time to split. See *(It's) time to run.*

It's time we should be going. a statement made by one member of a pair (or group) of guests to the other member(s). (Typically, a way for a husband or wife to signal the other spouse that it is time to leave.) □ *Mr. Franklin looked at his wife and said softly, "It's time we should be going."* □ TOM: *Well, I suppose it's time we should be going.* MARY: *Yes, we really should.* ALICE: *So early?*

it strikes me that it seems to me that. □ HENRY: *It strikes me that you are losing a little weight.* MARY: *Oh, I love you!* □ *"It strikes me that all this money we are spending is accomplishing very little," said Bill.*

(It) suits me (fine). It is fine with me. □ JOHN: *Is this one okay?* MARY: *Suits me.* □ JOHN: *I'd like to sit up front where I can hear better.* MARY: *Suits me fine.*

It's you! It suits you perfectly.; It is just your style. □ JOHN (trying on jacket): *How does this look?* SALLY: *It's you!* □ SUE: *I'm tak-*

ing a job with the candy company. I'll be managing a store on Maple Street. MARY: *It's you! It's you!*

It's your funeral. If that is what you are going to do, you will have to endure the consequences. □ TOM: *I'm going to call in sick and go to the ball game instead of to work today.* MARY: *Go ahead. It's your funeral.* □ BILL: *I'm going to take my car to the racetrack and see if I can race against someone.* SUE: *It's your funeral.*

(It) won't bother me any. AND **(It) won't bother me at all.** It will not trouble me at all.; I have no objection if you wish to do that. (Not very polite or cordial. See *(It) doesn't bother me any.* for the present tense of this expression.) □ JOHN: *Will you mind if I sit here?* JANE: *Won't bother me any.* □ SALLY (lighting a cigarette): *Do you mind if I smoke?* BILL: *It won't bother me at all.*

(It) won't bother me at all. See the previous entry.

(It) works for me. It is fine with me. (Slang. With stress on *works* and *me.* The answer to *Does it work for you?*) □ BOB: *Is it okay if I sign us up for the party?* SALLY: *It works for me.* □ TOM: *Is Friday all right for the party?* BILL: *Works for me.* BOB: *It works for me too.*

(I've) been getting by. a response to a greeting inquiry into one's well-being indicating that one is having a hard time surviving or that things are just all right, but they could be much better. (See also *(I'm) just getting by.*) □ JOHN: *How are things?* JANE: *Oh, I've been getting by.* □ SUE: *How are you doing?* MARY: *Been getting by. Things could be better.*

(I've) been keeping busy. AND **(I've been) keeping busy.** a response to a specific greeting inquiry asking what one has been doing. □ SUE: *What've you been doing?* JOHN: *Been keeping busy. And you?* SUE: *About the same.* □ MARY: *Been keeping busy?* BOB: *Yeah. Been keeping busy.*

(I've) been keeping cool. AND **(I've been) keeping cool.** an answer to a question about what one has been doing during very hot weather. □ JANE: *How do you like this hot weather?* BILL: *I've been keeping cool.* □ MARY: *Been keeping cool?* BOB: *Yeah. Been keeping cool.*

(I've) been keeping myself busy. AND **(I've been) keeping myself busy.** a typical response to a greeting inquiry asking what one has been doing. □ BILL: *What have you been doing?* BOB: *I've been* *keeping myself busy. What about you?* BILL: *About the same.* □ JOHN: *Yo! What have you been up to?* BILL: *Been keeping myself busy.*

(I've) been keeping out of trouble. AND **(I've been) keeping out of trouble.** a response to any greeting inquiry that asks what one has been doing. □ JOHN: *What have you been doing, Fred?* FRED: *Been keeping out of trouble.* JOHN: *Yeah. Me too.* □ MARY: *How are things, Tom?* TOM: *Oh, I've been keeping out of trouble.*

(I've) been okay. a response to any greeting inquiry that asks how one has been. □ BILL: *Well, how have you been, good buddy?* JOHN: *I've been okay.* □ SUE: *How you doing?* JANE: *Been okay. And you?* SUE: *The same.*

I've been there. I know exactly what you are talking about.; I know exactly what you are going through. □ JOHN: *Wow! Those sales meetings really wear me out!* JANE: *I know what you mean. I've been there.* □ SUE: *These employment interviews are very tiring.* BOB: *I know it! I've been there.*

(I've) been under the weather. a greeting response indicating that one has been ill. □ JOHN: *How have you been?* SALLY: *I've been under the weather, but I'm better.* □ DOCTOR: *How are you?* MARY: *I've been under the weather.* DOCTOR: *Maybe we can fix that. What seems to be the trouble?*

(I've) been up to no good. a vague greeting response indicating that one has been doing mischief. □ JOHN: *What have you been doing, Tom?* TOM: *Oh, I've been up to no good, as usual.* JOHN: *Yeah. Me too.* □ MARY: *Been keeping busy as usual?* SUE: *Yeah. Been up to no good, as usual.* MARY: *I should have known.*

(I've) better things to do. See the following entry.

(I've) (got) better things to do. There are better ways to spend my time.; I cannot waste any more time on this matter. (Either *I've got* or *I have*.) □ ANDREW: *Good-bye. I've got better things to do than stand around here listening to you brag.* HENRY: *Well, good-bye and good riddance.* □ MARY: *How did things go at your meeting with the zoning board?* SALLY: *I gave up. Can't fight city hall. Better things to do.*

(I've) got to be shoving off. See *(I) have to shove off.*

(I've) got to fly. a phrase announcing one's need to depart. (See *(I) have to shove off* for other possible variations.) □ BILL: *Well,* *time's up. I've got to fly.* BOB: *Oh, it's early yet. Stay a while.* BILL: *Sorry. I got to go.* □ *"It's past lunchtime. I've got to fly," said Alice.*

(I've) got to get moving. a phrase announcing one's need to depart. (See *(I) have to shove off* for other possible variations.) □ BILL: *Time to go. Got to get moving.* SALLY: *Bye, Tom.* □ MARY: *It's late and I've got to get moving.* SUE: *Well, if you must, okay. Come again sometime.* MARY: *Bye.*

(I've) got to go. a phrase announcing one's need to depart. (See *(I) have to shove off* for other possible variations.) □ ANDREW: *Bye, I've got to go.* RACHEL: *Bye, little brother. See you.* □ SALLY: *Ciao! Got to go.* SUE: *See ya! Take it easy.*

(I've) got to go home and get my beauty sleep. a phrase announcing one's need to depart. (See *(I) have to shove off* for other possible variations.) □ SUE: *Leaving so early?* JOHN: *I've got to go home and get my beauty sleep.* □ JANE: *I've got to go home and get my beauty sleep.* FRED: *Well, you look to me like you've had enough.* JANE: *Why, thank you.*

(I've) got to hit the road. See *(It's) time to hit the road.*

(I've) got to run. a phrase announcing one's need to depart. (See *(I) have to shove off* for other possible variations.) □ JOHN: *Got to run. It's late.* JANE: *Me too. Seeya, bye-bye.* □ MARY: *Want to watch another movie?* BILL: *No, thanks. I've got to run.*

(I've) got to shove off. See *(I) have to shove off.*

(I've) got to split. a phrase announcing one's need to depart. (See *(I) have to shove off* for other possible variations.) □ JANE: *Look at the time! Got to split.* MARY: *See you later, Jane.* □ BILL: *It's getting late. I've got to split.* SUE: *Okay, see you tomorrow.* BILL: *Good night.*

(I've) got to take off. a phrase announcing one's need to depart. (See *(I) have to shove off* for other possible variations.) □ MARY: *Got to take off. Bye.* BOB: *Leaving so soon?* MARY: *Yes. Time to go.* BOB: *Bye.* □ *"Look at the time. I've got to take off!" shrieked Alice.*

I've got work to do. **1.** I'm too busy to stay here any longer. □ JANE: *Time to go. I've got work to do.* JOHN: *Me too. See you.* □ BOB: *I have to leave now.* BILL: *So soon?* BOB: *Yes, I've got work to do.* **2.** Do not bother me. I'm busy. □ BILL: *Can I ask you a question?* JANE: *I've got work to do.* □ MARY: *There are some things we have to get straight-*

ened out on this Wilson contract. JOHN: *I've got work to do. It will have to wait.*

I've had a lovely time. AND **We've had a lovely time.** a polite expression said to a host or hostess on departure. □ BOB: *I've had a lovely time. Thanks for asking me.* FRED: *We're just delighted you could come. Good night.* BOB: *Good night.* □ SUE: *We've had a lovely time. Good night.* BILL: *Next time don't stay away so long. Good night.*

I've had enough of this! I will not take any more of this situation! □ SALLY: *I've had enough of this! I'm leaving!* FRED: *Me too!* □ JOHN (glaring at Tom): *I've had enough of this! Tom, you're fired!* TOM: *You can't fire me, I quit!*

I've had it up to here (with someone or something). I will not endure any more of someone or something. □ BILL: *I've had it up to here with your stupidity.* BOB: *Who's calling who stupid?* □ JOHN: *I've had it up to here with Tom.* MARY: *Are you going to fire him?* JOHN: *Yes.*

I've heard so much about you. a polite phrase said upon being introduced to someone you have heard about from a friend or the person's relatives. □ BILL: *This is my cousin Kate.* BOB: *Hello, Kate. I've heard so much about you.* □ SUE: *Hello, Bill. I've heard so much about you.* BILL: *Hello. Glad to meet you.*

(I've) never been better. AND **(I've) never felt better.** a response to a greeting inquiry into one's health or state of being. □ MARY: *How are you, Sally?* SALLY: *Never been better, sweetie.* □ DOCTOR: *How are you, Jane?* JANE: *Never felt better.* DOCTOR: *Then why are you here?*

(I've) never felt better. See *(I've) never been better.*

(I've) seen better. a noncommittal and not very positive judgment about something or someone. □ ALICE: *How did you like the movie?* JOHN: *I've seen better.* □ BILL: *What do you think about this weather?* BOB: *Seen better.*

(I've) seen worse. a noncommittal and not totally negative judgment about something or someone. □ ALICE: *How did you like the movie?* JOHN: *I've seen worse.* □ BILL: *What do you think about this weather?* BOB: *Seen worse. Can't remember when, though.*

(I was) just wondering. a comment made after hearing a response to a previous question. (See examples for typical patterns.) □

JOHN: *Do you always keep your film in the refrigerator?* MARY: *Yes, why?* JOHN: *I was just wondering.* □ BOB: *Did this cost a lot?* SUE: *I really don't think you need to know that.* BOB: *Sorry. Just wondering.*

I was up all night with a sick friend. an unlikely, but popular excuse for not being where one was supposed to be the night before. □ BILL: *Where in the world were you last night?* MARY: *Well, I was up all night with a sick friend.* □ *Mr. Franklin said rather sheepishly, "Would you believe I was up with a sick friend?"*

[I will] See the entries beginning with *I'll.*

I wish I'd said that. a comment of praise or admiration for someone's clever remark. □ MARY: *The weed of crime bears bitter fruit.* SUE: *I wish I'd said that.* MARY: *I wish I'd said it first.* □ JOHN: *Tom is simply not able to see through the airy persiflage of Mary's prolix declamation.* JANE: *I wish I'd said that.* JOHN: *I'm sorry I did.*

(I) wonder if a phrase introducing a hypothesis. □ HENRY: *I wonder if I could have another piece of cake.* SUE: *Sure. Help yourself.* □ ANDREW: *Wonder if it's stopped raining yet.* RACHEL: *Why don't you look out the window?* □ ANDREW: *I wonder if I'll pass algebra.* FATHER: *That thought is on all our minds.*

(I) won't breathe a word (of it). AND **(I) won't tell a soul.** I will not tell anyone your secret. □ BILL: *Don't tell anybody, but Sally is getting married.* MARY: *I won't breathe a word of it.* □ ALICE: *The Jacksons are going to have to sell their house. Don't spread it around.* MARY: *I won't tell a soul.*

I won't give up without a fight. I will not give in easily. (Compare to *Don't give up too eas(il)y.*) □ SUE: *Stick by your principles, Fred.* FRED: *Don't worry, I won't give up without a fight.* □ BOB: *The boss wants me to turn the Wilson project over to Tom.* SUE: *How can he do that?* BOB: *I don't know. All I know is that I won't give up without a fight.*

(I) won't tell a soul. See *(I) won't breathe a word (of it).*

[I would] See also the entries beginning with *I'd.*

(I) would if I could(, but I can't). I simply can't do it. □ JANE: *Can't you fix this yourself?* JOHN: *I would if I could, but I can't.* □ BOB: *Can you go to the dance? Hardly anyone is going.* ALICE: *Would if I could.*

I would like to introduce you to someone. See the following entry.

I would like you to meet someone. AND **I would like to introduce you to someone.** an expression used to introduce one person to another. □ MARY: *I would like you to meet my Uncle Bill.* SALLY: *Hello, Uncle Bill. Nice to meet you.* □ TOM: *I would like to introduce you to Bill Franklin.* JOHN: *Hello, Bill. Glad to meet you.* BILL: *Glad to meet you, John.*

(I) wouldn't bet on it. AND **(I) wouldn't count on it.** I do not believe that something will happen. (Also with *that* or some specific happening. See examples.) □ JOHN: *I'll be a vice president in a year or two.* MARY: *I wouldn't bet on that.* □ JOHN: *I'll pick up a turkey on the day before Thanksgiving.* MARY: *Did you order one ahead of time?* JOHN: *No.* MARY: *Then I wouldn't count on it.*

(I) wouldn't count on it. See the previous entry.

(I) wouldn't if I were you. a polite way to advise someone not to do something. □ MARY: *Do you think I should trade this car in on a new one?* SALLY: *I wouldn't if I were you.* □ BOB: *I'm going to plant nothing but corn this year.* SUE: *I wouldn't if I were you.* BOB: *Why?* SUE: *It's better to diversify.*

(I) wouldn't know. There is no way that I would know the answer to that question. □ JOHN: *When will the flight from Miami get in?* JANE: *Sorry, I wouldn't know.* □ BOB: *Are there many fish in the Amazon River?* MARY: *Gee, I wouldn't know.*

J

Just a minute. AND **Just a moment.; Just a second.; Wait a minute.; Wait a sec(ond).** **1.** Please wait a short time. □ JOHN: *Just a minute.* BOB: *What's the matter?* JOHN: *I dropped my wallet.* □ SUE: *Just a sec.* JOHN: *Why?* SUE: *I think we're going in the wrong direction. Let's look at the map.* **2.** Stop there.; *Hold it!* □ JOHN: *Just a minute!* MARY: *What's wrong?* JOHN: *That stick looked sort of like a snake. But it's all right.* MARY: *You scared me to death!* □ MARY: *Wait a minute!* BILL: *Why?* MARY: *We're leaving an hour earlier than we have to.*

Just a moment. See the previous entry.

Just a second. See *Just a minute.*

Just getting by. See *(I'm) just getting by.*

Just goes to show (you). See *(It) just goes to show (you) (something).*

just let me say See *let me (just) say.*

just like that in just the way it was stated; without any [further] discussion or comment. □ SUE: *You can't walk out on me just like that.* JOHN: *I can too. Just watch!* □ MARY: *And then she slapped him in the face, just like that!* SALLY: *She can be so rude.*

Just plugging along. See *(I'm) (just) plugging along.*

(just) taking care of business an answer to the question "What are you doing lately?" (Also abbreviated **T.C.B.**) □ BILL: *Hey, man. What you been doing?* TOM: *Just taking care of business.* □ ANDREW: *Look, officer, I'm just standing here, taking care of business, and this Tom guy comes up and tries to hit me for a loan.* TOM: *That's not true!*

(just) thinking out loud. See *(I'm) (just) thinking out loud.*

Just wait! See *You (just) wait (and see)!*

just want(ed) to See *(I) just want(ed) to.*

Just watch! See *(You) (just) watch!*

Just what you need. See *(It's) just what you need.*

Just wondering. See *(I was) just wondering.*

Just (you) wait (and see)! See *You (just) wait (and see)!*

K

Keeping busy. See *(I've) been keeping busy.; (Have you) been keeping busy?*

Keeping cool. See *(Have you) been keeping cool?; (I've) been keeping cool.*

Keeping myself busy. See *(I've) been keeping myself busy.*

Keeping out of trouble. See *(I've) been keeping out of trouble.*

keep in mind that See *keep (it) in mind that.*

Keep in there! Keep trying. □ ANDREW: *Don't give up, Sally. Keep in there!* SALLY: *I'm doing my best!* □ JOHN: *I'm not very good, but I keep trying.* FRED: *Just keep in there, John.*

Keep in touch. Please try to communicate occasionally. □ RACHEL: *Good-bye, Fred. Keep in touch.* FRED: *Bye, Rach.* □ SALLY (throwing kisses): *Good-bye, you two.* MARY (waving good-bye): *Be sure and write.* SUE: *Yes, keep in touch.*

keep (it) in mind that introduces something that the speaker wants remembered. □ BILL: *When we get there I want to take a long hot shower.* FATHER: *Keep it in mind that we are guests, and we have to fit in with the routines of the household.* □ SALLY: *Keep it in mind that you don't work here anymore, and you just can't go in and out of offices like that.* FRED: *I guess you're right.*

Keep it up! 1. *Keep up the good work!; Keep on doing it.; Keep (on) trying.* □ JANE: *I think I'm doing better in calculus.* JOHN: *Keep it up!* □ SALLY: *I can now jog for almost three miles.* FRED: *Great! Keep it up!* 2. Just keep acting that way and see what happens to you.

(Compare to *(Go ahead,) make my day!*) □ JOHN: *You're just not doing what is expected of you.* BILL: *Keep it up! Just keep it up, and I'll quit right when you need me most.* □ *"Your behavior is terrible, young man! You just keep it up and see what happens,"* warned Alice. *"Just keep it up!"*

Keep (on) trying. AND **Don't quit trying.** a phrase encouraging continued efforts. □ JANE: *I think I'm doing better in calculus.* JOHN: *Keep trying! You can get an A.* □ SUE: *I really want that promotion, but I keep getting turned down.* BILL: *Don't quit trying! You'll get it.*

Keep out of my way. AND **Stay out of my way.** **1.** Don't get in my pathway. □ JOHN: *Keep out of my way! I'm carrying a heavy load.* BILL: *Sorry.* □ *"Keep out of my way!"* shouted the piano mover. **2.** Don't cause me any trouble. □ HENRY: *I'm going to get even no matter what. Keep out of my way.* ANDREW: *Keep it up! You'll really get in trouble.* □ JOHN: *I intend to work my way to the top in this business.* MARY: *So do I, so just keep out of my way.*

Keep out of this! AND **Stay out of this!** This is not your business, so do not try to get involved. □ JOHN: *Now you listen to me, Fred!* MARY: *That's no way to talk to Fred!* JOHN: *Keep out of this, Mary! Mind your own business!* FRED: *Stay out of this, Mary!* MARY: *It's just as much my business as it is yours.*

Keep quiet. AND **Keep still.** Get quiet and stay that way. □ JOHN: *I'm going to go to the store.* BILL: *Keep quiet.* JOHN: *I just said. . .* BILL: *I said, keep quiet!* □ CHILD: *I want some candy!* MOTHER: *Keep still.*

Keep quiet about it. See *Keep still about it.*

Keep smiling. a parting phrase encouraging someone to have good spirits. □ JOHN: *Things are really getting tough.* SUE: *Well, just keep smiling. Things will get better.* □ BILL: *What a day! I'm exhausted and depressed.* BOB: *Not to worry. Keep smiling. Things will calm down.*

Keep still. See *Keep quiet.*

Keep still about it. AND **Keep quiet about it.** Don't tell it to anyone. □ BILL: *Are you really going to sell your car?* MARY: *Yes, but keep quiet about it.* □ JOHN: *Someone said you're looking for a new job.* SUE: *That's right, but keep still about it.*

Keep this to yourself. a phrase introducing something that is meant to be a secret. □ ANDREW: *Keep this to yourself, but I'm go-*

ing to Bora Bora on my vacation. HENRY: *Sounds great. Can I go too?* □ JOHN: *Keep this to yourself. Mary and I are breaking up.* SUE: *I won't tell a soul.*

Keep up the good work.   Please keep doing the good things that you are doing now. (A general phrase of encouragement.) □ FA-THER: *Your grades are fine, Bill. Keep up the good work.* BILL: *Thanks, Dad.* □ *"Nice play,"* said the coach. *"Keep up the good work!"*

Keep your chin up.   an expression of encouragement to someone who has to bear some emotional burdens. □ FRED: *I really can't take much more of this.* JANE: *Keep your chin up. Things will get better.* □ JOHN: *Smile, Fred. Keep your chin up.* FRED: *I guess you're right. I just get so depressed when I think of this mess I'm in.*

Keep your mouth shut (about someone or something).   Do not tell anyone about someone or something. □ BOB: *Are you going to see the doctor?* MARY: *Yes, but keep your mouth shut about it.* □ BOB: *Isn't Tom's uncle in tax trouble?* JANE: *Yes, but keep your mouth shut about him.*

Keep your nose out of my business.   See *Mind your own business.*

Keep your opinions to yourself!   I do not want to hear your opin-ions! □ JANE: *I think this room looks drab.* SUE: *Keep your opinions to yourself! I like it this way!* □ SALLY: *You really ought to do something about your hair. It looks like it was hit by a truck.* JOHN: *Keep your opinions to yourself. This is the latest style where I come from.* SALLY: *I won't suggest where that might be.*

Keep your shirt on!   Be patient!; Just wait a minute! (Colloquial.) □ JOHN: *Hey, hurry up! Finish this!* BILL: *Keep your shirt on! I'll do it when I'm good and ready.* □ JOHN: *Waiter! We've been waiting fifteen minutes! What sort of place is this?* WAITER: *Keep your shirt on!* JOHN (quietly): *Now I know what sort of place this is.*

Kind of.   See *Sort of.*

Knock it off!   *Be quiet!*; *Stop that noise!* (Slang.) □ JOHN: *Hey, you guys! Knock it off!* BOB: *Sorry.* BILL: *Sorry. I guess we got a little car-ried away.* □ SUE: *All right. Knock it off!* BILL: *Yeah. Let's get down to business.*

Know something? See *(Do you) want to know something?*

Know what? See *(Do you) know what?*

Know what I mean? See *(Do you) know what I'm saying?*

Know what I'm saying? See *(Do you) know what I'm saying?*

L

Ladies first. an expression indicating that women should go first, as in going through a doorway. ☐ *Bob stepped back and made a motion with his hand indicating that Mary should go first. "Ladies first," smiled Bob.* ☐ BOB: *It's time to get in the food line. Who's going to go first?* BILL: *Ladies first, Mary.* MARY: *Why not gentlemen first?* BOB: *Looks like nobody's going first.*

Later. See *I will see you later.*

Later, alligator. See *See you later, alligator.*

Leave it to me. I will attend to it by myself.; I will do it. ☐ JOHN: *This whole business needs to be straightened out.* SUE: *Leave it to me. I'll get it done.* ☐ JANE: *Will you do this as soon as possible?* MARY: *Leave it to me.*

Leave me alone! Stop harassing me!; *Don't bother me!* ☐ JOHN: *You did it. You're the one who always does it.* BILL: *Leave me alone! I never did it.* ☐ FRED: *Let's give Bill a dunk in the pool.* BILL: *Leave me alone!*

Leaving so soon? See *(Are you) leaving so soon?*

Let it be. Leave the situation alone as it is. ☐ ALICE: *I can't get over the way he just left me there on the street and drove off. What an arrogant pig!* MARY: *Oh, Alice, let it be. You'll figure out some way to get even.* ☐ JOHN: *You can't!* BILL: *Can too!* JOHN: *Can't!* BILL: *Can too!* JANE: *Stop! Let it be! That's enough!*

Let me get back to you (on that). See *I'll get back to you (on that).*

Let me have it! AND **Let's have it!** Tell me the news. ☐ BILL: *I'm afraid there's some bad news.* BOB: *Okay. Let me have it! Don't waste time!* BILL: *The plans we made did away with your job.* BOB: *What?* ☐ JOHN: *I didn't want to be the one to tell you this.* BOB: *What is it? Let's have it!* JOHN: *Your cat was just run over.* BOB: *Never mind that, what's the bad news?*

let me (just) say AND **just let me say** a phrase introducing something that the speaker thinks is important. ☐ RACHEL: *Let me say how pleased we all are with your efforts.* HENRY: *Why, thank you very much.* ☐ BOB: *Just let me say that we're extremely pleased with your activity.* BILL: *Thanks loads. I did what I could.*

Let's call it a day. Let us end what we are doing for the day. ☐ MARY: *Well, that's the end of the reports. Nothing else to do.* SUE: *Let's call it a day.* ☐ BOB: *Let's call it a day. I'm tired.* TOM: *Me too. Let's get out of here.*

Let's do lunch (sometime). See *We('ll) have to do lunch sometime.*

Let's do this again (sometime). AND **We must do this again (sometime).** an expression indicating that one member of a group or pair has enjoyed doing something and would like to do it again. ☐ BILL: *What a nice evening.* MARY: *Yes, let's do this again sometime.* BILL: *Bye.* MARY: *Bye, Bill.* ☐ SUE (saying good night): *So nice to see both of you.* MARY: *Oh, yes. We must do this again sometime.*

Let's eat. **1.** an announcement that a meal is ready to be eaten. ☐ FATHER: *It's all ready now. Let's eat.* BILL: *Great! I'm starved.* ☐ JOHN: *Soup's on! Let's eat!* BILL: *Come on, everybody. Let's eat!* **2.** AND **Let's eat something.** a suggestion that it is time to eat. ☐ MARY: *Look at the clock. We only have a few minutes before the show. Let's eat.* ☐ BILL: *What should we do? We have some time to spare.* SUE: *Let's eat something.* BILL: *Good idea.* SUE: *Food is always a good idea with you.*

Let's eat something. See the previous entry.

Let's get down to business. a phrase marking a transition to a business discussion or serious talk. ☐ JOHN: *Okay, enough small talk. Let's get down to business.* MARY: *Good idea.* ☐ *"All right, ladies and gentlemen, let's get down to business,"* said the president of the board.

Let's get out of here. Let us leave (and go somewhere else). ☐ ALICE: *It's really hot in this room. Let's get out of here.* JOHN: *I'm with* *you. Let's go.* □ BILL: *This crowd is getting sort of angry.* BOB: *I noticed that too. Let's get out of here.*

Let's get together (sometime). a vague invitation to meet again, usually said upon departing. (The *sometime* can be a particular time or the word *sometime*.) □ BILL: *Good-bye, Bob.* BOB: *See you, Bill. Let's get together sometime.* □ JANE: *We need to discuss this matter.* JOHN: *Yes, let's get together next week.*

Let's go somewhere where it's (more) quiet. Let us continue our conversation where there is less noise or where we will not be disturbed. □ TOM: *Hi, Mary. It's sure crowded here.* MARY: *Yes, let's go somewhere where it's quiet.* □ BILL: *We need to talk.* SALLY: *Yes, we do. Let's go somewhere where it's more quiet.*

Let's have it! See *Let me have it!*

Let's not go through all that again. We are not going to discuss that matter again. (Compare to *Do we have to go through all that again?*) □ BILL: *Now, I still want to explain again about last night.* SALLY: *Let's not go through all that again!* □ SALLY: *I can't get over the way you spoke to me at our own dinner table.* FRED: *I was only kidding! I said I was sorry. Let's not go through all that again!*

Let's shake on it. Let us mark this agreement by shaking hands on it. □ BOB: *Do you agree?* MARY: *I agree. Let's shake on it.* BOB: *Okay.* □ BILL: *Good idea. Sounds fine.* BOB (extending his hand): *Okay, let's shake on it.* BILL (shaking hands with Bob): *Great!*

Let's talk (about it). Let us talk about the problem and try to settle things. □ TOM: *Bill! Bill! I'm sorry about our argument. Let's talk.* BILL: *Get lost!* □ SALLY: *I've got a real problem.* BOB: *Let's talk about it.*

[let us] See the entries beginning with *Let's*.

Like it or lump it! There is no other choice. Take that or none. (Slang.) □ JOHN: *I don't like this room. It's too small.* BILL: *Like it or lump it. That's all we've got.* □ JANE: *I don't want to be talked to like that.* SUE: *Well, like it or lump it! That's the way we talk around here.*

like I was saying See *as I was saying*.

Likewise(, I'm sure). The same from my point of view. (A hackneyed phrase said in the greeting sequence. See examples.) □ ALICE: *I'm delighted to make your acquaintance.* BOB: *Likewise, I'm sure.*

☐ JOHN: *How nice to see you!* SUE: *Likewise.* JOHN: *Where are you from, Sue?*

like you say See *as you say.*

Long time no see. I have not seen you in a long time.; We have not seen each other in a long time. ☐ TOM: *Hi, Fred. Where have you been keeping yourself?* FRED: *Good to see you, Tom. Long time no see.* ☐ JOHN: *It's Bob! Hi, Bob!* BOB: *Hi, John! Long time no see.*

look a sentence opener seeking the attention of the person spoken to. (Words such as this often use intonation to convey the connotation of the sentence that is to follow. The brief intonation pattern accompanying the word may indicate sarcasm, disagreement, caution, consolation, sternness, etc. See also *look here.*) ☐ SUE: *How could you!* FRED: *Look, I didn't mean to.* ☐ ANDREW: *Look, can't we talk about it?* SUE: *There's no more to be said.* ☐ JOHN: *I'm so sorry!* ANDREW: *Look, we all make mistakes.* ☐ *"Look, let me try again,"* said Fred. ☐ ANDREW: *Look, I've just about had it with you!* SALLY: *And I've had it with you.* ☐ ANDREW: *Look, that can't be right.* RACHEL: *But it is.*

Look alive! Act alert and responsive! ☐ *"Come on, Fred! Get moving! Look alive!"* shouted the coach, who was not happy with Fred's performance. ☐ BILL: *Look alive, Bob!* BOB: *I'm doing the best I can.*

Look (at) what the cat dragged in! *Look who's here!* (A good-humored and familiar way of showing surprise at someone's presence in a place, especially if the person looks a little rumpled. Compare to *(Someone) looks like something the cat dragged in.*) ☐ *Bob and Mary were standing near the doorway talking when Tom came in. "Look what the cat dragged in!" announced Bob.* ☐ MARY: *Hello, everybody. I'm here!* JANE: *Look at what the cat dragged in!*

look here a phrase emphasizing the point that follows. (Can show some impatience. See also *look.*) ☐ HENRY: *Look here, I want to try to help you, but you're not making it easy for me.* RACHEL: *I'm just so upset.* ☐ ANDREW: *Look here, I just asked you a simple question!* BOB: *As I told you in the beginning, there are no simple answers.*

Look me up when you're in town. When you next come to my town, try to find me (and we will get together). (A vague and perhaps insincere invitation.) ☐ BOB: *Nice to see you, Tom. Bye now.* TOM: *Yes, indeed. Look me up when you're in town. Bye.* ☐ SALLY (on the phone): *Bye. Nice talking to you.* MARY: *Bye, Sally. Sorry we can't talk more. Look me up when you're in town.*

Look out! AND **Watch out!** *Be careful; Be aware of the danger near you!* □ *Bob saw the scenery starting to fall on Tom. "Look out!" cried Bob.* □ *"Watch out! That sidewalk is really slick with ice!" warned Sally.*

Looks like something the cat dragged in. See *(Someone) looks like something the cat dragged in.*

Look who's here! an expression drawing attention to someone present at a place. □ BILL: *Look who's here! My old friend Fred. How goes it, Fred?* FRED: *Hi, there, Bill! What's new?* BILL: *Nothing much.* □ BILL: *Look who's here!* MARY: *Yeah. Isn't that Fred Morgan?*

Look who's talking! You are guilty of doing what you have criticized someone else for doing or accused someone else of doing. □ ANDREW: *You criticize me for being late! Look who's talking! You just missed your flight!* JANE: *Well, nobody's perfect.* □ MARY: *You just talk and talk, you go on much too long about practically nothing, and you never give a chance for anyone else to talk, and you just don't know when to stop!* SALLY: *Look who's talking!*

Lord knows I've tried. I certainly have tried very hard. □ ALICE: *Why don't you get Bill to fix this fence?* MARY: *Lord knows I've tried. I must have asked him a dozen times—this year alone.* □ SUE: *I can't seem to get to class on time.* RACHEL: *That's just awful.* SUE: *Lord knows I've tried. I just can't do it.*

lose one's train of thought to forget what one was talking about. □ ANDREW: *I had something important on my mind, but that telephone call made me lose my train of thought.* MARY: *Did it have anything to do with money, such as the money you owe me?* ANDREW: *I can't remember.* □ TOM: *Now, let's take a look at, uh. Well, next I want to talk about something that is very important.* MARY: *I think you lost your train of thought.* TOM: *Don't interrupt. You'll make me forget what I'm saying.*

Lots of luck! I wish you luck; you will need it, but it probably will not do any good. □ BILL: *I'm going to try to get my tax bill lowered.* TOM: *Lots of luck!* □ MARY: *I'll go in there and get him to change his mind, you just watch!* SALLY: *Lots of luck!*

Love it! See *(I) love it!*

Lovely weather for ducks. a greeting phrase meaning that this unpleasant rainy weather must be good for something. □ BILL: *Hi, Bob. How do you like this weather?* BOB: *Lovely weather for ducks.* □ SALLY: *What a lot of rain!* TOM: *Yeah. Lovely weather for ducks. Don't care for it much myself.*

lucky for you a phrase introducing a description of an event that favors the person being spoken to. □ ANDREW: *Lucky for you the train was delayed. Otherwise you'd have to wait till tomorrow morning for the next one.* FRED: *That's luck, all right. I'd hate to have to sleep in the station.* □ JANE: *I hope I'm not too late.* SUE: *Lucky for you, everyone else is late too.*

M

Ma'am? **1.** Did you call me, ma'am? [said to a woman] □
MOTHER: *Tom!* TOM: *Ma'am?* MOTHER: *Come take out the garbage.*
TOM: *Yuck!* □ DOCTOR: *Now, Bill, I need you to do something for me.*
BILL: *Ma'am?* DOCTOR: *Stick out your tongue.* **2.** Will you please re-
peat what you said, ma'am? □ SALLY: *Bring it to me, please.* BILL:
Ma'am? SALLY: *Bring it to me.* □ *Uncle Fred turned his good ear to the
clerk and said, "Ma'am?"*

Make a lap. Sit down. (Slang.) □ ANDREW: *Hey, you're in the way,
Tom! Make a lap, why don't you?* TOM: *Sorry.* □ RACHEL: *Come over
here and make a lap. You make me tired, standing there like that.* JOHN: *You
just want me to sit by you.* RACHEL: *That's right.*

Make it snappy! *Hurry up!;* Move quickly and smartly. □ AN-
DREW: *Make it snappy! I haven't got all day.* BOB: *Don't rush me.* □
MARY: *Do you mind if I stop here and get some film?* BOB: *Not if you make
it snappy!* MARY: *Don't worry. I'll hurry.*

make it (to something) to manage to attend something; to manage
to attend some event. □ *"I'm sorry," said Mary, "I won't be able to
make it to your party."* □ RACHEL: *Can you come to the rally on Saturday?* ANDREW: *Sorry. I can't make it.*

Make it two. I wish to order the thing that someone else just now
ordered. (Said to food or drink service personnel.) □ BILL
(speaking to the waiter): *I'll have the roast chicken.* MARY: *Make it two.*
□ WAITER: *Would you like something to drink?* TOM: *Just a beer.*
WAITER (turning to Mary): *And you?* MARY: *Make it two.*

Make mine something.   I wish to have *something*. (The *something* can be a particular food or drink, a flavor of a food, a size of a garment, or a type of almost anything. Most typically used for food or drink.)   □   BILL: *I want some pie. Yes, I'd like apple.* TOM: *Make mine cherry.*   □   WAITER: *Would you care for some dessert? The ice cream is homemade.* TOM: *Yes, indeed. Make mine chocolate.*

Make my day!   See *(Go ahead,) make my day!*

Make no mistake (about it)!   Do not be mistaken!   □   SALLY: *I'm very angry with you! Make no mistake about it!* FRED: *Whatever it's about, I'm sorry.*   □   CLERK: *Make no mistake, this is the finest carpet available.* SALLY: *I'd like something a little less fine, I think.*

Makes me no difference.   See *(It) makes no difference to me.*

Makes me no nevermind.   See *(It) makes no difference to me.*

Makes no difference to me.   See *(It) makes no difference to me.*

Makes no nevermind to me.   See *(It) makes no difference to me.*

Make up your mind. AND **Make your mind up.**   Please make a decision.; Please choose.   □   HENRY: *I don't have all day. Make up your mind.* RACHEL: *Don't rush me.*   □   BOB: *Make your mind up. We have to catch the plane.* MARY: *I'm not sure I want to go.*

Make your mind up.   See the previous entry.

Make yourself at home.   Please make yourself comfortable in my home. (Also a signal that a guest can be less formal.)   □   ANDREW: *Please come in and make yourself at home.* SUE: *Thank you. I'd like to.*   □   BILL: *I hope I'm not too early.* BOB: *Not at all. Come in and make yourself at home. I've got a few little things to do.* BILL: *Nice place you've got here.*

[may]   See also the entries beginning with *could.*

may as well   See *might as well.*

Maybe some other time. AND **We'll try again some other time.**   a polite phrase said by a person whose invitation has just been turned down by another person.   □   BILL: *Do you think you can come to the party?* BOB: *I'll have to beg off. I have another engagement.* BILL: *Maybe some other time.*   □   JOHN: *Can you and Alice come over this Friday?* BILL: *Gee, sorry. We have something else on.* JOHN: *We'll try again some other time.*

May I help you?   See *How may I help you?*

May I speak to someone?   See *Could I speak to someone?*

might as well AND **may as well**   a phrase indicating that it is probably better to do something than not to do it.   □ BILL: *Should we
try to get there for the first showing of the film?* JANE: *Might as well. Nothing else to do.*   □ ANDREW: *May as well leave now. It doesn't matter if
we arrive a little bit early.* JANE: *Why do we always have to be the first
to arrive?*

Might be better.   See *(Things) could be better.*

mind if   See *(Do you) mind if?*

Mind if I join you?   See *Could I join you?*

Minding my own business.   See *(I'm just) minding my own
business.*

Mind your manners.   See under *Remember your manners.*

Mind your own business. AND **Get your nose out of my business.;
Keep your nose out of my business.**   Stop prying into my af-
fairs. (Not at all polite. The expressions with *get* and *keep* can have
the literal meanings of removing and keeping removed.)   □ AN-
DREW: *This is none of your affair. Mind your own business.* SUE: *I was
only trying to help.*   □ BOB: *How much did you pay in federal taxes last
year?* JANE: *Good grief, Bob! Keep your nose out of my business!*   □
TOM: *How much did it cost?* SUE: *Tom! Get your nose out of my business!*
□ *"Hey!" shrieked Sally, jerking the checkbook out of Sue's grasp. "Get
your nose out of my business!"*

more or less   somewhat. a vague phrase used to express vagueness or
uncertainty.   □ HENRY: *I think this one is what I want, more or less.*
CLERK: *A very wise choice, sir.*   □ HENRY: *Is this one the biggest, more
or less?* JOHN: *Oh, yes. It's the biggest there is.*

More power to you!   *Well done!;* You really stood up for yourself!;
You really did something for your own benefit! (The stress is on *to*,
and the *you* is usually "ya.")   □ BILL: *I finally told her off, but good.*

BOB: *More power to you!* □ SUE: *I spent years getting ready for that job, and I finally got it.* MARY: *More power to you!*

more than you('ll ever) know   A great deal, more than you suspect. □ BOB: *Why did you do it?* BILL: *I regret doing it. I regret it more than you know.* □ JOHN: *Oh, Mary, I love you.* MARY: *Oh, John, I love you more than you'll ever know.*

Morning.   See *(Good) morning.*

Mum's the word.   See *The word is mum.*

my   a sentence opener expressing a little surprise or amazement. (See also *my(, my)*. Words such as this often use intonation to convey the connotation of the sentence that is to follow. The brief intonation pattern accompanying the word may indicate sarcasm, disagreement, caution, consolation, sternness, etc.) □ *"My, what a nice place you have here,"* gloated Gloria. □ RACHEL: *My, it's getting late!* JOHN: *Gee, the evening is just beginning.* □ *"My, it's hot!"* said Fred, smoldering.

(My) goodness (gracious)!   a general expression of interest or mild amazement. □ BILL: *My goodness! The window is broken!* ANDREW: *I didn't do it!* BILL: *Who did, then?* □ *"Goodness! I'm late!"* said Kate, glancing at her watch. □ *"Goodness gracious! Are you hurt?"* asked Sue as she helped the fallen student to his feet.

(My) heavens!   a mild exclamation of surprise or amazement. □ BILL: *Heavens! The clock has stopped.* BOB: *Don't you have a watch?* □ SALLY: *The police are parked in our driveway, and one of them is getting out!* MARY: *My heavens!*

My house is your house. AND **Our house is your house.**   a polite expression said to make a guest feel at home. (From the Spanish phrase *Mi casa, su casa.*) □ BILL: *Hello, Tom.* TOM (entering): *So nice you can put me up for the night.* BILL: *My house is your house, make yourself at home.* □ MARY: *Come in, you two.* BILL: *Thanks.* SUE: *Yes, thank you.* MARY: *Well, what can I get you? My house is your house.*

(My,) how time flies.   **1.** Time has gone by quickly, it is time for me to go. □ BILL: *Look at the clock!* MARY: *How time flies! I guess you'll* *be going.* TOM: *Oh, no. I just noticed that it's time for the late show on television.* □ JOHN: *My watch says it's nearly midnight. How time flies!* JANE: *Yes, it's late. We really must go.* **2.** Time passes quickly. (Said especially when talking about how children grow and develop.) □ *"Look at how big Billy is getting,"* said Uncle Michael. *"My, how time flies."* □ TOM: *It seems it was just yesterday that I graduated from high school. Now I'm a grandfather.* MARY: *My, how time flies.*

My lips are sealed. I will tell no one this secret or this gossip. □ MARY: *I hope you don't tell anyone about this.* ALICE: *Don't worry. My lips are sealed.* □ BOB: *Don't you dare tell her I told you.* BILL: *My lips are sealed.*

My(, my). an expression of mild surprise or interest. (See also *my.*) □ FRED: *My, my! How you've grown, Bill.* BILL: *Of course! I'm a growing boy. Did you think I would shrink?* □ DOCTOR: *My, my, this is interesting.* JANE: *What's wrong?* DOCTOR: *Nothing that a little exercise won't fix.*

My pleasure. **1.** *You're welcome.*; It is my pleasure to do so. (From *It's my pleasure.* There is a stress on both words.) □ MARY: *Thank you for bringing this up here.* BILL: *My pleasure.* □ JANE: *Oh, doctor, you've really helped Tom. Thank you so much!* DOCTOR: *My pleasure.* **2.** Happy to meet you.; Happy to see you. □ SALLY: *Bill, meet Mary, my cousin.* BILL: *My pleasure.* □ BILL: *Good to see you again.* MARY: *My pleasure.*

N

Name your poison. See *What'll it be?*

need I remind you of See the following entry.

need I remind you that AND **need I remind you of** a phrase that introduces a reminder. (A little haughty or parental.) ☐ BILL: *Need I remind you that today is Friday?* BOB (sarcastically): *Gee, how else would I have known?* ☐ JOHN: *Need I remind you of our policy against smoking in the office?* JANE: *Sorry, I forgot.*

Need I say more? Is it necessary for me to say any more? ☐ MARY: *There's grass to be mowed, weeds to be pulled, dishes to be done, carpets to be vacuumed, and there you sit! Need I say more?* TOM: *I'll get right on it.* ☐ *"This project needs to be finished before anyone sleeps tonight," said Alice, hovering over the office staff. "Need I say more?"*

Neither can I. I cannot do that either. (Any subject pronoun can be used in place of *I*.) ☐ BILL: *No matter what they do to them, I just can't stand sweet potatoes!* BOB: *Neither can I.* ☐ JOHN: *Let's go. I cannot tolerate the smoke in here.* JANE: *Neither can I.*

Neither do I. I do not do that either. (Any subject pronoun can be used in place of *I*.) ☐ BILL: *No matter what they do to them, I just don't like sweet potatoes!* BOB: *Neither do I.* ☐ JANE: *I really don't like what the city council is doing.* FRED: *Neither do I.*

Never been better. See *(I've) never been better.*

Never felt better. See *(I've) never felt better.*

Never heard of such a thing. See *(I) never heard of such a thing.*

Never hurts to ask. See *(It) never hurts to ask.*

Never in a thousand years! See *Not in a thousand years!*

never in my life an emphatic expression showing the depth of the speaker's feelings. □ SALLY: *Never in my life have I seen such a mess!* JOHN: *Well, it's always this way. Where have you been all this time?* SALLY: *I just never noticed before, I suppose.* □ SUE: *Never will I go there again! Never in my life!* BOB: *That bad, huh?* SUE: *Yes! That bad and worse!*

Never mind! Forget it!; It's not important! □ SALLY: *What did you say?* JANE: *Never mind! It wasn't important.* □ JOHN: *I tried to get the book you wanted, but they didn't have it. Shall I try another store?* MARY: *No, never mind.* JOHN: *I'd be happy to give it a try.*

Never thought I'd see you here! See *(I) never thought I'd see you here!*

Next question. That is settled, let's move on to something else. (Usually a way of evading further discussion.) □ MARY: *When can I expect this construction noise to stop?* BOB: *In about a month. Next question.* □ BILL: *When will the board of directors raise the dividend again?* MARY: *Oh, quite soon. Next question.*

Nice going! AND **Good job!; Nice job!** **1.** That was done well. □ JOHN: *Well, I'm glad that's over.* SALLY: *Nice going, John! You did a good job.* □ TOM: *Nice job, Bill!* BILL: *Thanks, Tom!* **2.** That was done poorly. (Sarcastic.) □ FRED: *I guess I really messed it up.* BILL: *Nice job, Fred! You've now messed us all up!* FRED: *Well, I'm sorry.* □ *"Nice going," frowned Jane, as Tom upset the bowl of potato chips.*

Nice job! See the previous entry.

Nice place you have here. Your home is nice. (A compliment paid by a guest. The word *place* might be replaced with *home, house, room, apartment,* etc.) □ *Jane came in and looked around. "Nice place you have here," she said.* □ BOB: *Come in. Welcome.* MARY: *Nice place you have here.* BOB: *Thanks. We like it.*

Nice talking to you. See *(It's been) good talking to you.*

Nice to be here. See *(It's) good to be here.*

Nice to have you here. See *(It's) good to have you here.*

Nice to meet you. See *(It's) nice to meet you.*

Nice to see you. See *(It's) nice to see you.*

Nice weather we're having. **1.** Isn't the weather nice? (Sometimes used to start a conversation with a stranger.) □ BILL: *Nice weather we're having.* BOB: *Yeah. It's great.* □ *Mary glanced out the window and said to the lady sitting next to her, "Nice weather we're having."* **2.** Isn't this weather bad? (A sarcastic version of sense 1.) □ BILL: *Hi, Tom. Nice weather we're having, huh?* TOM: *Yeah. Gee, it's hot!* □ MARY: *Nice weather we're having!* SALLY: *Sure. Lovely weather for ducks.*

Night. See *(Good) night.*

Nighty-night. Good night. (As said to a child.) □ FATHER: *Nighty-night, Bill.* BILL: *Catch you later, Pop.* □ *The mother smiled at the tiny sleeping form and whispered, "Nighty-night, little one."*

No can do. I cannot do it. (The opposite of *Can do.*) □ BOB: *Can you do this now?* SALLY: *Sorry. No can do.* □ FRED: *Will you be able to fix this, or do I have to buy a new one?* ALICE: *No can do. You'll have to buy one.*

No chance. See *(There is) no chance.*

no doubt a transitional or interpretative phrase strengthening the rest of a previous sentence. □ SUE: *Mary is giving this party for herself?* RACHEL: *Yes. She'll expect us to bring gifts, no doubt.* □ MARY: *All this talk about war has my cousin very worried.* SUE: *No doubt. At his age, I don't wonder.*

No doubt about it. See *(There is) no doubt about it.*

No fair! That isn't fair! □ BILL: *No fair! You cheated!* BOB: *I did not!* □ *"No fair," shouted Tom. "You stepped over the line!"*

No kidding! **1.** You are not kidding me, are you? (An expression of mild surprise.) □ JANE: *I got elected vice president.* BILL: *No kidding! That's great!* **2.** Everyone already knows that! Did you just find that out? (Sarcastic.) □ SUE: *It looks like taxes will be increasing.* TOM: *No kidding! What do you expect?* □ ALICE: *I'm afraid I'm putting on a little weight.* JANE: *No kidding!*

No lie? You are not lying, are you? □ BILL: *A plane just landed on the interstate highway outside of town!* TOM: *No lie? Come on! It didn't really, did it?* BILL: *It did too!* TOM: *Let's go see it!* □ BOB: *I'm going to take a trip up the Amazon.* SUE: *No lie?*

No more than I have to. an answer to the greeting question "What are you doing?" □ BOB: *Hey, Fred. What you been doing?* FRED: *No more than I have to.* □ SUE: *Hi, Bill. How are you?* BILL: *Okay. What have you been doing?* SUE: *No more than I have to.*

No need (to). See *(There is) no need (to).*

None of your business! See *(It's) none of your business!*

No, no, a thousand times no! Very definitely, no! (Jocular.) □ BOB: *Here, have some sweet potatoes.* BILL: *No, thanks.* BOB: *Oh, come on!* BILL: *No, no, a thousand times no!* □ SUE: *The water is a little cold, but it's great. Come on in.* BILL: *How cold?* SUE: *Well, just above freezing, I guess. Come on in!* BILL: *No, no, a thousand times no!*

Nope. No. (Colloquial. The opposite of *Yup.*) □ BOB: *Tired?* BILL: *Nope.* □ BILL: *Are you sorry you asked about it?* MARY: *Nope.*

No problem. See *(That causes) no problem.*

No problem with that. See *(I have) no problem with that.*

No siree(, Bob)! Absolutely no! (Not necessarily said to a male, and rarely to any Bob.) □ BILL: *Do you want to sell this old rocking chair?* JANE: *No siree, Bob!* □ BILL: *You don't want sweet potatoes, do you?* FRED: *No siree!*

No skin off my nose. See *(That's) no skin off my nose.*

No skin off my teeth. See *(That's) no skin off my nose.*

No sweat. *(That causes) no problem.*; There is no difficulty. (Slang or colloquial.) □ TOM: *I'm sorry I'm late.* MARY: *No sweat. We're on a very flexible schedule.* □ BILL: *Thanks for carrying this up here.* BOB: *No sweat. Glad to help.*

Not a chance! There is no chance at all that something will happen. (A variation of *(There is) no chance.*) □ SALLY: *Do you think our team will win today?* MARY: *Not a chance!* □ JANE: *Can I have this delivered by Saturday?* CLERK: *Not a chance!*

Not again! I cannot believe that it happened again! □ MARY: *The sink is leaking again.* SALLY: *Not again!* MARY: *Yes, again.* □ FRED: *Here comes Tom with a new girlfriend.* SUE: *Not again!*

Not always. a conditional negative response. (See examples.) □ JOHN: *Do you come here every day?* JANE: *No, not always.* □ JOHN: *Do you find that this condition usually clears up by itself?* DOCTOR: *Not always.*

Not anymore. The facts you mentioned are no longer true.; A previous situation no longer exists. □ MARY: *This cup of coffee you asked me to bring you looks cold. Do you still want it?* SALLY: *Not anymore.* □ TOM: *Do the Wilsons live on Maple Street?* BOB: *Not anymore.*

Not at all. a very polite response to *Thank you*, or some other expression of gratitude. □ JOHN: *Thank you.* JANE: *Not at all.* □ MARY: *I want to thank you very much for all your help.* SUE: *Not at all. Happy to do it.*

Not bad. **1.** Someone or something is quite satisfactory. (Compare to *Not half bad.*) □ BILL: *How do you like your new teacher?* JANE: *Not bad.* □ BOB: *Is this one okay?* BILL: *I guess. Yeah. Not bad.* **2.** Someone or something is really quite good. (The person or thing can be named, as in the examples.) □ JOHN: *How do you like that new car of yours?* MARY: *Not bad. Not bad at all.* □ TOM: *This one looks great to me. What do you think?* SUE: *It's not bad.*

Not by a long shot. *under no circumstances; no chance.* (A negative characterization of one's appraisal of someone or something.) □ BILL: *Are you generally pleased with the new president?* MARY: *No, indeed, not by a long shot.* □ JOHN: *Do you find this acceptable?* BILL: *Good grief, no! Not by a long shot.*

Not for love nor money. *Absolutely not!; No way!* □ JOHN: *Would you be willing to drive through the night to get to Florida a day earlier?* MARY: *Not for love nor money!* □ JANE: *Someone needs to tell Sue that her favorite cat was just run over. Would you do it?* BOB: *Not for love nor money!*

Not for my money. Not *as far as I'm concerned.* (Has nothing to do with money or finance.) □ SUE: *Do you think it's a good idea to* *build all these office buildings in this part of the city?* MARY: *Not for my money. That's a real gamble.* □ JOHN: *We think that Fred is the best choice for the job. Do you think he is?* MARY: *Not for my money, he's not.*

Not half bad. See *(It's) not half bad.*

No, thanks. See *No, thank you.*

no thanks to you I cannot thank you for what happened, because you did not cause it.; I cannot thank you for your help, because you did not give it. □ BOB: *Well, despite our previous disagreement, he seemed to agree to all our demands.* ALICE: *Yes, no thanks to you. I wish you'd learn to keep your big mouth shut!* □ JANE: *It looks like the picnic wasn't ruined despite the fact that I forgot the potato salad.* MARY: *Yes, it was okay. No thanks to you, of course.*

No, thank you. AND **No, thanks.** a phrase used to decline something. □ BOB: *Would you care for some more coffee?* MARY: *No, thank you.* □ JOHN: *Do you want to go downtown tonight?* JANE: *No, thanks.*

Nothing. **1.** I did not say anything. □ MARY: *What did you say?* SUE: *Nothing.* □ TOM: *Did you have something to say? What do you want?* MARY: *Nothing.* **2.** a response to greeting inquiries into what one has been doing. □ BOB: *What you been doing?* MARY: *Nothing.* □ BILL: *What have you been up to?* MARY: *Nothing, really.*

Nothing doing! I will not permit it!; I will not participate in it! □ JOHN: *Can I put this box in your suitcase?* BILL: *Nothing doing! It's too heavy now.* □ SUE: *We decided that you should drive us to the airport. Do you mind?* JANE: *Nothing doing! I've got work to do.*

Nothing for me, thanks. I do not want any of what was offered. (Typically to decline a serving of food or drink.) □ WAITER: *Would you care for dessert?* BOB: *Nothing for me, thanks.* □ BOB: *We have beer and wine. Which would you like?* MARY: *Nothing for me, thanks.*

Nothing much. not much; hardly anything; nothing of importance. □ JOHN: *Hey, man! How's by you?* BOB: *Hiya! Nothing much.* □ BILL: *What have you been doing?* TOM: *Nothing much.*

Nothing to complain about. See *(I) can't complain.*

Nothing to it!   See *(There's) nothing to it!*

Not if I see you first.   See the following entry.

Not if I see you sooner. AND **Not if I see you first.**   a response to *I'll see you later.* (This means you will not see me if I see you first, because I will avoid you.) □ TOM: *See you later.* MARY: *Not if I see you sooner.* □ JOHN: *Okay. If you want to argue, I'll just leave. See you later.* MARY: *Not if I see you first.*

Not in a thousand years! AND **Never in a thousand years!**   No, never! □ JOHN: *Will you ever approve of her marriage to Tom?* SUE: *No, not in a thousand years.* □ MARY: *Will all this trouble ever subside?* JOHN: *Never in a thousand years.*

Not in my book.   Not according to my views. (Compare to *Not for my money.*) □ JOHN: *Is Fred okay for the job, do you think?* MARY: *No, not in my book.* □ SUE: *My meal is great! Is yours a real winner?* BOB: *Not in my book.*

Not likely.   That is probably not so. □ MARY: *Is it possible that you'll be able to fix this watch?* SUE: *Not likely, but we can always try.* □ SALLY: *Will John show up on time, do you think?* BOB: *Not likely.*

Not much.   See *Not (too) much.*

Not on your life!   No, *absolutely not!* □ SALLY: *Do you want to go downtown today?* BILL: *Not on your life! There's a parade this afternoon.* □ SUE: *I was cheated out of fifty dollars. Do you think I need to see a lawyer?* JOHN: *Not on your life! You'll pay more than that to walk through a lawyer's door.*

Not right now, thanks.   No for the present. (It is hoped that one will be asked again later. Usually used for a [temporary] refusal of a serving of food or drink. There is an implication that more will be wanted later.) □ WAITER: *Do you want some more coffee?* MARY: *Not right now, thanks.* □ JOHN: *Can I take your coat?* SUE: *Not right now, thanks. I'm still a little chilly.*

No trouble.   See *(It's) no trouble.*

Not supposed to.   See *(It's) not supposed to.*

Not (too) much.   a response to greeting inquiries into what one has been doing. □ JOHN: *What have you been doing?* MARY: *Not much.*

☐ SUE: *Been keeping busy? What are you up to?* BOB: *Not too much.* SUE: *Yeah. Me too.*

not to put too fine a point on it a phrase introducing a fine or important point, apologetically. ☐ RACHEL: *Not to put too fine a point on it, Mary, but you're still acting a little rude to Tom.* MARY: *I'm sorry, but that's the way I feel.* ☐ JOHN: *I think, not to put too fine a point on it, you ought to do exactly as you are told.* ANDREW: *And I think you ought to mind your own business.*

Not to worry. Please do not worry. ☐ BILL: *The rain is going to soak all our clothes.* TOM: *Not to worry, I put them all in plastic bags.* ☐ SUE: *I think we're about to run out of money.* BILL: *Not to worry. I have some more travelers checks.*

not under any circumstances See *under no circumstances.*

now a sentence opener having no specific meaning. (See the examples. See also *now, now.* Words such as this often use intonation to convey the connotation of the sentence that is to follow. The brief intonation pattern accompanying the word may indicate sarcasm, disagreement, caution, consolation, sternness, etc.) ☐ JOHN: *I'm totally disgusted with you.* BOB: *Now, don't get angry!* ☐ ANDREW: *I'm fighting mad. Why did you do that?* BILL: *Now, let's talk this over.* ☐ ANDREW: *Now, try it again, slowly this time.* SALLY: *How many times do I have to rehearse this piece?* ☐ FRED: *Now, who do you think you are?* TOM: *Well, who do you think you are, asking me that question?*

No way! No!; Absolutely not! ☐ BILL: *Will you take my calculus test for me?* BOB: *No way!* ☐ BOB: *You don't want any more sweet potatoes, do you?* JANE: *No way!*

No way, José! No! (Slang. An elaboration of *No. José* is pronounced with an initial *H.*) ☐ BOB: *Can I borrow a hundred bucks?* BILL: *No way, José!* ☐ SALLY: *Can I get you to take this nightgown back to the store for me and get me the same thing in a slightly smaller size?* BOB: *No way, José!*

No way to tell. See *(There's) no way to tell.*

now, now a calming and consoling phrase that introduces good advice. ☐ *"Now, now, don't cry,"* said the mother to the tiny baby. ☐ JANE: *I'm so upset!* ANDREW: *Now, now, everything will work out all right.*

now then a sentence opener indicating that a new topic is being opened or that the speaker is getting down to business. (Expressions such as this often use intonation to convey the connotation of the sentence that is to follow. The brief intonation pattern accompanying the expression may indicate sarcasm, disagreement, caution, consolation, sternness, etc.) ☐ *"Now then, where's the pain?"* asked the doctor. ☐ MARY: *Now then, let's talk about you and your interests.* BOB: *Oh, good. My favorite subject.* ☐ SUE: *Now then, what are your plans for the future?* ALICE: *I want to become a pilot.* ☐ *"Now then, what did you have in mind when you took this money?"* asked the police investigator.

Now what? AND **What now?** What is going to happen now?; What kind of new problem has arisen? ☐ *The doorbell rang urgently, and Tom said, rising from the chair, "Now what?"* ☐ BOB: *There's a serious problem—sort of an emergency—in the mail room.* SUE: *What now?* BOB: *They're out of stamps or something silly like that.*

Now you're cooking (with gas)! Now you are doing what you should be doing! ☐ *As Bob came to the end of the piece, the piano teacher said, "Now you're cooking with gas!"* ☐ TOM (painting a fence): *How am I doing with this painting? Any better?* JANE: *Now you're cooking.* TOM: *Want to try it?*

Now you're talking! Now you are saying the right things. ☐ TOM: *I won't put up with her behavior any longer. I'll tell her exactly what I think of it.* BILL: *Now you're talking!* ☐ JOHN: *When I get back to school, I'm going to study harder than ever.* MOTHER: *Now you're talking!*

O

Of all the nerve! See *What (a) nerve!*

of course yes; *Certainly!; For sure.* □ SALLY: *Are you ready to go?*
BOB: *Of course.* SALLY: *Then let's go.* □ JANE: *Are you coming with us?*
JOHN: *Of course. I wouldn't miss this for the world.* □ *"And you'll be
there, of course?" asked Alice.* □ *"I would be happy to help, of course,"
confided Tom, a little insincerely.*

off the top of one's head See *(right) off the top of one's head.*

Oh, boy. **1.** Wow! (Usually **Oh, boy!** An exclamation. It has nothing to do with boys.) □ BILL: *Oh, boy! An old-fashioned circus!* BOB:
So what? □ *"Oh, boy!" shouted John. "When do we eat?"* **2.** I dread
this!; This is going to be awful! □ *"Oh, boy!" moaned Fred, "Here
we go again."* □ DOCTOR: *It looks like something fairly serious.* JANE:
Oh, boy. DOCTOR: *But nothing modern medicine can't handle.*

Oh, sure (someone or something will)! a sarcastic expression
claiming that someone or something will do something or that
something will happen. □ ANDREW: *Don't worry. I'll do it.* RA-
CHEL: *Oh, sure you will. That's what you always say.* □ BOB: *I'll fix
this fence the first chance I get.* MARY: *Oh, sure. When will that be? Next
year?*

Oh, yeah? Is that what you think? (Rude and hostile.) □ TOM:
You're getting to be sort of a pest. BILL: *Oh, yeah?* TOM: *Yeah.* □ BOB:
This sauce tastes bad. I think you ruined it. BILL: *Oh, yeah? What makes
you think so?* BOB: *My tongue tells me!*

OK. See *Okay.*

Okay. AND **OK, O.K.** **1.** Yes.; *All right.* □ JOHN: *Can we go now?* SUE: *Okay. Let's go.* □ MARY: *Can I have one of these?* FRED: *Okay.* MARY: *Thanks.* **2.** an expression indicating that the speaker accepts the current situation. (Not an answer to a question.) □ *"Okay, we're all here. Let's go now," said Tom.* □ BILL: *Okay, I can see the house now.* RACHEL: *This must be where we turn then.* **3.** (usually **Okay?**) a question word asking if the person spoken to accepts the current situation. (Very close to sense 1.) □ BILL: *I'm going to turn here, okay?* RACHEL: *Sure. It looks like the right place.* □ ANDREW: *I'll take this one, okay?* MARY: *Yes, that's okay.*

Okay by me. See *(That's) fine with me.*

Okay with me. See *(That's) fine with me.*

on balance See *all in all.*

once and for all finally; permanently. □ SUE: *I'm going to get this place organized once and for all!* ALICE: *That'll be the day!* □ *"We need to get this straightened out once and for all," said Bob, for the fourth time today.*

once more AND **one more time** Please do it one more time. □ MARY: *You sang that line beautifully, Fred. Now, once more.* FRED: *I'm really tired of all this rehearsing.* □ JOHN (finishing practicing his speech): *How was that?* SUE: *Good! One more time, though.* JOHN: *I'm getting bored with it.*

one final thing See the following entry.

one final word AND **one final thing** a phrase introducing a parting comment or the last item in a list. □ JOHN: *One final word, keep your chin up.* MARY: *Good advice!* □ SUE: *And one final thing, don't haul around a lot of expensive camera stuff. It just tells the thieves who to rob.* JOHN: *There are thieves here?* SUE: *Yeah. Everywhere.*

One moment, please. Please wait a minute.; *Just a minute.* □ JOHN: *Can you help me?* CLERK: *One moment, please. I will be with you shortly.* □ BILL (answering the phone): *Hello?* BOB: *Hello. Can I speak to Tom?* BILL: *One moment, please.* (handing phone to Tom) *It's for you.* TOM: *Hello, this is Tom.*

one more thing See *one final word.*

one more time See *once more.*

one way or another somehow. □ TOM: *Can we fix this radio, or do I have to buy a new one?* MARY: *Don't fret! We'll get it repaired one way or another.* □ JOHN: *I think we're lost.* ALICE: *Don't worry. We'll get there one way or another.*

on the contrary a phrase disagreeing with a previous statement. □ TOM: *It's rather warm today.* BOB: *On the contrary, I find it too cool.* □ MARY: *I hear that you aren't too happy about my decision.* SUE: *On the contrary, I find it fair and reasonable.*

on the other hand a phrase introducing an alternate view. □ JOHN: *I'm ready to go; on the other hand, I'm perfectly comfortable here.* SALLY: *I'll let you know when I'm ready, then.* □ MARY: *I like this one. On the other hand, this is nice too.* SUE: *Why not get both?*

or what? a way of adding emphasis to a yes-or-no question the speaker has asked. (In effect, if it wasn't what I said, what is it?) □ BOB: *Now, is this a fine day or what?* JOHN: *Looks okay to me.* □ TOM: *Look at Bill and Mary. Do they make a fine couple or what?* BOB: *Sure, they look great.*

or words to that effect or similar words meaning about the same thing. □ JOHN: *It says right here in the contract, "You are expected to attend without fail," or words to that effect.* MARY: *That means I have to be there, huh?* JOHN: *You got it!* □ SALLY: *She said that I wasn't doing my job well, or words to that effect.* JANE: *Well, you ought to find out exactly what she means.* SALLY: *I'm afraid I know.*

Our house is your house. See *My house is your house.*

Out of the question. See *(It's) out of the question.*

Out, please. Please let me get out. (Said by someone trying to get out of an elevator. Compare to *Coming through(, please.)*) □ *The elevator stopped again, as it had at every floor, and someone said, "Out, please," as someone had said at every floor.* □ JANE: *Out, please. This is my floor.* JOHN: *I'll get out of your way.* JANE: *Thanks.*

Over my dead body! a defiant phrase indicating the strength of one's opposition to something. (A joking response is "That can be arranged.") □ SALLY: *Alice says she'll join the circus no matter what anybody says.* FATHER: *Over my dead body!* SALLY: *Now, now. You know how she is.* □ BILL: *I think I'll rent out our spare bedroom.* SUE: *Over my dead body!* BILL (smiling): *That can be arranged.*

P

Pardon (me). See *Excuse me.; Excuse me?*

Pardon me for living! a very indignant response to a criticism or rebuke. □ FRED: *Oh, I thought you had already taken yourself out of here!* SUE: *Well, pardon me for living!* □ TOM: *Butt out, Mary! Bill and I are talking.* MARY: *Pardon me for living!*

Perhaps a little later. Not now, but possibly later. □ WAITER: *Would you like your coffee now?* BOB: *Perhaps a little later.* WAITER: *All right.* □ SALLY: *Hey, Bill, how about a swim?* BOB: *Sounds good, but not now. Perhaps a little later.* SALLY: *Okay. See you later.*

Permit me. See *Allow me.*

Please. **1.** a response to a denial or refusal. □ BILL: *Can I go to the picnic on the Fourth of July?* MOTHER: *No, you can't go to the picnic.* BILL: *Please!* □ TOM: *No, Bill. You can't have a raise.* BILL: *Please. I can hardly afford to live.* TOM: *You'll manage.* **2.** You go first.; Give yourself priority.; Attend to your interests first. (See examples.) □ *Bob stepped back and made a motion with his hand indicating that Mary should go first. "Please," smiled Bob.* □ MARY: *Do you mind if I take the last piece of cake?* BOB: *Please.* MARY: *Thanks.* **3.** Please stop what you are doing.; Please do not do that.; Please do not say that. (Compare to *I beg your pardon.*) □ MARY: *You always make a mess wherever you go.* ALICE: *Please! I do not!* □ *Andrew kept bumping up against Mary in line. Finally Mary turned to him and said, "Please!"*

Pleased to meet you. See *(I'm) pleased to meet you.*

Please hold. See *Hold the wire(, please.)*

Plugging along.   See *(I'm) (just) plugging along.*

Pull up a chair.   Please get a chair and sit down and join us. (Assumes that there is seating available. The speaker does not necessarily mean that the person spoken to actually has to move a chair.)   □   TOM: *Well, hello, Bob!* BOB: *Hi, Tom. Pull up a chair.*   □ *The three men were sitting at a table for four. Bob came up and said hello. Bill said, "Pull up a chair." Bob sat in the fourth chair at the table.*

put another way   See *to put it another way.*

Put 'er there.   See *Put it there.*

Put it anywhere.   **1.** Set down your burden any place that is convenient. (Literal. Compare to the second sense.)   □   MARY: *What shall I do with this?* JANE: *Oh, put it anywhere.*   □   TOM: *Where does this lamp go, lady?* SUE: *Please put it anywhere. I'll move it later.* **2.** AND **Put it there.**   Sit down anywhere. (Literally, place your buttocks anywhere. Colloquial and very familiar.)   □   TOM: *Hi, Fred. Is there room for me here?* FRED: *Sure, man! Put it anywhere.*   □   BOB: *Come in and set a spell. We'll have a little talk.* JOHN: *Nice place you've got here.* BOB: *Put it there, old buddy. How you been?*

Put it there.   **1.** See under *Put it anywhere.* **2.** AND **Put 'er there.**   Shake hands with me. (Literally, put your hand there, in mine. Colloquial. The apostrophe on *'er* is not always used.)   □ BOB (extending his hand): *Sounds great to me, old buddy. Put it there.* FRED: *Thanks, Bob. I'm glad we could close the deal.*   □   BOB: *Good to see you, Fred.* FRED: *Put 'er there, Bob.*

Q

quite frankly   See *(speaking) (quite) frankly.*

R

Ready for this? See *(Are you) ready for this?*

Read you loud and clear. See *(I) read you loud and clear.*

Ready to order? See *(Are you) ready to order?*

Really. **1.** I agree with what you just said. □ RACHEL: *This cake is just too dry.* MARY: *Really. I guess it's getting stale.* □ HENRY: *Taxes are just too high.* MARY: *Really. It's out of hand.* **2.** (as a question, *Really?*) Do you really mean what you just said? □ HENRY: *I'm going to join the army.* MARY: *Really?* HENRY: *Yes, I'm really going to do it.* □ SALLY: *This will cost over two hundred dollars.* RACHEL: *Really? I paid half that the last time.* **3.** (usually **Really!**) I can't believe what has just been said or done.; I'm shocked. □ FRED: *Then I punched him in the nose.* HENRY: *Really!* FRED: *Well, I had too.* HENRY: *Really!* □ *"Really!" cried Sally, seeing the jogger knock down the elderly lady.*

Really doesn't matter to me. See *(It) (really) doesn't matter to me.*

Really must go. See *(I) really must go.*

Remember me to someone. Please carry my good wishes to someone. (The *someone* can be a person's name or a pronoun.) □ TOM: *My brother says hello.* BILL: *Oh, good. Please remember me to him.* TOM: *I will.* □ FRED: *Bye.* JOHN: *Good-bye, Fred. Remember me to your Uncle Tom.*

Remember to write. AND **Don't forget to write.** **1.** a final parting comment made to remind someone going on a journey to write to those remaining at home. □ ALICE: *Bye.* MARY: *Good-bye, Alice.*

Remember to write. ALICE: *I will. Bye.* ☐ SALLY: *Remember to write!* FRED: *I will!* SALLY: *I miss you already!* **2.** a parting comment made to someone in place of a regular good-bye. (Jocular.) ☐ JOHN: *See you tomorrow. Bye.* JANE: *See you. Remember to write.* ☐ JOHN: *Okay. See you after lunch.* JANE: *Yeah. Bye. Remember to write.*

Remember your manners. **1.** a parting instruction, usually to a child, encouraging proper behavior. ☐ *As Jimmy was going out the door, his mother said, "Have a good time and remember your manners."* ☐ JOHN: *It's time for me to go to the party, Mom.* MOTHER: *Yes, it is. Remember your manners. Good-bye.* **2.** AND **Mind your manners.** a comment intended to remind someone of proper behavior, such as saying *thank you* or *excuse me.* ☐ *After Mary gave a cookie to little Bobby, Bobby's mother said to him, "Remember your manners."* ☐ BOB: *Here, Jane. Have one of these.* JANE (taking one): *Wow!* BOB: *Okay. Have another.* MOTHER: *What do you say? Remember your manners.* JANE: *Thanks a lot!*

Right. Correct.; What you said is right. ☐ JANE: *It's really hot today.* JOHN: *Right.* JANE: *Keeping cool?* JOHN: *No way.* ☐ SALLY: *Let's go over to Fred's room and cheer him up.* SUE: *Right.*

Right away. I will do it right now. ☐ JOHN: *Take this over to Sue.* BILL: *Right away.* ☐ JOHN: *How soon can you do this?* SUE: *Right away.*

Righto. Yes.; I will comply. ☐ FRED: *Can you handle this project for me today?* SUE: *Righto.* ☐ JOHN: *Is that you, Tom?* TOM: *Righto. What do you want?*

(right) off the top of one's head without giving it too much thought or without the necessary knowledge. ☐ MARY: *How much do you think this car would be worth on a trade?* FRED: *Well, right off the top of my head, I'd say about a thousand.* ☐ TOM: *What time does the morning train come in?* BILL: *Off the top of my head, I don't know.*

Roger (wilco). Yes. (From aircraft radio communication. *Wilco* is "will comply.") ☐ JOHN: *Can you do this right now?* BOB: *Roger.* ☐ MARY: *I want you to take this over to the mayor's office.* BILL: *Roger wilco.*

Run it by (me) again. See the following entry.

Run that by (me) again. AND **Run it by (me) again.** Please repeat what you just said.; Please go over that one more time. (Slang.) ☐ ALICE: *Do you understand?* SUE: *No. I really didn't understand what you said. Run that by me again, if you don't mind.* ☐ JOHN: *Put this* *piece into the longer slot and the remaining piece into the slot on the bottom.* SUE: *Run that by again. I got lost just after* put. ☐ MARY: *Keep to the right, past the fork in the road, then turn right at the crossroads. Do you follow?* JANE: *No. Run it by me again.*

S

Same to you. See *(The) same to you.*

say a word used to catch someone's attention and announce that a sentence—probably a question—follows. (Words such as this often use intonation to convey the connotation of the sentence that is to follow. The brief intonation pattern accompanying the word may indicate sarcasm, disagreement, caution, consolation, sternness, etc.) □ BOB: *Say, don't I know you from somewhere?* RACHEL: *I hope not.* □ *"Say, why don't you stay on your side?" screamed Tom at the other boys.* □ ANDREW: *Say, where did I see that can opener?* RACHEL: *You saw it where you left it after you last used it.*

Say cheese! an expression used by photographers to get people to smile, which they must do while saying the word *cheese.* □ *"All of you please stand still and say cheese!" said the photographer.* □ *"Is everybody ready? Say cheese!" said Mary, holding the camera to her face.*

Say hello to someone (for me). Please convey my good wishes to *someone.* (The *someone* can be a person's name or a pronoun. See also *Give my best to someone.; Remember me to someone.*) □ ANDREW: *Good-bye, Tom. Say hello to your brother.* TOM: *Sure. Bye, Andy.* □ SALLY: *Well, good-bye.* MARY: *Bye.* SALLY: *And say hello to Jane.* MARY: *Sure. Bye-bye.*

Say no more. I agree.; I will do it; I concede, no need to continue talking. □ JOHN: *Someone ought to take this stuff outside.* BILL: *Say no more. Consider it done.* □ MARY: *Shouldn't we turn here if we plan to visit Jane?* ALICE: *Say no more. Here we go.*

Says me! the contentious response to *Says who?* ☐ BILL: *I think you're making a mess of this project.* BOB: *Says who?* BILL: *Says me!* ☐ JOHN: *What do you mean I shouldn't have done it? Says who?* MARY: *Says me!*

Says who? Who do you think you are to say that? ☐ TOM: *Fred, you sure can be dumb sometimes.* FRED: *Says who?* TOM: *Says me!* ☐ BILL: *You take this dog out of here right now!* BOB: *Says who?* BILL: *Says me!*

Says you! It is just you who are saying that, so it does not matter. ☐ BILL: *I think you're headed for some real trouble.* BOB: *Says you!* ☐ FRED: *Says who?* TOM: *Says me!* FRED: *Aw, says you!*

Say what? What did you say?; Please repeat what you said. ☐ SALLY: *Would you like some more salad?* FRED: *Say what?* SALLY: *Salad? Would you like some more salad?* ☐ JOHN: *Put this one over there.* SUE: *Say what?* JOHN: *Never mind, I'll do it.*

Say when. Tell me when I have given you enough of something, usually a liquid. (Sometimes answered with **When.**) ☐ TOM (pouring milk into Fred's glass): *Say when, Fred.* FRED: *When.* ☐ JOHN: *Do you want some more juice?* MARY: *Yes.* JOHN: *Okay. Say when.*

'Scuse (me). See *Excuse me.*

'Scuse me? See *Excuse me?*

'Scuse, please. See *Excuse me.*

Search me. I do not know.; You can search my clothing and my person, but you won't find the answer to your question anywhere near me. (Colloquial and not too polite. The two words have equal stress.) ☐ JANE: *What time does Mary's flight get in?* SALLY: *Search me.* ☐ JOHN: *What kind of paint should I use on this fence?* BILL: *Search me.*

See? See *(Don't you) see?*

See if I care! I do not care if you do it. ☐ MARY: *That does it! I'm going home to Mother!* JOHN: *See if I care!* ☐ SUE: *I'm putting the sofa here, whether you like it or not.* BILL: *Go ahead! See if I care!*

Seen better. See *(I've) seen better.*

Seen worse. See *(I've) seen worse.*

145

See ya! Good-bye! (Colloquial.) □ ANDREW: *Good-bye, Tom, see ya!* TOM: *Bye. Take it easy.* □ MARY: *Bye, Jane! See you later.* JANE: *See ya!*

See ya, bye-bye. Bye. (Colloquial and slang.) □ BILL: *I have to be off.* BOB: *See ya, bye-bye.* □ MARY: *See ya, bye-bye.* SUE: *Toodle-oo.*

See you. See *I will see you later.*

See you around. I will see you again somewhere. □ BOB: *Bye for now.* JANE: *See you around.* □ TOM: *See you around, Fred.* FRED: *Sure, Tom. See you.*

See you in a little while. See *(I'll) see you in a little while.*

(See you) later. See *I will see you later.*

See you later, alligator. AND **Later, alligator.** *Good-bye.* (A natural mate to *After while(, crocodile.)*) □ BOB: *See you later, alligator.* JANE: *After while, crocodile.* □ BOB: *Bye, Tom.* TOM: *See you later, alligator.* BOB: *Later.*

See you next year. See *(I'll) see you next year.*

See you (real) soon. See *(I'll) see you (real) soon.*

See you soon. See *(I will) see you (real) soon.*

See you then. See *(I'll) see you then.*

See you tomorrow. See *(I'll) see you tomorrow.*

Shake it (up)! *Hurry up!; Move faster!; Run faster!* □ FRED: *Move it, Tom! Shake it up!* TOM: *I can't go any faster!* □ JANE: *Move, you guys. Shake it!* BILL: *Hey, I'm doing the best I can!*

Shake the lead out! See *Get the lead out.*

Shame on you! a phrase scolding someone for being naughty. (Typically said to a child or to an adult for a childish infraction.) □ JOHN: *I think I broke one of your figurines.* MARY: *Shame on you!* JOHN:

I'll replace it, of course. MARY: *Thanks, I sort of liked it.* □ *"Shame on you!" said Mary. "You should have known better!"*

Shoot! Say what you have to say!; Ask your question! □ BOB: *Can I ask you a question?* BILL: *Sure. Shoot!* □ MARY: *There are a few things I want to say before we go on.* TOM: *Shoot!*

Shut up! Be quiet! (Impolite.) □ BOB: *And another thing.* BILL: *Oh, shut up, Bob!* □ ANDREW: *Shut up! I've heard enough!* BOB: *But I have more to say!* □ *"Shut up! I can't hear anything because of all your noise!" shouted the director.*

Shut up about it. Do not tell anyone about it. □ BILL: *I heard that you had a little trouble with the police.* TOM: *Just shut up about it! Do you hear?* □ ANDREW: *Didn't you once appear in a movie?* ALICE: *Shut up about it. No one has to know.*

Shut your face! Be quiet!; *Shut up!* (Rude.) □ HENRY: *Shut your face! I'm tired of your constant chatter.* BOB: *I didn't say a single word!* □ MARY: *You make me sick!* SALLY: *Shut your face!*

Since when? When was that decided?; *That's news to me.*; When was that done? □ TOM: *You've been assigned to the night shift.* JOHN: *Since when?* □ JANE: *Fred is now the assistant manager.* BILL: *Since when?* JANE: *Since I appointed him, that's when.*

Sir? **1.** Did you call me, sir? (Compare to *Ma'am.*) □ JOHN: *Tom!* TOM: *Sir?* JOHN: *Get over here!* □ FRED: *Bill!* BILL: *Sir? Did you call me?* FRED: *Yes. Have a seat. I want to talk to you.* **2.** I did not hear what you said, sir. □ JOHN: *I want you to take this to Mr. Franklin.* CHILD: *Sir?* JOHN: *Please take this to Mr. Franklin.* □ BOB: *Can you wait on me?* CLERK: *Sir?* BOB: *Can you wait on me?* CLERK: *Oh, yes, sir.*

Skin me! See *Give me five!*

Skip it! *Never mind!*; *Forget it!* (Shows impatience or disappointment.) □ JOHN: *I need some help on this project.* MARY: *What?* JOHN: *Oh, skip it!* □ JANE: *Will you be able to do this, or should I get someone with more experience?* BOB: *What did you say?* JANE: *Oh, skip it!*

Skoal! See *Bottoms up.*

Slip me five! See *Give me five!*

Slip me some skin! See *Give me five!*

Smile when you say that. I will be happy to interpret that remark as a joke or as kidding. □ JOHN: *You're a real pain in the neck.* BOB: *Smile when you say that.* □ SUE: *I'm going to bop you on the head!* JOHN: *Smile when you say that!*

Snap it up! *Hurry up!* (Colloquial.) □ JOHN: *Come on, Fred. Snap it up!* FRED: *I'm hurrying! I'm hurrying!* □ SALLY: *Snap it up! You're going to make us late.* JOHN: *That's exactly what I had in mind.*

Snap to it! Move faster!; Look alert! □ BILL: *Snap to it!* MARY: *Don't rush me!* □ JOHN: *Get in line there. Snap to it!* SALLY: *What is this, the army? You just wait till I'm ready!*

So? See *So (what)?*

so 1. a sentence opener used to break a silence in a conversation or aggressively start a new topic. (Words such as this often use intonation to convey the connotation of the sentence that is to follow. The brief intonation pattern accompanying the word may indicate sarcasm, disagreement, caution, consolation, sternness, etc.) □ ANDREW: *So, I'm new around here. Where's the fun?* BOB: *You must be new. There's never been any fun around here.* □ *"So, how are you?" asked Kate.* □ ANDREW: *So, when do we eat?* RACHEL: *Don't you have any manners?* □ BOB: *So, what you been doing?* BILL: *Not much.* □ ANDREW: *So, been keeping busy?* BOB: *No. I been taking it easy.* 2. a defensive sentence opener that takes an offensive tone. □ FRED: *So I made a mistake. So what?* JOHN: *It caused us all a lot of trouble. That's what.* □ ALICE: *So I'm not perfect! What does that prove?* ANDREW: *Nothing, I guess.*

So do I. I do too. □ MARY: *I want some more cake.* SALLY: *So do I.* □ BOB: *I have to go home now.* TOM: *So do I.* BOB: *Bye.*

(Someone had) better keep quiet about it. See under *(Someone had) better keep still about it.*

(Someone had) better keep still about it. AND **(Someone had) better keep quiet about it.** an admonition that a particular person ought not to tell about or discuss something. (The *someone* can stand for any person's name, any pronoun, or even the word *someone* meaning "you-know-who." If there is no *Someone had*, the

phrase is a mild admonition to keep quiet about something.) □
MARY: *I saw you with Bill last night.* JANE: *You'd better keep quiet about it.* □ JANE: *Tom found out what you're giving Sally for her birthday.* BILL: *He had better keep quiet about it!*

(Someone) looks like something the cat dragged in. Someone looks rumpled or worn out. (Jocular. Compare to *Look (at) what the cat dragged in!*) □ ALICE: *Tom just came in. He looks like something the cat dragged in. What do you suppose happened to him?* □ RACHEL: *Wow! Did you see Sue?* JANE: *Yes. Looks like something the cat dragged in.*

(Someone or something is) supposed to. an expression meaning that someone or something was meant to do something. (Frequently, in speech, *supposed* is reduced to *'sposed.* The words *someone* or *something* can be replaced with nouns or pronouns, or used themselves.) □ MARY: *They didn't deliver the flowers we ordered.* SUE: *Supposed to. Give them a call.* □ SALLY: *This screw doesn't fit into hole number seven in the way the instructions say it should.* BILL: *It's supposed to. Something's wrong.*

(Someone's) not supposed to. See *(It's) not supposed to.*

(Someone will) be with you in a minute. AND **With you in a minute.** Please be patient, someone will attend to you very soon. (The *someone* can be any person's name or a pronoun, typically *I.* If there is no one mentioned, *I* is implied. The *minute* can be replaced by *moment* or *second.*) □ SUE: *Oh, Miss?* CLERK: *Someone will be with you in a minute.* □ BILL: *Please wait here. I'll be with you in a minute.* BOB: *Please hurry.*

Some people (just) don't know when to give up. See the following entry.

Some people (just) don't know when to quit. AND **Some people (just) don't know when to give up.** **1.** You, or someone being talked about, should stop doing something, such as talking, arguing, scolding, etc. (Often directed toward the person being addressed.) □ BILL: *I hate to say it again, but that lipstick is all wrong for you. It brings out the wrong color in your eyes, and it makes your mouth larger than it really is.* JANE: *Oh, stop, stop! That's enough! Some people* *just don't know when to quit.* □ JOHN: *Those bushes out in the backyard need trimming.* SALLY: *You keep criticizing! Is there no end to it? Some people don't know when to stop!* **2.** Some people do not know when to slow down and stop working so hard. □ BOB: *We were afraid that John had had a heart attack.* BILL: *I'm not surprised. He works so hard. Some people don't know when to quit.* □ JANE: *He just kept on gambling. Finally, he had no money left.* SALLY: *Some people don't know when to quit.*

Something's got to give. Emotions or tempers are strained, and there is going to be an outburst. □ ALICE: *There are serious problems with Mary and Tom. They fight and fight.* SUE: *Yes, something's got to give. It can't go on like this.* □ BILL: *Things are getting difficult at the office. Something's got to give.* MARY: *Just stay clear of all the bickering.*

So much for that. That is the end of that.; We will not be dealing with that anymore. □ *John tossed the stub of a pencil into the trash. "So much for that," he muttered, fishing through his drawer for another.* □ MOTHER: *Here, try some carrots.* CHILD (brushing the spoon aside): *No! No!* MOTHER: *Well, so much for that.*

Sooner than you think. an expression stating when something will happen. □ SALLY: *I'm going to have to stop pretty soon for a rest.* MARY: *Sooner than you think, I'd say. I think one of our tires is low.* □ TOM: *The stock market is bound to run out of steam pretty soon.* BOB: *Sooner than you think from the look of today's news.*

Sorry. See *(I'm) sorry.*

Sorry (that) I asked. Now that I have heard the answer, I regret asking the question. □ ALICE: *Can we get a new car soon? The old one is a wreck.* JOHN: *Are you kidding? There's no way that we could ever afford a new car!* ALICE: *Sorry I asked.* □ *After he heard the long list of all the reasons he wouldn't be allowed to go to the concert, Fred just shrugged and said, "Sorry that I asked."*

Sorry to hear that. See *(I'm) sorry to hear that.*

Sorry you asked? See *(Are you) sorry you asked?*; *(I'm) sorry you asked (that).*

Sort of. AND **Kind of.** Yes, but only to a small degree. □ BOB: *Do you like what you're doing in school?* ALICE: *Kind of.* □ HENRY: *What do you think about all these new laws? Do they worry you?* JOHN: *Sort of.*

Soup's on! The meal is ready to eat. (Said for any food, not just soup.) □ TOM: *Soup's on!* BILL: *The camp chef has dished up another disaster. Come on, we might as well face the music.* □ JOHN: *Soup's on! Come and get it!* MARY: *Well, I guess it's time to eat again.* SUE: *Yeah, no way to avoid it, I guess.*

So (what)? Why does that matter? (Colloquial or familiar. Can be considered rude.) □ BOB: *Your attitude always seems to lack sincerity.* MARY: *So what?* □ JOHN: *Your car sure is dusty.* SUE: *So?*

(So) what else is new? This isn't new. It has happened before; Not this again. □ MARY: *Taxes are going up again.* BOB: *So what else is new?* □ JOHN: *Gee, my pants are getting tight. Maybe I'm putting on a little weight.* SALLY: *What else is new?*

Speaking. AND **This is someone.** I am the person you have just asked for (on the telephone). (The *someone* can be a person's name or *he* or *she*.) □ TOM: *Hello?* MARY: *Is Tom there?* TOM: *Speaking.* □ TOM: *Hello?* MARY: *Is Tom there?* TOM: *This is he.*

speaking (quite) candidly an expression introducing a frank or forthright statement. □ *"Speaking quite candidly, I find your behavior a bit offensive,"* stated Frank, obviously offended. □ MARY: *Tell me what you really think about this skirt.* SALLY: *Speaking candidly, I think you should get your money back.*

(speaking) (quite) frankly AND **frankly speaking** a transitional phrase announcing that the speaker is going to talk in a more familiar and totally forthright manner. □ TOM: *Speaking quite frankly, I'm not certain she's the one for the job.* MARY: *I agree.* □ BOB: *We ought to be looking at housing in a lower price bracket.* BILL: *Quite frankly, I agree.* □ *"Frankly speaking,"* said John, *"I think you're out of your mind!"*

Speak of the devil. a phrase said when someone whose name has just been mentioned suddenly appears on the scene. (Compare to *We were just talking about you.*) □ TOM: *Speak of the devil, here comes Bill.* MARY: *We were just talking about you, Bill.* □ JOHN: *I wonder how Fred is doing in his new job.* FRED: *Hi, you two. What's up?* JOHN: *Speak of the devil. Look who's here!*

Speak up. Please speak louder.; Do not be shy, speak louder. □ *"Speak up. I can hardly hear you,"* said Uncle Henry, cupping his hand to *his ear.* □ MARY: *I'm sorry.* TEACHER: *Speak up.* MARY: *I'm sorry, ma'am. I won't do it again.*

'Spose not. See under *I guess not.*

'Spose so. See under *I guess (so).*

Stay out of my way. See *Keep out of my way.*

Stay out of this! See *Keep out of this!*

Step aside. Please move out of the way so there is a pathway. □ *"Step aside. Let the mayor through, please,"* called out the mayor's bodyguard. □ TOM (blocking the boss's door): *Just a moment, sir.* BOSS (trying to exit): *Step aside, please.* TOM: *But, sir!* BOSS: *Step aside, please.* TOM: *But, sir, the tax people are here with an arrest warrant.*

Stick with it. Do not give up. Stay with your task. □ BILL: *I'm really tired of calculus.* FATHER: *Stick with it. You'll be a better person for it.* □ BILL: *This job is getting to be such a pain.* SUE: *True, but it pays well, doesn't it? Stick with it.*

Stop the music! AND **Stop the presses!** Stop everything!; *Hold it!* (*Presses* refers to the printing presses used to print newspapers. This means that there is recent news of such magnitude that the presses must be stopped so a new edition can be printed immediately.) □ JOHN (entering the room): *Stop the music! There's a fire in the kitchen!* MARY: *Good grief! Let's get out of here!* □ *"Stop the presses!"* shouted Jane. *"I have an announcement."*

Stop the presses! See the previous entry.

Stuff a sock in it! *Shut up!*; Stop talking! (Literally, stuff a sock in your mouth to stop the noise.) □ TOM: *Hey, Henry! Can you hear me?* HENRY: *Be quiet, Tom. Stuff a sock in it!* □ FRED: *Hey, you still here? I want to tell you a few things!* JOHN: *Oh, stuff a sock in it! You're a pain.*

Suits me (fine). See *(It) suits me (fine).*

Suit yourself. You decide the way you want it.; *Have it your way.* □ MARY: *I think I want the red one.* TOM: *Suit yourself.* □ JOHN (reading the menu): *The steak sounds good, but I'm helpless in the face of fried chicken.* SALLY: *Suit yourself. I'll have the steak.*

suppose See *supposing.*

Supposed to. See *(Someone or something is) supposed to.*

Suppose I do? AND **Supposing I do?** And what does it matter if I do, and what are you going to do about it? (Not usually with question intonation.) □ ALICE: *Do you really think it's right to do something like that?* SUE: *Suppose I do?* □ FRED: *Are you going to drive up into the mountains as you said you would?* SALLY: *Supposing I do?* FRED: *I'm just asking.*

Suppose I don't? AND **Supposing I don't?** And what will happen if I don't? (Not usually with question intonation.) □ BILL: *You'd better get yourself over to the main office.* TOM: *Suppose I don't?* □ FATHER: *You simply must do better in school.* TOM: *Supposing I don't?* FATHER: *Your clothing and personal belongings will be placed on the curb for the garbage pickup, and we will have the locks changed. Next question.*

supposing AND **suppose** a word introducing a hypothesis. □ FRED: *Supposing I was to walk right out of here, just like that.* MARY: *I'd say good-bye and good riddance.* □ SUE: *Suppose all the electricity suddenly stopped. What would we do?* BOB: *It doesn't matter, the television can run on batteries too.*

Supposing I do? See *Suppose I do?*

Supposing I don't? See *Suppose I don't?*

Sure. Yes, certainly. (See also *Oh, sure (someone or something will).*) □ MARY: *This okay?* JANE: *Sure.* □ BILL: *Want to go to a movie with me Saturday?* SUE: *Sure, why not?*

Sure as shooting! Absolutely yes! (An elaboration of *Sure.*) □ BILL: *Are you going to be there Monday night?* BOB: *Sure as shooting!* □ BOB: *Will you take this over to the main office?* BILL: *Sure as shooting!*

Sure thing. I certainly will. □ SUE: *Will you be at the reception?* BOB: *Sure thing.* □ BILL: *You remember my cousin, Tom, don't you?* BOB: *Sure thing. Hi, Tom.*

T

Tah-dah! a phrase introducing or pointing to something that is supposed to be exciting. □ *"Tah-dah," said Alice, pretending to be a trumpet. "This is my new car!"* □ BILL: *Tah-dah! Everyone, meet Mrs. Wilson!* MARY: *Hello, Mrs. Wilson.*

Take care (of yourself). **1.** Good-bye and keep yourself healthy. □ JOHN: *I'll see you next month. Good-bye.* BOB: *Good-bye, John. Take care of yourself.* □ MARY: *Take care.* SUE: *Okay. See you later.* **2.** Take care of your health and get well. □ MARY: *Don't worry. I'll get better soon.* SUE: *Well, take care of yourself. Bye.* □ JANE: *I'm sorry you're ill.* BOB: *Oh, it's nothing.* JANE: *Well, take care of yourself.*

Take it easy. **1.** Good-bye and be careful. □ MARY: *Bye-bye.* BILL: *See you, Mary. Take it easy.* □ SUE: *Take it easy, Tom. Don't do anything I wouldn't do.* TOM: *Could you give me a short list of things you wouldn't do?* **2.** Be gentle.; Treat someone carefully. □ SUE: *Then I want you to move the piano and turn all the mattresses.* ANDREW: *Come on. Take it easy! I'm not made of steel, you know.* □ HENRY: *Oh, I'm pooped.* ALICE: *You just need a little rest and you'll feel as good as new. Just take it easy.* **3.** Calm down.; Relax.; Do not get excited. □ ANDREW: *I am so mad I could blow my top!* RACHEL: *Now, now. Take it easy. What's wrong?* □ *Mary could see that Sally was very upset at the news. "Now, just take it easy," said Mary. "It can't be all that bad."*

Take it or leave it. That is all there is. There is no choice. Take this one or none. □ BILL: *That's my final offer. Take it or leave it.* BOB: *Aw, come on! Take off a few bucks.* □ BILL: *Aw, I want eggs for breakfast, Mom.* MOTHER: *There's only Sweet Wheets left. Take it or leave it.*

Take my word for it.   Believe me.; *Trust me*, I am telling you the truth.   □ BILL: *Take my word for it. These are the best encyclopedias you can buy.* BOB: *But I don't need any encyclopedias.*   □ RACHEL: *No one can cook better than Fred. Take my word for it.* BILL: *Really?* FRED: *Oh, yes. It's true.*

taking care of business   See *(just) taking care of business.*

talk through one's hat   to brag or boast; to tell small lies casually.   □ MARY: *I've got the fastest feet in the dorm and they're going to carry me all the way to the Olympics.* SALLY: *Oh, Mary, you're just talking through your hat.*   □ *"Bill is always talking through his hat," said Fred. "Don't pay any attention to his bragging."*

Talk to you soon.   See *(I will) talk to you soon.*

Ta-ta.   See *Toodle-oo.*

T.C.B.   See under *(just) taking care of business.*

Tell me another (one)!   What you just told me was a lie, so tell me another lie!   □ BILL: *Did you know that the football coach was once a dancer in a movie?* TOM: *Go on! Tell me another one!*   □ *"Tell me another one!" laughed Bill at Tom's latest exaggeration.*

Thank goodness! AND **Thank heavens!**   Oh, I am so thankful!   □ JOHN: *Well, we finally got here. Sorry we're so late.* MOTHER: *Thank goodness! We were all so worried.*   □ JANE: *There was a fire on Maple Street, but no one was hurt.* BILL: *Thank heavens!*

Thank heavens!   See the previous entry.

Thanks.   See *Thanks (a lot)* and the entries beginning with *Thank you.*

Thanks (a lot). AND **Thank you a lot.**   **1.** Thank you, I am grateful.   □ BILL: *Here, take mine.* BOB: *Thanks a lot.*   □ MARY: *Well, here's your pizza.* BILL: *Thanks.* **2.** That is not worth much.; That is nothing to be grateful for. (Sarcasm is indicated by the tone of voice used with this expression.)   □ JOHN: *I'm afraid that you're going to have to work the night shift.* BOB: *Thanks a lot.*   □ FRED: *Here's* *your share of the money. We had to take out nearly half to make up for the damage you did to the car.* BILL: *Thanks a lot.*

Thanks a million. *Thank you a lot.* □ BILL: *Oh, thanks a million. You were very helpful.* BOB: *Just glad I could help.* □ JOHN: *Here's your book.* JANE: *Thanks a million. Sorry I needed it back in such a rush.*

Thanks awfully. *Thank you very much.* □ JOHN: *Here's one for you.* JANE: *Thanks awfully.* □ MARY: *Here, let me help you with all that stuff.* SUE: *Thanks awfully.*

Thanks, but no thanks. *Thank you, but I am not interested.* (A way of turning down something that is not very desirable.) □ ALICE: *How would you like to buy my old car?* JANE: *Thanks, but no thanks.* □ JOHN: *What do you think about a trip over to see the Wilsons?* SALLY: *Thanks, but no thanks. We don't get along.*

Thanks for having me. See *Thank you for inviting me.*

Thanks for the lift. See the following entry.

Thanks for the ride. AND **Thanks for the lift.** Thank you for giving me a ride in your car. □ JOHN (stopping the car): *Here we are.* BOB: *Thanks for the ride. Bye.* JOHN: *Later.* □ *As Fred got out of the car, he said, "Thanks for the lift."*

Thanks loads. *Thanks a lot.* (Colloquial.) □ MARY: *Here, you can have these. And take these too.* SALLY: *Thanks loads.* □ JOHN: *Wow! You look great!* SALLY: *Thanks loads. I try.*

Thank you. I am grateful to you and offer you my thanks. □ BILL: *Here, have some more cake.* BOB: *Thank you.* □ JOHN: *Your hair looks nice.* MARY: *Thank you.*

Thank you a lot. See *Thanks (a lot).*

Thank you for a lovely evening. an expression said by a departing guest to the host or hostess at the end of an evening. (Other adjectives, such as *nice*, can be used in place of *lovely*.) □ MARY: *Thank you for a lovely evening.* JOHN: *Will I see you again?* □ BILL: *Thank you for a nice evening.* MARY: *Thank you so much for coming. Good night.*

Thank you for a lovely time. an expression said by a departing guest to the host or hostess. (Other adjectives, such as *nice*, can be used in place of *lovely*.) □ BILL: *Thank you for a nice time.* MARY: *Thank you so much for coming. Bye now.* □ JOHN: *Thank you so much for coming.* JANE: *Well, thank you for a lovely time.* JOHN: *Don't stay away so long next time.*

Thank you for calling. Thank you for calling on the telephone. (Said when the call is helpful or a bother to the caller.) □ MARY: *Good-bye.* SUE: *Good-bye, thanks for calling.* □ JOHN: *Okay. Well, I have to get off the phone. I just wanted you to know what was happening with your order.* JANE: *Okay. Bye. Thanks for calling.*

Thank you for inviting me. AND **Thank you for inviting us.; Thank you for having me.; Thank you for having us.** a polite expression said to a host or hostess on departure. □ MARY: *Good-bye, glad you could come.* BILL: *I had a great time. Thank you for inviting me.* □ JOHN: *I had a good time. Thank you for inviting me.* SALLY: *Come back again, John. It was good talking to you.*

Thank you for inviting us. See the previous entry.

Thank you so much. See the following entry.

Thank you very much. AND **Thank you so much.** a more polite and emphatic way of saying *Thank you.* □ TOM: *Welcome. Come in.* BOB: *Thank you very much.* □ BILL: *Here's the book I promised you.* SUE: *Thank you so much.*

That ain't the way I heard it. That is not the way I heard the story told. (A catch phrase. The grammar error, *ain't*, is built into the expression.) □ JOHN: *It seemed like a real riot, then Sally called the police and things calmed down.* SUE: *That ain't the way I heard it.* JOHN: *What?* SUE: *Somebody said the neighbors called the police.* □ FRED: *Four of us went fishing and were staying in this cabin. These women stopped and said they were having car trouble. What could we do?* SALLY: *That ain't the way I heard it.*

That (all) depends. My answer depends on factors that have yet to be discussed. □ TOM: *Will you be able to come to the meeting on Thursday night?* MARY: *That all depends.* □ BOB: *Can I see you again?* SALLY: *That depends.*

That beats everything! See *If that don't beat all!*

That brings me to the (main) point. a transitional expression that introduces the main point of a conversation. (See also *which brings me to the (main) point.*) □ FATHER: *It's true. All of us had to go through something like this when we were young, and that brings me to the point. Aren't you old enough to be living on your own and making your own decisions and supporting yourself?* TOM: *Well, yes, I guess so.* □ FRED: *Yes, things are very expensive these days, and that brings me to the main point. You simply have to cut back on spending.* BILL: *You're right. I'll do it!*

(That causes) no problem. That will not cause a problem for me or anyone else. □ MARY: *Do you mind waiting for just a little while?* BOB: *No problem.* □ SUE: *Does this block your light? Can you still read?* JANE: *That causes no problem.*

That does it! **1.** That completes it!; It is now done just right! □ *When Jane got the last piece put into the puzzle, she said, "That does it!"* □ JOHN (signing a paper): *Well, that's the last one! That does it!* BILL: *I thought we'd never finish.* **2.** That's the last straw!; Enough is enough! □ BILL: *We're still not totally pleased with your work.* BOB: *That does it! I quit!* □ SALLY: *That does it! I never want to see you again!* FRED: *I only put my arm around you!*

[that is] See the entries beginning with *that's.*

That'll be the day! It will be an unusually amazing day when that happens! □ BILL: *I think I'll fix that lamp now.* ANDREW: *When you finally get around to fixing that lamp, that'll be the day!* □ SUE: *I'm going to get this place organized once and for all!* ALICE: *That'll be the day!*

That'll teach someone! What happened to *someone* is a suitable punishment! (The *someone* is usually a pronoun.) □ BILL: *Tom, who has cheated on his taxes for years, finally got caught.* SUE: *That'll teach him.* □ BILL: *Gee, I got a ticket for speeding.* FRED: *That'll teach you!*

That (really) burns me (up)! That makes me very angry! □ BOB: *Did you hear that interest rates are going back up?* MARY: *That really burns me up!* □ SUE: *Fred is telling everyone that you are the one who lost the party money.* MARY: *That burns me! It was John who had the money in the first place.*

That's about the size of it. That is the way it is. □ BOB: *We only have grocery money left in the bank.* SALLY: *That means that there isn't enough money for us to go to Jamaica?* BOB: *That's about the size of it.* □

BOB: *I'm supposed to take this bill to the county clerk's office and pay them four hundred dollars?* SALLY: *That's about the size of it.*

That's all someone needs. AND **It's all someone needs.; (It's) just what you need.; That's just what you need.** *Someone* does not need that at all.; *That's the last straw!* (Always sarcastic. The *someone* can be a person's name or a pronoun.) ☐ JANE: *The dog died and the basement is just starting to flood.* FRED: *That's all we need.* ☐ SALLY: *Bill, the check you wrote to the Internal Revenue Service was returned. There's no more money in the bank.* BILL: *That's all we need.* ☐ BOB: *On top of all that, now I have car trouble!* MARY: *That's just what you need!*

That's a new one on me! I had not heard that before. ☐ BOB: *Did you hear? They're building a new highway that will bypass the town.* FRED: *That's a new one on me! That's terrible!* ☐ SUE: *All of us will have to pay our taxes monthly from now on.* MARY: *That's a new one on me!*

That's easy for you to say. You can say that easily because it really does not affect you the way it affects others. ☐ WAITER: *Here's your check.* MARY: *Thanks.* (turning to others) *I'm willing to just split the check evenly.* BOB: *That's easy for you to say. You had lobster!* ☐ SALLY: *Let's each chip in ten bucks and buy him a sweater.* SUE: *That's easy for you to say. You've got ten bucks to spare.*

That's enough! No more!; Stop that! ☐ SUE: *Here, I'll stack another one on top.* MARY: *That's enough! It will fall.* ☐ JOHN: *I could go on with complaint after complaint. I could talk all week, in fact.* BOB: *That's enough!*

That's enough for now. No more of that for now.; Please stop for a while. ☐ MARY: *Here, have some more cake. Do you want a larger piece?* BILL: *Oh, no. That's enough for now.* ☐ BILL: *Shall I cut a little more off this tree, lady, or save the rest till spring?* JANE: *No, that's enough for now.*

(That's) enough (of this) foolishness! **1.** Stop this foolishness. ☐ BILL: *Enough of this foolishness. Stop it!* SALLY: *Sorry.* ☐ FATHER: *That's enough of this foolishness. You two stop fighting over nothing.* BOB: *Okay.* BILL: *Sorry.* **2.** I have had enough of this. (Does not refer to something that is actual foolishness.) ☐ ANDREW: *Enough of this* *foolishness. I hate ballet. I'm leaving.* SUE: *Well, sneak out quietly.* ANDREW: *No, I'll lead an exodus.* □ SALLY: *That's enough foolishness. I'm leaving and I never want to see you again!* BOB: *Come on! I was only teasing.*

(That's) fine by me. See the following entry.

(That's) fine with me. AND **(That's) fine by me.; (That's) okay by me.; (That's) okay with me.** That is agreeable as far as I am concerned. (The expressions with *by* are colloquial.) □ SUE: *I'm giving away your old coat.* BOB: *That's fine with me.* □ SALLY: *Can I take twenty dollars out of your wallet?* FRED: *That's okay by me—if you can find it, of course.*

That's funny. That is strange or peculiar. □ BILL: *Tom just called from Detroit and says he's coming back tomorrow.* MARY: *That's funny. He's not supposed to.* □ SUE: *The sky is turning very gray.* MARY: *That's funny. There's no bad weather forecast.*

That's (just) too much! **1.** That is unpleasant and unacceptable!; That is more than I can bear! □ *"That's just too much!" exclaimed Sue, and she walked out.* □ BILL: *I'm afraid this movie isn't what we thought it was going to be.* SUE: *Did you see that? That's too much! Let's go!* **2.** That is just too funny. (Compare to *You're too much.*) □ *After Fred finished the joke, and Bill had stopped howling with laughter, Bill said, "That's too much! Tell a sad one for a change."* □ *When Tom stopped laughing, his sides ached and he had tears in his eyes. "Oh, that's too much!" he moaned.*

That's just what you need. See *That's all someone needs.*

That's more like it. That is better.; That is a better response this time. □ WAITER: *Here is your order, sir. Roast chicken as you requested. Sorry about the mix-up.* JOHN: *That's more like it.* □ CLERK: *Now, here's one that you might like.* SALLY: *Now, that's more like it!*

That's news to me. I did not know that.; I had not been informed of that. □ BILL: *They've blocked off Maple Street for some repairs.* TOM: *That's news to me.* □ SALLY: *The telephones are out. None of them work.* BILL: *That's news to me.*

(That's) no skin off my nose. AND **(That's) no skin off my teeth.** That does not embarrass me.; That causes me no difficulty or harm. (Colloquial. The second form is borrowed from the metaphor *by the skin of someone's teeth* meaning "just barely." The

first form has additional variations—most of them vulgar.) □
BILL: *Everybody around here seems to think you're the one to blame.* BOB: *So what? I'm not to blame. That's no skin off my teeth, whatever they think.*
□ BILL: *Sally is going to quit her job and go to Tampa.* BOB: *No skin off my nose! I don't care what she does.*

(That's) okay by me. See *(That's) fine with me.*

(That's) okay with me. See *(That's) fine with me.*

That's that! That is the end of that! Nothing more can be done. □
TOM: *Well, that's that! I can do no more.* SALLY: *That's the way it goes.*
□ DOCTOR (finishing an operation): *That's that! Would you close for me, Sue?* SUE: *Nice job, doctor. Yes, I'll close.*

That's the last straw! That is going too far!; Something will have to be done. □ BOB: *Now they say I have to have a tutor to pass calculus.*
MARY: *That's the last straw! I'm going straight up to that school and find out what they aren't doing right.* □ *"That's the last straw!" cried Fred when he got another special tax bill from the city.*

That's the stuff! That is the right attitude or action. □ BOB: *I'm sure I can do it!* FRED: *That's the stuff!* □ *"That's the stuff!" cried the coach as Mary crossed the finish line.*

That's the ticket! That is what is required! □ MARY: *I'll just get ready and drive the letter directly to the airport!* SUE: *That's the ticket. Take it right to the airport post office.* □ BOB: *I've got it! I'll buy a new computer!* BILL: *That's the ticket!*

That's the way it goes. That is fate. □ MARY: *All my roses died in the cold weather.* SUE: *That's the way it goes.* □ SALLY: *Someone stole all the candy we left out in the front office.* JANE: *That's the way it goes.*

That's the way the ball bounces. See the following entry.

That's the way the cookie crumbles. AND **That's the way the ball bounces.; That's the way the mop flops.** That is life.; *That's the way it goes.* □ SUE: *I lost out on the chance for a promotion.*
ALICE: *That's the way the cookie crumbles.* □ JOHN: *This entire week was spent on this project. Then they canceled it.* SALLY: *That's the way the ball bounces.*

That's the way the mop flops. See the previous entry.

(That's the) way to go! a phrase encouraging someone to continue the good work. □ *As John ran over the finish line, everyone cried, "That's the way to go!"* □ *"Way to go!" said Mary when Bob finally got the car started.*

(That's) too bad. It is unfortunate.; *I'm sorry to hear that.* □ TOM: *I hurt my foot on our little hike.* FRED: *That's too bad. Can I get you something for it?* TOM: *No, I'll live.* □ BOB: *My uncle just passed away.* TOM: *That's too bad. I'm sorry to hear that.* BOB: *Thanks.*

That's what I say. I agree with what was just said. □ TOM: *We've got to get in there and stand up for our rights!* MARY: *That's what I say.* □ BOB: *They shouldn't do that!* MARY: *That's what I say!* BOB: *They should be put in jail!* MARY: *That's what I say!*

that's why! a tag on the end of a statement that is an answer to a question beginning with *why*. (Shows a little impatience.) □ SUE: *Why do you always put your right shoe on first?* BOB: *Because, when I get ready to put on my shoes, I always pick up the right one first, that's why!* □ MARY: *Why do you eat that awful peppermint candy?* TOM: *Because I like it, that's why!*

That takes the cake! **1.** That is good, and it wins the prize! (Assuming that the prize is a cake.) □ *"What a performance!" cheered John. "That takes the cake!"* □ SUE: *Wow! That takes the cake! What a dive!* RACHEL: *She sure can dive!* **2.** That is the end!; *That does it!* □ BOB: *What a dumb thing to do, Fred!* BILL: *Yeah, Fred. That takes the cake!* □ BOB: *Wow! That takes the cake!* BILL: *What is it? Why are you slowing down?* BOB: *That stupid driver in front of me just hit the car on the left and then swung over and hit the car on the right.*

That tears it! That's the absolute end!; *That does it!* (*Tears* rhymes with *stairs*.) □ RACHEL: *Okay, that tears it! I'm going to complain to the landlord. Those people make noise day and night!* SUE: *Yes, this is too much.* □ TOM: *The boss thinks maybe you should work on the night shift.* MARY: *That tears it! I quit!*

[that will] See the entries beginning with *that'll*.

(The) best of luck (to someone). I wish good luck to someone. □ ALICE: *Good-bye, Bill.* BILL: *Goodbye, Alice. Best of luck.* ALICE:

Thanks. Bye. □ *"Good-bye, and the best of luck to you," shouted Mary, waving and crying at the same time.*

then as a consequence; therefore; because of that. (Often this word seems to be filler with no clear or needed meaning.) □ BILL: *I've taken a job in New York.* ALICE: *You'll be leaving Toledo then?* BILL: *Yes, I have to move.* □ *"All right then, what sort of car were you thinking about?" asked the sales manager.*

(There is) no chance. There is no chance that something will happen. □ TOM: *Do you think that some little country like that will actually attack England?* JOHN: *There's no chance.* □ BILL: *No chance you can lend me a few bucks, is there?* BILL: *Nope. No chance.*

(There is) no doubt about it. It cannot be doubted.; It is obvious. □ JANE: *It's really cold today.* FRED: *No doubt about it!* □ SUE: *Things seem to be getting more and more expensive.* TOM: *There's no doubt about that. Look at the price of oranges!*

(There is) no need (to). You do not have to.; It is not necessary. □ MARY: *Shall I try to save all this wrapping paper?* SUE: *No need. It's all torn.* □ BOB: *Would you like me to have it repaired? I'm so sorry I broke it.* BILL: *There is no need to. I can just glue it, thanks.*

(There's) nothing to it! It is easy! □ JOHN: *Is it hard to learn to fly a small plane?* SUE: *There's nothing to it!* □ BILL: *Me? I can't dive off a board that high! I can hardly dive off the side of the pool!* BOB: *Aw, come on! Nothing to it!*

(There's) no way to tell. No one can find out the answer. □ TOM: *How long are we likely to have to wait before the plane takes off?* CLERK: *Sorry, sir. There's no way to tell.* □ BILL: *Will the banks be open when we arrive?* BOB: *No way to tell. They don't keep regular hours.*

The rest is history. Everyone knows the rest of the story that I am telling. □ BILL: *Then they arrested all the officers of the corporation, and the rest is history.* SUE: *Can't trust anybody these days.* □ BOB: *Hey, what happened between you and Sue?* BILL: *Finally we realized that we could never get along, and the rest is history.*

There will be hell to pay. There will be a lot of trouble if something is done or if something is not done. □ FRED: *If you break another window, there will be hell to pay.* ANDREW: *I didn't do it! I didn't.* □ BILL: *I'm afraid there's no time to do this one. I'm going to skip it.* BOB: *There will be hell to pay if you do.*

There you are. That's the way things are.; This is the way things have worked out. (A fatalistic dismissal.) □ *"There's nothing more that can be done. We've done what we could. So there you are,"* said Fred, dejected. □ ANDREW: *Then what happened?* BOB: *Then they put me in a cell until they found I was innocent. Somebody stole my watch in there, and I cut myself on a broken wine bottle left on a bench. And now I've got lice. All because of mistaken identity. So there you are.*

There you go! Now you are doing it right!; Now you have the right attitude! □ ALICE: *I know I can do it. I just need to try harder.* JANE: *There you go!* □ BOB: *I'll devote my full time to studying and stop messing around.* FATHER: *There you go! That's great!*

The same for me. See *I'll have the same.*

(The) same to you. **1.** AND **You too.** a polite way of returning good wishes to someone. □ CLERK: *Have a nice day.* SALLY: *The same to you.* □ BOB: *I hope things work out for you. Happy New Year!* BILL: *You to. Bye.* **2.** (often **Same to ya.**) an impolite way of returning a curse or epithet to someone. (Slang. In *Same to ya.* the stress is on *to.*) □ TOM: *You're such a pest!* BILL: *Same to ya!* □ TOM: *I hope you go out and fall in a hole.* BILL: *You too.*

The shame of it (all)! That is so shameful!; I am so embarrassed. (Considerable use as a parody. Compare to *For shame!*) □ JOHN: *Good grief! I have a pimple! Always, just before a date.* ANDREW: *The shame of it all!* □ TOM: *John claims that he cheated on his taxes.* BILL: *Golly! The shame of it!*

The sooner the better. The sooner something gets done, the better things will be. (A cliché.) □ BOB: *When do you need this?* MARY: *The sooner the better.* □ BOB: *Please get the oil changed in the station wagon. The sooner the better.* ALICE: *I'll do it today.*

the way I see it See *from my perspective.*

The word is mum. AND **Mum's the word.** a pledge not to reveal a secret or to tell about something or someone. □ BOB: *I hope you won't tell all this to anyone.* BILL: *Don't worry, the word is mum.* □ *"The word is mum,"* said Jane to ease Mary's mind about the secret.

They must have seen you coming. You were really cheated.; They saw you coming and decided they could cheat you easily. □ ANDREW: *It cost two hundred dollars.* RACHEL: *You paid two hundred dollars for that thing? Boy, they must have seen you coming.* □ BOB: *Do you*

think I paid too much for this car? It's not as good as I thought it was.
TOM: *It's almost a wreck. They must have seen you coming.*

(Things) could be better. AND **(I) could be better.; (Things) might be better.** a greeting inquiry response meaning "My state is not as good as it might be." (Not necessarily a direct answer.) □ JOHN: *How are things going, Fred?* FRED: *Things could be better. And you?* JOHN: *About the same.* □ BOB: *Hi, Bill! How are you?* BILL: *I could be better. What's new with you?* BOB: *Nothing much.*

(Things) could be worse. AND **(I) could be worse.** a greeting inquiry response meaning "My state is not as bad as it might be." (Not necessarily a direct answer.) □ JOHN: *How are you, Fred?* FRED: *Things could be worse. And you?* JOHN: *Okay, I guess.* □ BOB: *Hi, Bob! What's happening?* BOB: *I could be worse. What's new with you?*

Things getting you down? See *(Are) things getting you down?*

Things haven't been easy. See *(It) hasn't been easy.*

(Things) might be better. See *(Things) could be better.*

Things will work out (all right). AND **Everything will work out (all right.); Everything will work out for the best.; Things will work out for the best.** The situation will reach a satisfactory conclusion.; The problem(s) will be resolved. □ *"Cheer up!" Mary said to a gloomy Fred, "Things will work out all right."* □ MARY: *Oh, I'm so miserable!* BILL: *Don't worry. Everything will work out for the best.* □ *"Now, now, don't cry. Things will work out," consoled Sally, hoping that what she was saying was really true.*

Things will work out for the best. See the previous entry.

thinking out loud See *(I'm) (just) thinking out loud.*

Think nothing of it. AND **Don't give it another thought.; Don't give it a (second) thought.** 1. *You're welcome.; It was nothing.; I was glad to do it.* □ MARY: *Thank you so much for driving me home.* JOHN: *Think nothing of it.* □ SUE: *It was very kind of you to bring these all the way out here.* ALICE: *Think nothing of it. I was delighted* *to do it.* **2.** You did no harm at all. (A very polite way of reassuring someone that an action has not caused any great harm or hurt the speaker.) □ SUE: *Oh, sorry. I didn't mean to bump you!* BOB: *Think nothing of it.* □ JANE: *I hope I didn't hurt your feelings when I said you were too loud.* BILL: *Don't give it a second thought. I was too loud.*

This doesn't quite suit me. AND **It doesn't quite suit me.** This is not quite what I want.; This does not please me. (Compare to *(It) suits me (fine).*) □ CLERK: *How do you like this one?* MARY: *It doesn't quite suit me.* □ BOB: *This doesn't quite suit me. Let me see something a little darker.* CLERK: *How's this?* BOB: *Better.*

This is it! I have discovered the right thing!; This is the one! □ *"This is it!" shouted the scientist, holding a test tube in the air.* □ SUE: *This is it! This is the book that has all the shrimp recipes.* MARY: *Well, happy birthday! I never saw anybody get so happy about shrimp.*

This is my floor. a phrase said by someone at the back of an elevator suggesting that people make way for an exit at a particular floor. □ *Mary said, "This is my floor," and everyone made room for her to get out of the elevator.* □ *"Out, please," said Tom loudly. "This is my floor!"*

This is someone. See *Speaking.*

This is where I came in. I have heard all this before. (When someone begins watching a film after it has begun, this phrase is said when the reshowing of the film reaches familiar scenes.) □ *John sat through a few minutes of the argument, and when Tom and Alice kept saying the same thing over and over John said, "This is where I came in," and left the room.* □ *The speaker stood up and asked again for a new vote on the proposal. "This is where I came in," muttered Jane as she headed for the door.*

This one's on me. I will pay for the treat this time. (Usually said in reference to buying drinks. Compare to *It's on me.*) □ *As the waiter set down the glasses, Fred said, "This one's on me."* □ JOHN: *Check, please.* BILL: *No, this one's on me.*

This taken? See *(Is) this (seat) taken?*

Till later. See *(Good-bye) until then.*

Till next time. See *Good-bye for now.*

Till then. See *(Good-bye) until then.*

Till we meet again. See *Good-bye for now.*

Time for a change. See *(It's) time for a change.*

Time (out)! Stop everything for just a minute! □ *"Hey, stop a minute! Time out!" yelled Mary as the argument grew in intensity.* □ *Right in the middle of the discussion, Alice said, "Time!" Then she announced that dinner was ready.*

Times are changing. a response to a surprising piece of news from someone. □ SUE: *They paid nearly five hundred thousand for their first house!* RACHEL: *Well, I shouldn't be so surprised. Times are changing, I guess.* □ *"Times are changing," warned Mary. "You can't expect the world to stand still."*

Time to call it a day. It's time to quit for the day. □ JANE: *Well, I'm done. Time to call it a day.* SUE: *Yes, let's get out of here.* □ JANE: *Well, I've done too much work.* SUE: *Yes, it's late. Time to call it a day.*

Time to call it a night. It's time to quit one's activities for the night. (Can refer to work or partying.) □ BOB: *Wow, it's late! Time to call it a night.* MARY: *Yes, it's really dark! Good night.* □ FRED: *Gee, I'm tired. Look at the time!* JANE: *Yes, it's time to call it a night.*

Time to go. See *(It's) time to go.*

Time to hit the road. See *(It's) time to hit the road.*

Time to move along. See *(It's) time to run.*

Time to push along. See *(It's) time to run.*

Time to push off. See *(It's) time to run.*

Time to run. See *(It's) time to run.*

Time to shove off. See *(I) have to shove off.*

Time to split. See *(It's) time to run.*

(To) hell with that! I reject that! □ MARY: *I think we ought to go to the dance Friday night.* TOM: *To hell with that!* □ FRED: *Don't you want to drive me down to school?* JOHN: *To hell with that!*

Too bad. See *(That's) too bad.*

Toodle-oo. AND **Ta-ta.; Toodles.** *Good-bye.* ☐ FRED: *Bye, you guys. See you.* SALLY: *It's been. Really it has. Toodle-oo.* ☐ MARY: *See ya, bye-bye.* SUE: *Ta-ta.*

Toodles. See *Toodle-oo.*

Took the words right out of my mouth. See *(You) took the words right out of my mouth.*

to put it another way AND **put another way** a phrase introducing a restatement of what someone, usually the speaker, has just said. ☐ FATHER: *You're still very young, Tom. To put it another way, you don't have any idea about what you're getting into.* TOM: *But I still want to get married, so can I borrow fifty dollars?* ☐ JOHN: *Could you go back to your own room now, Tom? I have to study.* TOM: (no answer) JOHN: *Put another way, get out of here!* TOM: *Okay, okay. Don't get your bowels in an uproar!*

to the best of my knowledge See *(as) far as I know.*

Tout suite! right away; with all haste. (From French *Toute de Suite.* Pronounced "toot sweet.") ☐ JOHN: *Come on, get this finished!* BOB: *I'm trying.* JOHN: *Tout suite! Get moving!* ☐ *"I want this mess cleaned up, tout suite!" shouted Sally, hands on her hips and steaming with rage.*

Trust me! I am telling you the truth. Please believe me. ☐ *Tom said with great conviction, "Trust me! I know exactly what to do!"* ☐ MARY: *Do you really think we can keep this party a secret until Thursday?* SALLY: *Trust me! I know how to plan a surprise party.*

try as I may a phrase that introduces an expression of regret or failure. ☐ BILL: *Try as I may, I cannot get this thing put together right.* ANDREW: *Did you read the instructions?* ☐ RACHEL: *Wow! This place is a mess!* MOTHER: *Try as I may, I can't get Andrew to clean up after himself.*

Try to catch you later. See *(I'll) try to catch you some other time.*

Try to catch you some other time. See *(I'll) try to catch you some other time.*

Tsup? *What's up?* (Slang.) ☐ BILL: *Tsup?* TOM: *Nothing. What's new with you?* BILL: *Nothing.* ☐ BOB: *Tsup?* FRED: *I'm getting a new car.* BOB: *Excellent!*

U

under no circumstances AND **not under any circumstances**   never.
□ ANDREW: *Under no circumstances will I ever go back there again!* RA-
CHEL: *Why? What happened?* □ SUE: *Can I talk you into serving as a
referee again?* MARY: *Heavens, no! Not under any circumstances!*

under normal circumstances   normally; usually; typically.   □
*"We'd be able to keep the dog at home under normal circumstances," said
Mary to the vet.* □ *"Under normal circumstances you'd be able to return to
work in a week," explained the doctor.*

Until later.   See *(Good-bye) until then.*

Until next time.   See *Good-bye for now.*

Until then.   See *(Good-bye) until then.*

Until we meet again.   See *Good-bye for now.*

Use your head! AND **Use your noggin!; Use your noodle!**   Start
thinking!; Use your brain.   □ TOM: *I just don't know what to do.*
MARY: *Use your head! You'll figure out something.* □ ANDREW: *Come
on, John, you can figure it out. A kindergartner could do it. Use your noggin!* JOHN: *I'm doing my best.*

Use your noggin!   See the previous entry.

Use your noodle!   See *Use your head!*

V

Vamoose! Get out!; Go away! (From Spanish *vamos,* "let's go.") □
BOB: *Go on. Get out of here! Vamoose!* BILL: *I'm going! I'm going!* □
TOM: *Go away!* BILL: *What?* BOB: *Vamoose! Scram! Beat it!* BILL:
Why? BOB: *Because you're a pain.*

Very glad to meet you. See *(I'm) (very) glad to meet you.*

Very good. **1.** It is good. □ JOHN: *How do you like your lobster?*
ALICE: *Mmm. Very good.* □ JANE: *What did you think of the movie?*
FRED: *Very good.* JANE: *Is that all?* FRED: *Yeah.* **2.** as you say; Thank
you for your instructions. (Typically said by someone in a serving
role, such as a clerk, waiter, waitress, butler, maid, etc.) □
WAITER: *What are you drinking, madam?* SUE: *It's just soda. No more,*
thanks. WAITER: *Very good.* □ MARY: *Would you charge this to my ac-*
count? CLERK: *Very good.*

W

Wait a minute. See *Just a minute.*

Wait a sec(ond). See *Just a minute.*

Wait up (a minute)! Wait for me while I catch up with you! □ *Tom, who was following Mary down the street, said, "Wait up a minute! I need to talk to you."* □ JOHN: *Hey, Sally! Wait up!* SALLY: *What's happening?*

Want to know something? See *(Do you) want to know something?*

Want to make something of it? See *(Do you) want to make something of it?*

Watch! See *(You) (just) watch!*

Watch it! **1.** Be careful. □ RACHEL: *Watch it! There's a broken stair there.* JANE: *Gee, thanks.* □ MARY: *Watch it! There's a pothole in the street.* BOB: *Thanks.* **2.** Do not act or talk that way. □ SALLY: *I really hate John!* SUE: *Watch it! He's my brother!* □ BILL: *You girls always seem to take so long to do a simple thing like getting dressed.* MARY: *Watch it!*

Watch out! See *Look out!*

Watch your mouth! See the following entry.

Watch your tongue! AND **Watch your mouth!** Do not talk like that!; Do not say those things!; Do not say those bad words! □ ANDREW: *Don't talk to me like that! Watch your tongue!* BILL: *I'll talk to you any way I want.* □ *"Watch your mouth!" warned Sue. "I will not listen to any more of this slime!"*

171

Way to go!   See *(That's the) way to go!*

We aim to please.   We are happy to try to please you. (Usually a commercial slogan, but can be said in jest by one person, often in response to *Thank you*.) □ MARY: *This meal is absolutely delicious!* WAITER: *We aim to please.* □ TOM: *Well, Sue, here's the laundry detergent you wanted from the store.* SUE: *Oh, thanks loads. You saved me a trip.* TOM: *We aim to please.*

[we are]   See the entries beginning with *we're*.

(We) don't see you much around here anymore. AND **(We) don't see you around here much anymore.**   We haven't seen you for a long time. (The *we* can be replaced with *I*.) □ BILL: *Hello, Tom. Long time no see.* TOM: *Yes, Bill. We don't see you much around here anymore.* □ *"We don't see you around here much anymore," said the old pharmacist to John, who had just come home from college.*

We had a lovely time.   See *I had a lovely time.*

Welcome.   Come into this place. You are welcome here. □ MARY: *Welcome. Please come in.* TOM: *Thank you so much.* □ BILL: *I'm glad you could make it. Come in. Welcome.* MARY: *Thanks. My, what a nice place you have here.*

Welcome to our house.   an expression said by a host or hostess when greeting guests and bringing them into the house. □ ANDREW: *Hello, Sally. Welcome to our house. Come on in.* SALLY: *Thanks. It's good to be here.* □ TOM: *Welcome to our house. Make yourself at home.* HENRY: *Thanks, I'm really tired.*

well   a sentence opener, having no specific meaning, sometimes expressing reservation or indecision. (Words such as this often use intonation to convey the connotation of the sentence that is to follow. The brief intonation pattern accompanying the word may indicate sarcasm, disagreement, caution, consolation, sternness, etc.) □ SALLY: *Can you take this downtown for me?* ANDREW: *Well, I don't know.* □ *"Well, I guess," answered Tom, sort of unsure of himself.* □ *"Well, if you think you can treat me that way, you've got another think coming," raged Betty.* □ BILL: *What do you think about my haircut?* JANE: *Well, it looks okay to me.* □ SUE: *I've decided to sell my car.* MARY: *Well, if that's what you want.* □ *"Well, hello," smiled Kate.*

Well done! You did that nicely! □ SALLY: *Well done, Tom. Excellent speech.* TOM: *Thanks.* □ *In the lobby after the play, Tom was met with a chorus of well-wishers saying, "Well done, Tom!"*

We('ll) have to do lunch sometime. AND **Let's do lunch (sometime).** We must have lunch together sometime. (A vague statement that may lead to lunch plans.) □ RACHEL: *Nice to talk to you, Tom. We have to do lunch sometime.* TOM: *Yes, good to see you. I'll give you a ring.* □ TOM: *Can't talk to you now. Catch you later.* MARY: *We'll have to do lunch sometime.* □ JOHN: *Good to see you, Tom.* TOM: *Right. Let's do lunch sometime.* JOHN: *Good idea. I'll call you. Bye.* TOM: *Right. Bye.* □ MARY: *Catch you later.* SUE: *Sure. Let's do lunch.* MARY: *Okay. Call me. Bye.*

(Well,) I never! **1.** I have never been so insulted! □ BILL: *Just pack up your things and get out!* JANE: *Well, I never!* □ TOM: *Look, your manners with the customers are atrocious!* JANE: *Well, I never!* **2.** I never heard of such a thing. □ TOM: *Now they have machines that will do all those things at the press of a button.* SALLY: *Well, I never! I had no idea!* □ JOHN: *Would you believe I have a whole computer in this pocket?* ALICE: *I never!*

Well said. You said that very well, and I agree. □ *As Sally sat down, Mary complimented her, "Well said, Sally. You made your point very well."* □ JOHN: *And I for one will never stand for this kind of encroachment on my rights again!* MARY: *Well said!* BOB: *Well said, John!* FRED: *Yes, well said.*

We'll try again some other time. See *Maybe some other time.*

(Well,) what do you know! a way of expressing surprise at finding something that is unexpected; an expression of mild surprise at something someone has said. (No answer is expected or desired.) □ ANDREW: *Well, what do you know! Here's a brand new shirt in this old trunk.* BOB: *I wonder how it got there.* □ TOM: *These two things fit together like this.* JOHN: *Well, what do you know!*

We must do this again (sometime). See *Let's do this again (sometime).*

We need to talk about something. an expression inviting someone to discuss something. □ BILL: *Can I come over tonight? We need to talk about something.* MARY: *I guess so.* □ *"Mr. Franklin," said Bill's* *boss sort of sternly, "I want to see you in my office for a minute. We need to talk about something."*

(We're) delighted to have you.   See *(I'm) delighted to have you.*

(We're) glad you could come.   See *(I'm) glad you could come.*

(We're) glad you could drop by.   See *(I'm) glad you could drop by.*

(We're) glad you could stop by.   See *(I'm) glad you could drop by.*

Were you born in a barn?   an expression chiding someone who has left a door open or who is disorderly.   □ ANDREW: *Close the door! Were you born in a barn?* BOB: *Sorry.*   □ FRED: *Can't you clean this place up a little? Were you born in a barn?* BOB: *I call it the messy look.*

We've had a lovely time.   See *I've had a lovely time.*

We were just talking about you.   a phrase said when a person being discussed appears on the scene. (Compare to *Speak of the devil.*)   □ TOM: *Speak of the devil, here comes Bill.* MARY: *We were just talking about you, Bill.*   □ SALLY (approaching Tom and Bill): *Hi, Tom. Hi, Bill. What's new?* BILL: *Oh, Sally! We were just talking about you.*

[we will]   See the entries beginning with *we'll.*

What about it?   *So what?*; Do you want to argue about it? (Contentious.)   □ BILL: *I heard you were the one accused of breaking the window.* TOM: *Yeah? So, what about it?*   □ MARY: *Your piece of cake is bigger than mine.* SUE: *What about it?*

What about you?   **1.** What is your choice? (Compare to *How about you?*)   □ TOM: *I'm having the pot roast and a cup of coffee. What about you?* MARY: *I want something fattening and unhealthy.*   □ SALLY: *I prefer reds and purple for this room. What about you?* MARY: *Well, purple's okay, but reds are a little warm for this room.* **2.** What will happen to you?   □ MARY: *My parents are taking my brothers to the circus.* SUE: *What about you?* MARY: *I have a piano lesson.*   □ MARY: *All my friends have been accepted to colleges.* SUE: *What about you?* MARY: *Oh, I'm accepted too.*

What (a) nerve! AND **Of all the nerve!**   How rude!   □ BOB: *Lady, get the devil out of my way!* MARY: *What a nerve!*   □ JANE: *You can't have that one! I saw it first!* SUE: *Of all the nerve! I can too have it!*

What a pity! AND **What a shame!**   an expression of consolation meaning *That's too bad.* (Can also be used sarcastically.)   □

BILL: *I'm sorry to tell you that the cat died today.* MARY: *What a pity!* ☐ MARY: *The cake is ruined!* SALLY: *What a shame!*

What are you drinking?   **1.** a phrase inquiring what someone is already drinking so that the person who asks the question can offer another drink of the same thing. ☐ BILL: *Hi, Tom. Nice to see you. Can I get you something to drink?* TOM: *Sure. What are you drinking?* BILL: *Scotch and water.* TOM: *That works for me.* ☐ WAITER: *What are you drinking, madam?* SUE: *It's just soda. No more, thanks.* WAITER: *Very good.* **2.** a phrase inquiring what is being drunk at a particular gathering, so that the person asking can request the same drink. (A way of finding out what drinks are available.) ☐ MARY: *Do you want a drink?* SUE: *Yes, thanks. Say, that looks good. What are you drinking?* MARY: *It's just ginger ale.* ☐ BILL: *Can I get you something to drink?* JANE: *What are you drinking?* BILL: *I'm having gin and tonic.* JANE: *I'll have that too, thanks.*

What are you having?   What food or drink are you planning to order? (Either part of a conversation or a request from food service personnel. In a restaurant, sometimes the waiter or waitress will signal to a guest to order first by saying this. Sometimes a guest will ask this of a host or hostess to determine the price range that is appropriate.) ☐ WAITER: *Would you care to order now?* TOM: *What are you having?* MARY: *You order. I haven't made up my mind.* ☐ WAITER: *May I help you?* TOM: *What are you having, Pop?* FATHER: *I'll have the roast chicken, I think, with fries.* TOM: *I'll have the same.*

What a shame!   See *What a pity!*

What brings you here?   What is your reason for being here? (A polite request for this information. More polite than "Why are you here?") ☐ TOM: *Hello, Mary. What brings you here?* MARY: *I was invited, just like you.* ☐ DOCTOR: *Well, John, what brings you here?* JOHN: *I've had this cough for nearly a month, and I think it needs looking into.*

What can I do you for?   See *How may I help you?*

What can I say?   I have no explanation or excuse.; What do you expect me to say? (See also *What do you want me to say?*) ☐ BILL: *Why on earth did you lose that big order?* SALLY: *What can I say? I'm sorry!*

☐ Bob: *You're going to have to act more aggressive if you want to make sales. You're just too timid.* Tom: *What can I say? I am what I am.*

What can I tell you? **1.** What kind of information do you want? ☐ Bill: *I have a question.* Bob: *What can I tell you?* Bill: *When do we arrive at Chicago?* ☐ Mary: *I would like to ask a question about the quiz tomorrow.* Bill: *What can I tell you?* Mary: *The answers, if you know them.* **2.** I haven't any idea of what to say. (Compare to *What can I say?*) ☐ John: *Why on earth did you do a dumb thing like that?* Bill: *What can I tell you? I just did it, that's all.* ☐ Mary: *I'm so disappointed with you, Fred.* Fred: *What can I tell you? I am too.*

What does that prove? *So what?;* that does not mean anything. (A defensive expression. The heaviest stress is on *that.* Often with *so,* as in the examples.) ☐ Tom: *It seems that you were in the apartment the same night that it was robbed.* Bob: *So, what does that prove?* Tom: *Nothing, really. It's just something we need to keep in mind.* ☐ Rachel: *You're late again on your car payment.* Jane: *What does that prove?* Rachel: *Simply that you can't afford the car, and we are going to repossess it.*

What do you know? a typical greeting inquiry. (Informal. A specific answer is not expected. Often pronounced Wha-da-ya know?) ☐ Bob: *Hey, Tom! What do you know?* Tom: *Look who's here! Hi, Bob!* ☐ John: *What do you know?* Mary: *Nothing. How are you?* John: *Okay.*

What do you know for sure? *How are you?; What do you know?* (Familiar. An elaboration of *What do you know?* Does not require a direct answer.) ☐ Tom: *Hey, man! What do you know for sure?* Bill: *Howdy, Tom. What's new?* ☐ John: *How are you doing, old buddy?* Bill: *Great, you ugly beast!* John: *What do you know for sure?* Bill: *Nothing.*

What do you say? **1.** Hello, how are you? (Informal.) ☐ Bob: *What do you say, Tom?* Tom: *Hey, man. How are you doing?* ☐ Bill: *What do you say, man?* Fred: *What's the good word, you old so-and-so?* **2.** What is your answer or decision? ☐ Bill: *I need an answer from you now. What do you say?* Bob: *Don't rush me!* ☐ Sue: *I can offer you seven hundred dollars for your old car. What do you say?* Bob: *I'll take it!* **3.** an expression urging a child to say *Thank you* or *please.* ☐ *When Aunt Sally gave Billy some candy, his mother said to Billy, "What do you* *say?"* *"Thank you,"* said Billy. □ MOTHER: *Here's a nice glass of milk.* CHILD: *Good.* MOTHER: *What do you say?* CHILD: *Very good.* MOTHER: *No. What do you say?* CHILD: *Thank you.*

What do you think? What is your opinion? □ MARY: *This is our new company stationery. What do you think?* BILL: *Stunning. Simply stunning.* □ MARY: *We're considering moving out into the country. What do you think?* SUE: *Sounds good to me.*

What do you think about that? See the following entry.

What do you think of that? AND **What do you think about that?** Isn't that remarkable?; What is your opinion of that? □ BOB: *I'm leaving tomorrow and taking all these books with me. What do you think of that?* MARY: *Not much.* □ SUE: *I'm going to start taking cooking lessons. What do you think about that?* BILL: *I'm overjoyed!* JOHN: *Thank heavens!* MARY: *Fortune has smiled on us, indeed!*

What do you think of this weather? an expression used to open a conversation with someone, often someone one has just met. □ SUE: *Glad to meet you, Mary.* MARY: *What do you think about this weather?* SUE: *I've seen better.* □ BILL: *What do you think about this weather?* JANE: *Lovely weather for ducks.*

What do you think you are doing here? Why are you in this place? (Stern and threatening.) □ JOHN: *Mary!* MARY: *John!* JOHN: *What do you think you're doing here?* □ *"What do you think you're doing here?"* said Fred to a frightened rabbit trapped in the garage.

What do you want me to say? I have no response.; I have no answer, do you have one for me to say? (Almost the same as *What can I say?; What can I tell you?*) □ TOM: *You've really made a mess of all of this!* BILL: *Sorry. What do you want me to say?* □ BOB: *All of these problems should have been settled some time ago. Why are they still plaguing us?* TOM: *What do you want me to say?*

What else can I do? See *What more can I do?*

What else can I do for you? In what other way can I serve you? (Said by shopkeepers, clerks, and service personnel.) □ BILL: *What else can I do for you?* BOB: *Please check the oil.* □ *"Here's your prescription. What else can I do for you?"* said the pharmacist.

What else is new? See *(So) what else is new?*

Whatever.   Anything, it doesn't matter.; Either one.   □ BOB: *Which do you want, red or green?* TOM: *Whatever.*   □ MARY: *Do you want to go with me to the seashore or stay here?* JANE: *Whatever.*

Whatever turns you on.   **1.** Whatever pleases or excites you is okay.   □ MARY: *Do you mind if I buy some of these flowers?* BILL: *Whatever turns you on.*   □ MARY: *I just love to hear a raucous saxophone play some smooth jazz.* BOB: *Whatever turns you on, baby.* **2.** a comment implying that it is strange to get so excited about something. (Essentially sarcastic.)   □ BOB: *I just go wild whenever I see pink gloves on a woman. I don't understand it.* BILL: *Whatever turns you on.*   □ JANE: *You see, I never told anybody this, but whenever I see dirty snow at the side of the road, I just go sort of wild inside.* SUE: *Weird, Jane, weird. But, whatever turns you on.*

What gives?   *What happened?;* What went wrong?; What's the problem?   □ BILL: *Hi, you guys. What gives?* BOB: *Nothing, just a little misunderstanding. Tom's a little angry.*   □ BOB: *Where's my wallet? What gives?* TOM: *I think one of those roughnecks who just walked by us has borrowed it for a little while.*

What happened?   What went wrong here?   □ BOB (approaching a crowd): *What happened?* TOM (with Bob): *What's wrong?* BYSTANDER: *Just a little mix-up. A car wanted to drive on the sidewalk, that's all.*   □ *There was a terrible noise, an explosion that shook the house. Bob looked at Jane and said, "What happened?"*

What (have) you been up to?   a greeting inquiry. (A detailed answer may be expected.)   □ MARY: *Hello, Jane. What have you been up to?* JANE: *Been up to no good. What about you?* MARY: *Yeah. Me too.*   □ JOHN: *Bill, baby! What you been up to?* BILL: *Nothing really. What about you?* JOHN: *The same, I guess.*

What if I do?   Does it matter to you if I do it?; What difference does it make if I do it? (Saucy and colloquial.)   □ TOM: *Are you really going to sell your leather coat?* BOB: *What if I do?*   □ JANE: *You're not going to go out dressed like that, are you?* SUE: *So what if I do?*

What if I don't?   Does it matter to you if I do not do it?; What difference does it make if I do not do it? (Saucy and colloquial.)   □ BOB: *You're certainly going to tidy up a bit before going out, aren't you?*

TOM: *What if I don't?* □ FATHER: *You are going to get in by midnight tonight or you're grounded.* FRED: *So what if I don't?* FATHER: *That's enough! You're grounded as of this minute!*

[what is] See also the entries beginning with *what's*.

What is it? What do you want from me?; Why do you want to get my attention? (There is also a literal meaning.) □ TOM: *John, can I talk to you for a minute?* JOHN: *What is it?* □ SUE: *Jane?* JANE: *What is it?* SUE: *Close the door, please.*

What'll it be? AND **Name your poison.; What'll you have?; What's yours?** What do you want to drink?; What do you want?; How can I serve you? (Typically said by a bartender or bar waiter or waitress.) □ TOM: *What'll it be, friend?* BILL: *I'll just have a Coke, if you don't mind.* □ WAITRESS: *What'll you have?* BOB: *Nothing, thanks.*

What'll you have? See the previous entry.

What makes you think so? **1.** Why do you think that?; What is your evidence for that conclusion? □ TOM: *This bread may be a little old.* ALICE: *What makes you think so?* TOM: *The green spots on the edges.* □ BOB: *Congress is in session again.* TOM: *What makes you think so?* BOB: *My wallet's empty.* **2.** Is that not totally obvious? (Sarcastic.) □ JOHN: *I think I'm putting on a little weight.* MARY: *Oh, yeah? What makes you think so?* □ MARY (shivering): *Gee, I think it's going to be winter soon.* MARY (also shivering): *Yeah? What makes you think so?*

What more can I do? AND **What else can I do?** I am at a loss to know what else to do. Is there any thing else I can do? (An expression of desperation, not an inquiry.) □ BOB: *Did you hear about the death in the Wilson family?* BILL: *Yes, I feel so helpless. I sent flowers. What more can I do?* □ BILL: *Is your child still sick?* MARY: *Yes. I'm giving her the right medicine. What more can I do?*

What now? See *Now what?*

What number are you calling? an expression used when one suspects that a telephone caller may have gotten the wrong number.

☐ Bob (on the telephone): *Hello? *Mary*: Hello, is Sally there? *Bob*: Uh, what number are you calling? *Mary*: I guess I have the wrong number. Sorry. *Bob*: No problem. Good-bye. ☐ When the receptionist asked, "What number are you calling?" I realized I had made a mistake.*

What of it? What does it matter?; Why treat it as if it were important?; Why do you think that this is any of your business? (Colloquial and a bit contentious.) ☐ John: *I hear you've been having a little trouble at the office. *Bob*: What of it? ☐ Sue*: *You missed a spot shaving. *Fred*: What of it?*

What say? What did you say? (Widely used.) ☐ Tom: *My coat is there on the chair. Could you hand it to me? *Bob*: What say? *Tom* (pointing): Could you hand me my coat? ☐ Sue*: *Here's your paper. *Fred*: What say? *Sue* (louder): Here is your newspaper!*

What's coming off? AND **What's going down?** What is happening here?; What is going to happen? (Slang. Also a greeting inquiry.) ☐ Bill: *Hey, man! What's coming off? *Tom*: Oh, nothing, just a little car fire. ☐ Bob*: *Hey, we just got here! What's going down? *Bill*: What does it look like? This is a party, dude!*

What's cooking? What is happening?; How are you? (Colloquial or slang.) ☐ Bob: *Hi, Fred! What's cooking? *Fred*: How are you doing, Bob? ☐ Bob*: *Hi, Fred! What's cooking? *Fred*: Nothing. Anything happening with you?*

What's eating someone? What is bothering someone? (Slang.) ☐ Tom: *Go away! *Bob*: Gee, Tom, what's eating you? ☐ Bill*: *Tom's so grouchy lately. What's eating him? *Bob*: Beats me!*

What's going down? See *What's coming off?*

What's going on (around here)? What is happening in this place?; What is the explanation for the strange things that are happening here? ☐ Bill: *There was an accident in the factory this morning. *Bob*: That's the second one this week. What's going on around here? ☐ Mary*: *What's all the noise? What's going on? *Sue*: We're just having a little party.*

What's happening? a general and vague greeting inquiry. (Colloquial.) ☐ Bob: *Hey, man! What's happening? *Bill*: Nothing. How you be? ☐ Bill*: *Hi, Tom. *Tom*: Hi, Bill, what's happening? *Bill*: Nothing much.*

What's in it for me? What is the benefit for me in this scheme? □ BOB: *Now that plan is just what is needed.* BILL: *What's in it for me? What do I get out of it?* □ SUE: *We signed the Wilson contract yesterday.* MARY: *That's great! What's in it for me?*

What's it to you? Why does it matter to you?; It's none of your business. (Colloquial and a bit contentious.) □ TOM: *Where are you going?* JANE: *What's it to you?* □ MARY: *Bill's pants don't match his shirt.* JANE: *Does it matter? What's it to you?*

What's keeping someone? What is delaying someone? (The *someone* is replaced by a person's name or a pronoun.) □ BOB: *Wasn't Mary supposed to be here?* BILL: *I thought so.* BOB: *Well, what's keeping her?* BILL: *How should I know?* □ BILL: *I've been waiting here for an hour for Sally.* SUE: *What's keeping her?*

What's new? What things have happened since we last met? □ MARY: *Greetings, Jane. What's new?* JANE: *Nothing much.* □ BOB: *What's new?* TOM: *Not a whole lot.*

What's new with you? a typical response to *What's new?* □ MARY: *What's new with you?* SALLY: *Oh, nothing. What's new with you?* MARY: *The same.* □ FRED: *Hi, John! How you doing?* JOHN: *Great! What's new with you?*

What's on tap for today? What is on the schedule for today?; What is going to happen today? (As a beer that is on tap and ready to be served.) □ TOM: *Good morning, Fred.* FRED: *Morning. What's on tap for today?* TOM: *Trouble in the morning and difficulty in the afternoon.* FRED: *So nothing's new.* □ SALLY: *Can we have lunch today?* SUE: *I'll have to look at my schedule and see what's on tap for today.*

What's the catch? What is the drawback?; What are the negative factors? (Colloquial.) □ BILL: *How would you like to have these seven books for your very own?* SALLY: *What's the catch?* BILL: *There's no catch. You have to pay for them, but there's no catch.* □ BOB: *Here, take this dollar bill.* SUE: *So, what's the catch?* BOB: *No catch. It's counterfeit.*

What's the damage? What are the charges?; How much is the bill? (Slang.) □ BILL: *That was delicious. Waiter, what's the damage?* WAITER: *I'll get the check, sir.* □ WAITER: *Your check, sir.* TOM:

Thanks. BILL: *What's the damage, Tom? Let my pay my share.* TOM: *Nonsense, I'll get it.* BILL: *Okay this time, but I owe you one.*

What's the deal?   *What's going on?;* Why are you doing this?   □ MARY: *What's the deal?* SUE: *Oh, hi, Mary. We're just cleaning out the closet.*   □   BILL: *Hi, you guys. What's the deal?* BOB: *Nothing, just a little misunderstanding between Fred and Jane.*

What's the drill?   **1.** What is going on here?   □   BILL: *I just came in. What's the drill?* TOM: *We have to carry all this stuff out to the truck.*   □   *"What's the drill?" asked Mary. "Why are all these people sitting around like this?"* **2.** What are the rules and procedures for doing this?   □ BILL: *I need to apply for new license plates. What's the drill? Is there a lot of paper work?* CLERK: *Yes, there is.*   □   BILL: *I have to get my computer repaired. Who do I talk to? What's the drill?* BOB: *You have to get a purchase order from Fred.*

What's the good word?   a vague greeting inquiry. (Colloquial and familiar. A direct answer is not expected.)   □   BOB: *Hey, Tom! What's the good word?* TOM: *Hi, Bob! How are you doing?*   □   SUE: *What's happening?* JANE: *Hi, Sue. What's the good word?*

What's the matter (with you)?   **1.** Is there something wrong with you?; Are you ill?   □   BILL: *What's the matter with you?* FRED: *I have this funny feeling in my chest.* BILL: *Sounds serious.*   □   BOB: *I have to stay home again today.* BILL: *What's the matter with you? Have you seen a doctor?*   □   MARY: *Oh, I'm so miserable!* SUE: *What's the matter?* MARY: *I lost my contact lenses and my glasses.*   □   JOHN: *Ouch!* ALICE: *What's the matter?* JOHN: *I bit my tongue.* **2.** How very stupid of you! How can you be so stupid? (Usually said in anger.)   □   *As Fred stumbled over the step and dumped the birthday cake on the floor, Jane screamed, "What's the matter with you? The party is in fifteen minutes and we have no cake!"*   □   MARY: *I think I just lost the Wilson account.* SUE: *What! What's the matter with you? That account pays your salary!*

What's the problem?   **1.** What problem are you presenting to me?   □   BILL (coming in): *I need to talk to you about something.* TOM: *What's the problem, Bill?*   □   *"What's the problem?" said Mary, peering at her secretary over her glasses.* **2.** a question asking what the problem is and implying that there should not be a problem.   □   CHILD (crying): *He hit me!* FATHER: *What's the problem?* CHILD: *He hit me!*

FATHER: *Are you hurt?* CHILD: *No.* FATHER: *Then stop crying.* □
BOB: *Hi, Fred.* FRED: *What's the problem?* BOB: *There's no problem.
Why do you ask?* FRED: *I've had nothing but problems today.*

What's (there) to know? This doesn't require any special knowledge, so what are you talking about? □ BILL: *Do you know how to
wind a watch?* BOB: *Wind a watch? What's there to know?* □ SUE: *We
must find someone who knows how to repair a broken lawn mower.* TOM:
What's to know? Just a little tightening here and there. That's all it needs.

What's the scam? What's happening around here? (Slang.) □
TOM: *Hey, man! What's the scam?* BILL: *Greetings, oh ugly one! What's
happening?* TOM: *Not much. Want to order a pizza?* BILL: *Always.* □
*John burst into the room and shouted, "Yo! What's the scam?" It took the
prayer meeting a little time to get reorganized.*

What's the scoop? What is the news?; *What's new with you?*
(Slang.) □ BOB: *Did you hear about Tom?* MARY: *No, what's the
scoop?* □ *"Hi, you guys!" beamed John's little brother. "What's the
scoop?"*

What's to know? See *What's (there) to know?*

What's up? What is happening?; What are you doing lately? □
BOB: *Hi, Bill. What's up?* BILL: *Yo, Bob! Nothing going on around here.*
□ TOM (answering the telephone): *Hello.* BILL: *Hi, this is Bill.*
TOM: *What's up?* BILL: *You want to go camping?* TOM: *Sure.*

What's with someone or something? Why is someone or something in that condition?; What's going on with someone or something? □ MARY: *What's with Tom? He looks depressed.* BILL: *He broke
up with Sally.* □ *"What's with this stupid coffee pot? It won't get hot!"
groused Alice.*

What's wrong? There is something wrong here. What has happened? □ MARY: *Oh, good grief!* BILL: *What's wrong?* MARY: *I forgot to feed the cat.* □ SUE (crying): *Hello, Sally?* SALLY: *Sue, what's
wrong?* SALLY: *Oh, nothing. Tom left me.*

What's yours? See *What'll it be?*

What was the name again? Please tell me your name again. (More
typical of a clerk than of someone just introduced.) □ CLERK:
What was the name again? BILL: *Bill.* □ *"What was the name again? I
didn't write it down," confessed Fred.*

[what will] See also the entries beginning with *what'll*.

What would you like to drink? an offer to prepare an alcoholic drink. □ BILL: *Come in and sit down. What would you like to drink?* ANDREW: *Nothing, thanks. I just need to relax a moment.* □ WAITER: *What would you like to drink?* ALICE: *Do you have any grape soda?* WAITER: *I'll bring you some ginger ale, if that's all right.* ALICE: *Well, okay. I guess.*

what would you say if? an expression introducing a request for an opinion or a judgment. □ BILL: *What would you say if I ate the last piece of cake?* BOB: *Go ahead. I don't care.* □ MARY: *What would you say if we left a little early?* SALLY: *It's okay with me.*

What you been up to? See *What (have) you been up to?*

When. See under *Say when*.

When do we eat? What time is the next meal served? (Familiar. The speaker is hungry.) □ BILL: *This is a lovely view, and your apartment is great. When do we eat?* MARY: *We've already eaten. Weren't you just leaving?* BILL: *I guess I was.* □ ANDREW: *Wow! Something really smells good! When do we eat?* RACHEL: *Oh, mind your manners.*

Whenever. At whatever time, it really doesn't matter. □ BILL: *When should I pick you up?* SUE: *Oh, whenever. I don't care. Just come on up, and we'll take it from there.* □ MARY: *Well, Uncle Harry, how nice to have you for a visit. We need to book your return flight. When will you be leaving?* UNCLE: *Oh, whenever.*

when I'm good and ready not until I want to and no sooner. (A bit contentious.) □ MARY: *When are you going to rake the leaves?* FATHER: *When I'm good and ready.* □ BOB: *When are you going to help me move this piano?* FRED: *When I'm good and ready and not a minute before.*

when you get a chance See the following entry.

when you get a minute AND **when you get a chance** a phrase introducing a request. □ BILL: *Tom?* TOM: *Yes.* BILL: *When you get a minute, I'd like to have a word with you.* □ *"Please drop over for a chat when you get a chance," said Fred to Bill.*

Where can I wash up? AND **Is there some place I can wash up?** a way of asking where the toilet or bathroom is without referring to one's need to use it. (Of course, this is also appropriate to ask where one can wash one's hands.) □ *The minute he got to the house, he asked Fred, "Where can I wash up?"* □ FRED: *Welcome. Come in.* BILL: *Oh, is there some place I can wash up?*

Where have you been all my life? an expression of admiration usually said to a lover. □ MARY: *I feel very happy when I'm with you.* JOHN: *Oh, Mary, where have you been all my life?* □ *John, who always seemed to sound like a paperback novel, grasped her hand, stared directly at her left ear, and stuttered, "Where have you been all my life?"*

Where (have) you been keeping yourself? I haven't seen you for a long time. Where have you been? □ BILL: *Hi, Alice! Where you been keeping yourself?* ALICE: *Oh, I've been around. How are you doing?* BILL: *Okay.* □ JOHN: *Tsup?* BILL: *Hi, man. Where you been keeping yourself?* JOHN: *Oh, I've been busy.*

Where is the rest room? the appropriate way of asking for the toilet in a public building. □ BOB: *'Scuse me.* WAITER: *Yes, sir.* BOB: *Where is the rest room?* WAITER: *To your left, sir.* □ MARY: *Where is the rest room, please?* CLERK: *Behind the elevators, ma'am.*

Where is your powder room? See *Could I use your powder room?*

Where's the fire? Where are you going in such a hurry? (Typically said by a police officer to a speeding driver.) □ OFFICER: *Okay, where's the fire?* MARY: *Was I going a little fast?* □ *"Where's the fire?" Bob called ahead to Sue, who had gotten well ahead of him in her excitement.*

Where will I find you? Please give me directions for finding you. (Said when people are arranging a meeting somewhere.) □ SUE: *Where will I find you?* BOB: *I'll be sitting in the third row somewhere.* □ TOM: *We'll get to the farm about noon. Where will we find you?* SALLY: *Probably in the barn. If you can't find me, just go up to the house and make yourself comfortable on the porch.*

which brings me to the (main) point a transitional phrase that introduces the main point of a discussion. □ BILL: *Keeping safe at times like this is very important—which brings me to the main point. Does your house have an adequate burglar alarm?* SALLY: *I knew you were trying to sell me something! Out!* □ LECTURER: *. . . which brings me to the point.* JOHN (whispering): *Thank heavens! I knew there was a point to all this.*

Whoa! Stop! (An instruction—usually said to a horse—to stop, said to a person.) □ BOB: *First, slip the disk into this slot and then do a* *directory command to see what's on it.* JOHN: *Whoa! You lost me back at "slip the disk. . . ."* □ *"Whoa!" shouted Tom at Bill. "Don't move any more in that direction. The floor is rotten there."*

Who cares? Does anyone really care?; It is of no consequence. □ JOHN: *I have some advice for you. It will make things easier for you.* BOB: *Who cares?* JOHN: *You might.* □ SUE: *You missed a spot shaving.* FRED: *Who cares?*

who could have thought? See *who would have thought?*

Who do you think you are? Why do you think you can lord it over people that way?; Why are you so arrogant? (Usually in anger.) □ TOM: *Just a minute! Who do you think you are? You can't talk to me that way!* BOB: *Says who?* □ *"Who do you think you are, bursting in here like that?" sputtered the doorman as Fred bolted into the club lobby.*

Who do you think you're kidding? You aren't fooling anyone.; Surely, you do not think you can fool me, do you? □ BILL: *I must pull down about eighty thou a year.* BOB: *You? Who do you think you're kidding?* □ MARY: *This carpet was made in Persia by children.* TOM: *Who do you think you're kidding?*

Who do you think you're talking to? Why do you think you can address me in that manner?; You can't talk to me that way! □ TOM: *Get out of the way!* SUE: *Who do you think you're talking to?* TOM: *Then move please.* □ CLERK: *Look, take it or leave it. Isn't it good enough for you?* SUE: *Who do you think you're talking to? I want to see the manager!*

Who do you want to speak to? See the following entry.

Who do you want (to talk to)? AND **Who do you want to speak to?; Who do you wish to speak to?; Who do you wish to talk to?** Who do you want to speak to over the telephone? (All these questions can also begin with *whom*. Compare to *With whom do you wish to speak?*) □ SUE: *Wilson residence. Who do you want to speak to?* BILL: *Hi, Sue. I want to talk to you.* □ TOM (answering the phone): *Hello?* SUE: *Hello, who is this?* TOM: *Who do you wish to speak to?* SUE: *Is Sally there?* TOM: *Just a minute.*

Who do you wish to speak to? See the previous entry.

Who do you wish to talk to? See *Who do you want (to talk to)?*

Who is it? See *Who's there?*

Who is this? Who is making this telephone call?; Who is on the other end of this telephone line? □ TOM (answering the phone): *Hello?* FRED: *Hello. Do you have any fresh turkeys?* TOM: *Who is this?* FRED: *Isn't this the Harrison Poultry Shop?* TOM: *No.* FRED: *I guess I have the wrong number.* □ MARY (answering the phone): *Hello?* SUE: *Hello, who is this?* MARY: *Well, who did you want?* SUE: *I want Grandma.* MARY: *I'm sorry, I think you have the wrong number.*

Who knows? Who knows the answer to that question? □ TOM: *When will this train get in?* RACHEL: *Who knows?* □ ANDREW: *Why can't someone put this stuff away?* RACHEL: *Who knows? Why don't you put it away?*

Whoops! a phrase indicating that an error has been made by the previous speaker or someone else. □ *"Whoops! I think you meant flout, not flaunt," corrected Sally.* □ *"Whoops! I meant to say 'mature,' not 'old,'" said Kate.*

Who's calling(, please)? Who is this making this telephone call? □ RACHEL: *Yes, Tom is here. Who's calling, please?* TOM: *Who is it?* RACHEL: *It's Fred.* □ FRED (answering the phone): *Hello?* TOM: *Hello, is Bill there?* FRED: *Who's calling, please?* TOM: *This is Tom Wilson returning his call.*

Who's on the line? See the following entry.

Who's on the phone? AND **Who's on the line?** Who is on the telephone line now?; Who just called on the telephone? (The caller may still be waiting.) □ *Bill was on the telephone, and Mary walked by. "Who's on the phone?" asked Mary, hoping the call was for her.* □ *Tom asked, "Who's on the line?" Mary covered the receiver and said, "None of your business!"*

Who's there? AND **Who is it?** a question asking who is on the other side of a door or concealed in some other place. □ *Hearing a noise, Tom called out in the darkness, "Who's there?"* □ *Hearing a knock on the door, Mary went to the door and said, "Who is it?"*

Who's your friend? Who is that following along behind you? □ JOHN: *Hi, Tom. Who's your friend?* TOM: *Oh, this is my little brother, Willie.* JOHN: *Hi, Willie.* □ *Looking at the little dog almost glued to Bob's pants cuff, Sally asked, "Who's your friend?"*

Who was it? Who called on the telephone or who was at the door? (Assumes that the caller is not waiting on the telephone or at the door.) □ SUE (as Mary hangs up the telephone): *Who was it?* MARY: *None of your business.* □ BILL (as he leaves the door): *What a pest!* SUE: *Who was it?* BILL: *Some silly survey.*

who would have thought? AND **who could have thought?** a question phrase indicating surprise or amazement. (No answer is expected.) □ TOM: *Fred just quit his job and went to Africa.* BILL: *Who would have thought he could do such a thing?* □ ANDREW: *They say Bill jogs and runs in his spare time.* RACHEL: *Who would have thought?*

why a sentence opener expressing surprise. (The *why* is pronounced like the name of the letter *Y*.) □ *"Why, it's just a little boy!" said the old sea captain.* □ BOB: *Why, what are you doing here?* MARY: *I was going to ask you the same thing.* □ MARY: *Why, your hair has turned white!* ANDREW: *No, I'm in the school play. This is just temporary.* □ RACHEL: *Why, this page is torn!* ANDREW: *I didn't do it!*

why don't you? a question tag that is put onto the end of a command. □ ANDREW: *Make a lap, why don't you?* BOB: *Okay. Sorry. I didn't know I was in the way.* □ *"Just keep bugging me, why don't you?" threatened Wally.* □ ANDREW: *Try it again, why don't you?* SUE: *I hope I get it right this time.*

Why not? **1.** Please explain your negative answer. □ MARY: *No, you can't.* MOLLY: *Why not?* □ SUE: *Could I have another piece of cake?* MARY: *No.* SUE: *Why not?* MARY: *I want it.* **2.** I cannot think of a reason not to, so yes. □ BOB: *You want to go to see a movie next Friday?* JANE: *Why not?* □ FRED: *Do you feel like wandering over to the bowling alley?* TOM: *Why not?*

Will I see you again? a question asked toward the end of a date implying that further dating would please the speaker if it would please the other party. (This question seeks to find out if there is interest in another date, leaving it open to the other party to confirm that the interest is mutual by requesting a further date. Compare to *Can I see you again?*) □ TOM: *I had a wonderful time tonight, Mary. Good night.* MARY: *Will I see you again?* TOM: *That would be nice. Can I call you tomorrow?* MARY: *That would be nice.* □ *"Will I see you again?" asked Sally, cautiously and hopefully.*

[will not] See the entries beginning with *won't*.

Will that be all? See the following entry.

(Will there be) anything else? AND **Is that everything?; Is there anything else?; Will that be all?** Is there anything else you want?; Is there any other matter you wish to discuss?; Is there any other request? (These phrases are used by shopkeepers, clerks, and food service personnel to find out if the customer wants anything more.) □ CLERK: *Here's the roast you ordered. Will there be anything else?* RACHEL: *No, that's all.* □ WAITER: *Anything else?* BILL: *Just coffee.* □ *The clerk rang up the last item and asked, "Anything else?"* □ WAITER: *Anything else?* JANE: *No, that's everything.*

Will you excuse us, please? See *Could you excuse us, please?*

Will you hold? See *Could you hold?*

Win a few, lose a few. Sometimes one succeeds, and sometimes one fails. □ TOM: *Well, I lost out on that Wilson contract, but I got the Jones job.* SALLY: *That's life. Win a few, lose a few.* □ *"Win a few, lose a few," said Fred, staring at yesterday's stock prices.*

Wish you were here. See *(I) wish you were here.*

with my blessing a phrase expressing consent or agreement; yes. □ BOB: *Can I take this old coat down to the rummage sale?* SUE: *With my blessing.* □ MARY: *Shall I drive Uncle Tom to the airport a few hours early?* SUE: *Oh, yes! With my blessing!*

without a doubt a phrase expressing certainty or agreement; yes. □ JOHN: *This cheese is as hard as a rock. It must have been in the fridge for weeks.* FRED: *Without a doubt.* □ MARY: *Taxes will surely go up before I retire.* JANE: *Without a doubt!*

With pleasure. a phrase indicating eager consent to do something. □ FRED: *Would you please take this note over to the woman in the red dress?* WAITER: *With pleasure, sir.* □ SUE: *Would you kindly bring in the champagne now?* JANE: *With pleasure.*

With whom do you wish to speak? a polite phrase used by telephone answerers to find out whom the caller wants to speak to. (Compare to *Who do you want to talk to?*) □ *John answered the* *telephone and then said, "With whom do you wish to speak?"* □ TOM (answering the phone): *Good morning, Acme Air Products. With whom do you wish to speak?* SUE: *Sorry, I have the wrong number.* TOM: *That's perfectly all right. Have a nice day.*

With you in a minute. See under *(Someone will) be with you in a minute.*

wonder if See *(I) wonder if.*

Won't bother me any. See *(It) won't bother me any.*

Won't breathe a word (of it). See *(I) won't breathe a word (of it).*

Won't tell a soul. See *(I) won't breathe a word (of it).*

Won't you come in? the standard phrase used to invite someone into one's home or office. □ BILL: *Won't you come in?* MARY: *I hope I'm not early.* □ *Tom stood in the doorway of Mr. Franklin's office for a moment. "Won't you come in?" said Mr. Franklin without looking up.*

Works for me. See *(It) works for me.*

Would if I could(, but I can't). See *(I) would if I could(, but I can't).*

Wouldn't bet on it. See *(I) wouldn't bet on it.*

Wouldn't count on it. See *(I) wouldn't bet on it.*

Wouldn't if I were you. See *(I) wouldn't if I were you.*

Wouldn't know. See *(I) wouldn't know.*

Would you believe! Isn't that unbelievable?; How shocking! □ TOM: *Jane has run off and married Fred!* SALLY: *Would you believe!* □ JANE: *Then the manager came out and asked us to leave. Would you believe?* MARY: *It sounds just awful. I'd sue.*

(Would you) care for another (one)? Do you want another drink or serving? □ *Tom stood there with an almost empty glass. Bill said,*

"Would you care for another one?" □ WAITER: *Care for another one, madam?* SUE: *No, thank you.*

(would you) care to? a polite phrase introducing an inquiry as to whether someone wishes to do something. □ JOHN: *Would you care to step out for some air?* JANE: *Oh, I'd love it.* □ SUE: *Care to go for a swim?* MARY: *Not now, thanks.*

(Would you) care to dance? Do you want to dance with me?; Would you please dance with me? □ JOHN: *Would you care to dance?* MARY: *I don't dance, but thank you for asking.* □ *"Care to dance?" asked Bill, politely, hoping desperately that the answer would be no, preferably an emphatic and devastating no that would send him to the sidelines, crushed.*

(Would you) care to join us? Do you want to join us? □ *Tom and Mary saw Fred and Sally sitting at another table in the restaurant. Tom went over to them and said, "Would you care to join us?"* □ MARY: *Isn't that Bill and Sue over there?* JOHN: *Yes, it is. Shall I ask them to join us?* MARY: *Why not?* JOHN (after reaching the other table): *Hi, you guys! Care to join us?* BILL: *Love to, but Sue's mom is going to be along any minute. Thanks anyway.*

Would you excuse me? **1.** a polite question that essentially announces one's departure. (Compare to *Could I be excused?; Excuse me.*) □ JANE: *Would you excuse me? I have to get home now.* ANDREW: *Oh, sure. I'll see you to the door.* □ *Rising to leave, Jane said, "Would you excuse me?" and left by the rear door.* **2.** a polite way to request passage through or by a group of people; a way to request space to exit an elevator. □ *There were two people talking in the corridor, blocking it. Tom said, "Would you excuse me?" They stepped aside.* □ FRED: *Would you excuse me? This is my floor.* SALLY: *Sure. It's mine too.*

Would you excuse us, please? See *Could you excuse us, please?*

Would you please? a phrase that agrees that what was offered to be done should be done. □ BILL: *Do you want me to take this over to the bank?* MARY: *Would you please?* □ TOM: *Can I take your coat?* SALLY: *Would you please?*

Wow! an exclamation of surprise and amazement. □ *"Wow! A real shark!" said Billy.* □ SALLY: *Wow! I won the contest! What do I get?* RACHEL: *A stuffed doll.* SALLY: *Oh, goodie.* □ JANE: *Wow! I just made it. I thought I would miss this flight for sure.* SUE: *Well, you almost did.*

Y

Yes siree(, Bob)! *Absolutely!; Without a doubt!* (Not necessarily said to a male and not necessarily to Bob.) □ MARY: *Do you want some more cake?* TOM: *Yes siree, Bob!* □ *"That was a fine turkey dinner. Yes siree!" said Uncle Henry.*

Yesterday wouldn't be too soon. an answer to the question "When do you want this?" □ MARY: *Mr. Franklin, when do you want this?* FRED: *Well, yesterday wouldn't be too soon.* □ ALICE: *When am I supposed to have this finished?* SUE: *Yesterday wouldn't be too soon.*

yo a word used to get someone's attention or signal that the speaker is in a particular location. □ ANDREW: *Yo, Tom. I'm over here!* TOM: *I can't see you. Oh, there you are!* □ BOB: *Let's see who's here. I'll call the roll. Bill Franklin.* BILL: *Yo!*

You ain't seen nothing yet! The best, most exciting, or cleverest part is yet to come! (The use of *ain't* is a fixed part of this idiomatic expression.) □ ALICE: *Well, the first act was simply divine.* SUE: *Stick around. You ain't seen nothing yet!* □ MARY: *This part of the city is really beautiful.* BILL: *You ain't seen nothing yet!*

You (always) give up too eas(il)y. You don't stand up for your rights.; You give up without a fight. □ BILL: *Well, I guess she was right.* BOB: *No, she was wrong. You always give up too easily.* □ BOB: *I asked her to go out with me Friday, but she said she thought she was busy.* TOM: *Ask her again. You give up too easy.*

You and what army? See the following entry.

You and who else? AND **You and what army?** a phrase that responds to a threat by implying that the threat is a weak one. □

BILL: *I'm going to punch you in the nose!* BOB: *Yeah? You and who else?*
□ TOM: *Our team is going to slaughter your team.* BILL: *You and what army?* □ BILL: *If you don't stop doing that, I'm going to hit you.* TOM: *You and who else?*

[you are] See the entries beginning with *you're*.

You are something else (again)! You are amazing or entertaining!
□ *After Sally finished telling her joke, everyone laughed and someone said, "Oh, Sally, you are something else!"* □ *"You are something else again," said Fred, admiring Sue's presentation.*

You asked for it! **1.** You are getting what you requested! □ *The waiter set a huge bowl of ice cream, strawberries, and whipped cream in front of Mary, saying apologetically, "You asked for it!"* □ BILL: *Gee, this escargot stuff is gross!* MARY: *You asked for it!* **2.** You are getting the punishment you deserve! □ BILL: *The tax people just ordered me to pay a big fine.* BOB: *The careless way you do your tax forms caused it. You asked for it!* □ MOTHER: *I'm sorry to have to punish you in this fashion, but you asked for it!* BILL: *I did not!*

You been keeping busy? See *(Have you) been keeping busy?*

You been keeping cool? See *(Have you) been keeping cool?*

You been keeping out of trouble? See *(Have you) been keeping out of trouble?*

You been okay? See *(Have you) been okay?*

You bet. AND **You betcha.** You can be quite certain. □ BILL: *Can I take one of these apples?* BOB: *You bet.* □ BILL: *Do you like this movie?* TOM: *You betcha.*

You betcha. See the previous entry.

You bet your boots! See *You bet your (sweet) life!*

You bet your life! See *You bet your (sweet) life.*

You bet your (sweet) bippy. See the following entry.

You bet your (sweet) life! AND **You bet your boots!; You bet your life!; You bet your (sweet) bippy.** You can be absolutely certain of something! (Informal and colloquial.) □ MARY: *Will I need a coat today?* BILL: *You bet your sweet life! It's colder than an iceberg out there.* □ BILL: *Will you be at the game Saturday?* TOM: *You bet your boots!*

You called? **1.** a phrase used when returning a telephone call, meaning "What did you want to talk about when you called before?" □ BILL (answering the phone): *Hello?* BOB: *This is Bob. You called?* □ TOM: *You called? It's Tom.* MARY: *Hi, Tom. Yes, I wanted to ask you about these estimates.* **2.** a phrase said by someone who has been summoned into a person's presence. (Often used in jest, in the way a servant might answer an employer.) □ MARY: *Oh, Tom. Come over here a minute.* TOM (coming to where Mary is standing): *You called?* □ TOM: *Bill! Bill! Over here, Bill, across the street.* BILL (panting from running and with mock deference): *You called?*

You can say that again! That is so true or so insightful that it bears repeating. □ BILL: *Gee, it's cold today!* MARY: *You can say that again!* □ BILL: *This cake sure is good.* FATHER: *You can say that again.*

(You) can't AND **(You) cannot!** You are wrong, you cannot!; Don't say you can, because you cannot. (The second form is the typical response to *(I) can too.*) □ BILL: *Don't tell me I can't, because I can!* BOB: *Cannot!* BILL: *Can too!* BOB: *Cannot!* BILL: *Can too!* □ TOM: *I want to go to the rock concert. Bill can go and so can I, can't I?* MOTHER: *No, you can't!*

(You) can't beat that. AND **(You) can't top that.** No one can do better than that. (This *you* represents both personal and impersonal antecedents. That is, it means second person singular or plural, and *anyone.*) □ MARY: *Wow! Look at the size of that lobster! It looks yummy!* BILL: *Yeah. You can't beat that. I wonder what it's going to cost.* □ *"What a view! Nothing like it anywhere! You can't top this!" said Jeff, admiring the view he was paying two hundred dollars a night for.*

You can't expect me to believe that. AND **You don't expect me to believe that.** That is so outrageous that no one could believe it. □ BILL: *My father is running for president.* BOB: *You can't expect me to* *believe that.* □ JANE: *Everyone in our family has one extra toe.* MARY: *You don't expect me to believe that!*

(You) can't fight city hall. There is no way to win in a battle against a bureaucracy. □ BILL: *I guess I'll go ahead and pay the tax bill.* BOB: *Might as well. You can't fight city hall.* □ MARY: *How did things go at your meeting with the zoning board?* SALLY: *I gave up. Can't fight city hall. Better things to do.*

(You) can't get there from here. a catch phrase said jokingly when someone asks directions to get to a place that can be reached only by a circuitous route. □ BILL: *How far is it to Adamsville?* TOM: *Adamsville? Oh, that's too bad. You can't get there from here.* □ *"Galesburg? Galesburg, you say?" said the farmer. "By golly, you can't get there from here!"*

You can't mean that! Surely you do not mean what you said! □ BILL: *I hate you! I hate you! I hate you!* MARY: *You can't mean that.* □ SALLY: *The cake burned and there's no time to start another before the party.* MARY: *You can't mean that!*

(You) can't take it with you. Since you cannot take your wealth with you when you die, you ought to enjoy it while you're alive. (A proverb.) □ JANE: *Go ahead, enjoy it while you've got it. You can't take it with you.* ANDREW: *I love logic like that.* □ HENRY: *Sure, I spent a fortune on this car. Can't take it with you, you know.* RACHEL: *And this way, you can share it with your friends.*

(You) can't top that. See under *(You) can't beat that.*

(You) can't win them all. AND **(You) can't win 'em all.** a catch phrase said when someone, including the speaker, has lost in a contest or failed at something. (The *you* is impersonal, meaning *one, anyone.* The apostrophe on *'em* is not always used.) □ MARY: *Gee, I came in last again!* JANE: *Oh, well. You can't win them all.* □ *"Can't win 'em all," muttered Alice as she left the boss's office with nothing accomplished.*

You changed your mind? See *(Have you) changed your mind?*

(You) could have fooled me. I would have thought otherwise.; I would have thought the opposite. □ HENRY: *Did you know that this land is among the most productive in the entire state?* JANE: *You could have fooled me. It looks quite barren.* □ JOHN: *I really do like Mary.* ANDREW: *Could have fooled me. You treat her rather badly sometimes.*

You could have knocked me over with a feather. I was extremely surprised.; I was so surprised that I was disoriented and could have been knocked over easily. □ ANDREW: *When she told me she was going to get married, you could have knocked me over with a feather.* SALLY: *I can see why.* □ JOHN: *Did you hear that they are going to tear down city hall and build a new one—price tag twelve million dollars?* SALLY: *Yes, and when I did, you could have knocked me over with a feather.*

You couldn't (do that)! AND **You wouldn't (do that)!** an indication of disbelief that someone might do something. □ BILL: *I'm going to run away from home!* JANE: *You couldn't!* □ BILL: *I get so mad at my brother, I could just strangle him.* TOM: *You couldn't do that!*

You('d) better believe it! a way of emphasizing a previous statement. □ BILL: *Man, you're the best goalie this team has ever had!* TOM: *You better believe it!* □ BILL: *This food is so bad. It will probably stunt my growth.* TOM: *You'd better believe it!*

(You'd) better get moving. an expression encouraging someone to leave. □ JANE: *It's nearly dark. Better get moving.* MARY: *Okay. I'm leaving right now.* □ BOB: *I'm off. Good night.* BILL: *Yes, it's late. You'd better get moving.*

You doing okay? See *(Are you) doing okay?*

You don't expect me to believe that. See *You can't expect me to believe that.*

You don't know the half of it. You really don't know how bad it is.; You might think that what you have heard is bad, but you do not know the whole story. □ MARY: *They say you've been having a bad time at home.* SALLY: *You don't know the half of it.* □ SALLY: *The company has no cash, they are losing orders right and left, and the comptroller is cooking the books.* MARY: *Sounds bad.* SALLY: *You don't know the half of it.*

You don't know where it's been. It may be dirty, so do not touch it or put it in your mouth, because you do not know where it has been and what kind of dirt it has picked up. (Most often said to children.) □ MOTHER: *Don't put that money in your mouth. You don't know where it's been.* BILL: *Okay.* □ FATHER: *Take that stick out of your mouth. You don't know where it's been.* BOB: *It's been on the ground.*

You don't say. **1.** a general response to something that someone has said. (Expresses a little polite surprise or interest, but not disbelief.) □ BILL: *I'm starting work on a new job next Monday.* BOB: *You don't say.* □ SALLY: *The Jones boys are keeping a pet snake.* ALICE: *You don't say.* **2.** You have just said something that everybody already knows. □ BILL: *I think I'm beginning to put on a little weight.* JANE: *You don't say.* □ JOHN: *My goodness, prices are getting high.* SUE: *You don't say.*

You first. an invitation for someone to precede the speaker. (See the examples.) □ BILL: *Let's try some of this goose liver stuff.* JANE: *You first.* □ BILL: *The water sure looks cold. Let's jump in.* BOB: *You first.*

You got it! Good, you understand it!; Finally, you understand it! □ BILL: *Does that mean I can't have the car tonight?* FATHER: *You got it!* □ BOB: *You're fired! You don't work here any longer! There are no more paychecks coming to you.* BILL: *In other words, I'm out of a job.* BOB: *You got it!*

You got me beat! See *(It) beats me.*

You hear? See *(Do) you hear?*

You heard someone. Don't argue. You heard your instructions from someone. (The *someone* can be a person's name, a title, or a pronoun.) □ ANDREW: *You heard the man. Get moving.* HENRY: *Don't rush me!* □ BILL: *What makes her think she can tell me what to do?* BOB: *She's the boss. Do it! You heard her!*

You (just) wait (and see)! AND **Just (you) wait (and see)!** Wait and see what will happen.; If you wait, you will see that what I predict will be true. □ JOHN: *You'll get what you deserve! Just you wait!* JANE: *Mind your own business.* □ BILL: *Things will get better. Just wait!* SUE: *Sure, but when?*

(You) (just) watch! Just pay attention to what I do, and you will see that what I said is true! □ RACHEL: *I'll get her to change! You just watch!* ANDREW: *Good luck!* □ ANDREW: *You watch! You'll see I'm right.* SALLY: *Sure, you are.* □ BOB: *Watch! This is the way it's done.* BILL: *You don't know what you're doing.* BOB: *Just watch!*

you know an expression placed on the end of a statement for emphasis. (This expression is often overused, in which case it is totally meaningless and irritating.) □ ANDREW: *Sure, I spent a fortune on this car. Can't take it with you, you know.* RACHEL: *But there are* *better things to do with it here and now.* □ BILL: *Do you always lock your door?* TOM: *Usually. There's a lot of theft around here, you know.*

You know what? See *(Do you) know what?*

You know what I mean? See *(Do you) know what I'm saying?; You know (what I'm saying)?*

You know (what I'm saying)? AND **(You) know what I mean?; (You) know what I'm saying?** You can figure out what I'm trying to say, besides I forgot the right words, so I won't explain further. (The *You know* is frowned on by many people, especially when it is overused.) □ JOHN: *I'm going to Florida, on the gulf side. You know what I'm saying?* MARY: *Yeah, that's great!* □ FRED: *I've got to get some of those things that hold up the back of the car. You know what I mean.* BOB: *Yeah, springs. I need some too.*

You know what I'm saying? See *(Do you) know what I'm saying?; You know (what I'm saying)?*

You leaving so soon? See *(Are you) leaving so soon?*

You'll be sorry you asked. The answer to the question you just asked is so bad that you will be sorry you asked it. (Compare to *(Are you) sorry you asked?*) □ FATHER: *What are your grades going to be like this semester?* SALLY: *You'll be sorry you asked.* □ MARY: *How much did you pay for that lamp?* JANE: *You'll be sorry you asked.*

You'll be the death of me (yet). You and your problems may, in fact, kill me. (An exaggeration, of course.) □ HENRY: *You'll be the death of me yet. Why can't you ever do anything right?* ANDREW: *I got a talent for it, I guess.* □ BILL: *Mom, the teacher says you have to go to school again for a conference.* MOTHER: *Oh, Billy, you'll be the death of me.*

You'll get onto it. Don't worry. You will become more comfortable with this situation soon.; You will catch the spirit of the situation soon. □ BILL: *I just can't seem to do this right.* BOB: *You'll get onto it.* □ MARY: *How long does it take to learn to work this computer?* JANE: *Don't fret. You'll get onto it.*

You'll get the hang of it. Don't worry. You will learn soon how it is done. □ MARY: *It's harder than I thought to glue these things together.* TOM: *You'll get the hang of it.* □ BILL: *I can't seem to swing this club the way you showed me.* SALLY: *You'll get the hang of it. Don't worry. Golf is easy.*

You'll never get away with it. You will never succeed with that illegal or outrageous plan. □ BILL: *I have a plan to cheat on the exam.* MARY: *You'll never get away with it.* □ JANE: *I think I can trick everybody into walking out on the performance.* MARY: *That's awful. You'll never get away with it.*

You make me laugh! What you said is totally ridiculous.; You are totally ridiculous. (Compare to *Don't make me laugh!*) □ BILL: *I have this plan to make electricity from garbage.* SALLY: *What a dumb idea! You make me laugh!* □ BILL: *I'm really sorry. Give me another chance. I'll never do it again!* JANE: *You make me laugh!*

You mean to say? See *(Do) you mean to say?*

You mean to tell me something? See *(Do) you mean to tell me something?*

You (really) said a mouthful. You said exactly what needed to be said.; What you said was very meaningful and had great impact. (Colloquial and folksy.) □ BILL: *Did you hear what I said to her?* JANE: *Yes. You said a mouthful. Was she mad?* □ BILL: *This is the worst food I have ever eaten. It is either stale, wilted, dry, or soggy!* TOM: *You said a mouthful!*

You're dern tootin'! You are absolutely right! (Colloquial and folksy. Never the full form *tooting*.) □ TOM: *Are you really going to take up boxing?* BOB: *You're dern tootin'!* □ FATHER: *Do you really want to buy that droopy-looking puppy?* BILL: *You're dern tootin'!*

You're excused. **1.** You may leave the room, the table, etc. (Said in response to *May I be excused?*) □ MOTHER: *Are you finished, Tom?* TOM: *Yes, ma'am.* MOTHER: *You're excused.* □ BILL (raising his hand): *Can I leave the room? I have to go get my books off my bike.* TEACHER: *You're excused.* BILL: *Thanks.* **2.** You must leave the room or the premises. (Typically said at the end of a scolding.) □ FATHER: *I've heard quite enough of this nonsense, Tom. You're excused.* TOM: *Sorry.* □ ANDREW: *That is the end of this conversation. You're excused.* BOB: *But, there's more.* **3.** You are forgiven for belching or for some other breach of strict etiquette. (Said in response to *Excuse me.*) □ TOM (after belching): *Excuse me.* FATHER: *You're excused.* □ SALLY: *Excuse me for being so noisy.* MOTHER: *You're excused.*

You're (just) wasting my time. What you have to say is of no interest to me. □ RACHEL: *I've heard enough. You're just wasting my time. Good-bye.* MARY: *If that's the way you feel about it, good-bye.* □ FRED: *Come on, Bill. I'll show you what I mean.* BILL: *No, you're wasting my time.*

You're out of your mind! AND **You've got to be out of your mind!** You must be crazy for saying or doing that! (Said to someone who has said or done something silly or stupid.) □ ANDREW: *Go to the Amazon? You're out of your mind!* JANE: *Maybe so, but doesn't it sound like fun?* □ MARY: *Come on, Jane. Let's go swimming in the river.* JANE: *Look at that filthy water. Swim in it? You've got to be out of your mind!*

You're telling me! I know all too well the truth of what you are saying. □ TOM: *Man, it's hot today!* BOB: *You're telling me!* □ JANE: *This food is really terrible.* SALLY: *Wow! You're telling me!*

You're the doctor. You are in a position to tell me what to do.; I yield to you and your knowledge of this matter. (The person being addressed is most likely not a physician.) □ BILL: *Eat your dinner, then you'll feel more like playing ball. Get some energy!* TOM: *Okay, you're the doctor.* □ TEACHER: *You'd better study the first two chapters more thoroughly.* BOB: *You're the doctor.*

You're too much! **1.** You are too much of a problem for me. □ ANDREW: *You're too much! I'm going to report you to the head office!* BOB: *Go ahead. See if I care.* □ BOB: *Get out! Just go home! You're too much!* ANDREW: *What did I do?* BOB: *You're a pest!* **2.** You are just too funny, clever, entertaining, etc. □ ALICE: *Oh, Fred, that was really funny. You're too much!* FRED: *I do my best.* □ SALLY: *What a clever thing to say! You're too much!* ANDREW: *Actually, I didn't make it up myself.*

You're welcome. a phrase that follows *Thanks* or *Thank you.* (Made emphatic and more gracious with an adjective, such as *quite* or *very*.) □ FATHER: *Thank you.* MOTHER: *You're welcome.* □ BOB: *We all thank you very much.* SALLY: *You're quite welcome.*

Your guess is as good as mine. I really do not know.; You know as well as I do. □ MARY: *What time do we eat around here?* BOB: *Your guess is as good as mine.* □ BILL: *Why would anyone build a house like that way out here in the woods?* BOB: *Your guess is as good as mine.*

Your place or mine? an expression inquiry of someone about whose dwelling should be the site of a rendezvous. (Often associated with a sudden or spontaneous sexual encounter.) ☐ BILL: *So, do you want to go somewhere?* MARY: *Your place or mine?* ☐ BILL: *I was thinking of a movie. What's this "You're place or mine?"* MARY: *Okay, I'll rent the movie and we'll watch it at your place.*

Yourself? See *And you?*

You said a mouthful! See *You (really) said a mouthful!*

You said it! I agree with you entirely! (There is a stress on both *you* and *said*.) ☐ BILL: *Wow, it's really hot in here!* BOB: *You said it!* ☐ MARY: *Let's get out of here! I can't stand this movie.* SALLY: *You said it!*

You, too. See under *(The) same to you.*

(You) took the words right out of my mouth. You said exactly what I meant to say before I had a chance to say it, and, therefore, I agree with you very much. ☐ BILL: *I think she's old enough to know better.* TOM: *You took the words right out of my mouth.* ☐ MARY: *This movie is going to put me to sleep.* JANE (yawning): *You took the words right out of my mouth.*

You've got another think coming. You will have to rethink your position. (The second part of an expression something like, "If you think so-and-so, then *you've got another think coming.*" Also with *thing* rather than *think*.) ☐ RACHEL: *If you think I'm going to stand here and listen to your complaining all day, you've got another think coming!* BILL: *Frankly, I don't care what you do.* ☐ ANDREW: *If you think you can get away with it, you've got another think coming!* BOB: *Get away with what? I didn't do anything!*

(You've) got me stumped. I can't possibly figure out the answer to your question. ☐ BILL: *How long is the Amazon River?* JANE: *You've got me stumped.* ☐ BOB: *Do you know of a book that would interest a retired sea captain?* SALLY: *You've got me stumped.*

You've got to be kidding! This cannot be the truth. Surely you are kidding me! ☐ BOB: *Sally is getting married. Did you hear?* MARY: *You've got to be kidding!* ☐ BILL: *I think I swallowed my gold tooth!* MOTHER: *You've got to be kidding!*

You've got to be out of your mind! See *You're out of your mind!*

You wait! See *Just (you) wait!*

You want to know something? See *(Do you) want to know something?*

You want to make something of it? See *(Do you) want to make something of it?*

You want to step outside? See *(Do) you want to step outside?*

You watch! See *(You) (just) watch!*

[you will] See the entries beginning with *you'll.*

You wish! See *(Don't) you wish!*

[you would] See the entries beginning with *you'd.*

You wouldn't be trying to kid me, would you? You are not lying, are you? ☐ BILL: *There's a mouse sitting on the toe of your shoe.* TOM: *You wouldn't try to kid me, would you?* ☐ BILL: *The history final examination was changed to yesterday. Did they tell you?* BOB: *You wouldn't be trying to kid me, would you?*

You wouldn't dare (to do something)! an exclamation that shows disbelief about something that the speaker has stated an intention of doing. ☐ BILL: *I'm going to leave school.* TOM: *You wouldn't dare leave!* ☐ BILL: *Be quiet or I'll slap you.* JANE: *You wouldn't dare!*

You wouldn't (do that)! See *You couldn't (do that)!*

Yup. Yes. (Colloquial and folksy. Considered rude or disrespectful in some situations, such as a child speaking to an adult.) ☐ BILL: *Want some more?* TOM: *Yup.* ☐ MARY: *Tired?* JANE: *Yup.*

Z

Zip it up! See the following entry.

Zip (up) your lip! AND **Zip it up!** Be quiet!; Close your mouth and be quiet! (Slang and slightly rude.) □ *"I've heard enough. Zip your lip!" hollered the coach.* □ ANDREW: *All right, you guys. Shut up! Zip it up!* BOB: *Sorry.* BILL: *Be quiet.* ANDREW: *That's better.*

Phrase-Finder Index

Use this index to find the form of a phrase that you want to look up in the Dictionary. First, pick out any major word in the phrase you are seeking. Second, look that word up in this index to find the form of the phrase used in the Dictionary. Third, look up the phrase in the Dictionary. See **Uses** and **Hints** below. Single words should be looked up in the Dictionary directly.

Some of the words occurring in the Dictionary entries do not occur as entries in this index. Entries that are only single words are not indexed here. Some words are omitted because they occur so frequently that their lists cover many pages. In these instances, you should look up the phrase under some other word. The following words and the personal pronouns do not occur as entries in the index:

a
an
and
be
do
have
not
someone
something
that
this
to
will

Uses

This index provides a convenient way to find the words that follow the first word in a phrasal entry. Without the index there would be no way to find these "included" words.

Hints

1. When you are trying to find an expression in this index, look up the noun first, if there is one.

2. When you are looking for a noun, try first to find the singular form or the simplest form of the noun.

3. When you are looking for a verb, try first to find the present tense form or the simplest form of the verb.

4. In most expressions where a noun or pronoun is a variable part of an expression, it will be represented by the words "someone" or "something" in the form of the expression used in the Dictionary. If you do not find the noun you want in the index, it may, in fact, be a variable word.

5. This is an index of forms, not meanings. The expressions in an index entry do not usually have any meanings in common. Consult the Dictionary for information about meaning.

ABOUT

Better keep quiet about it. □ Better keep still about it. □ Don't even think about (doing) it. □ Don't even think about it (happening). □ Don't worry about a thing. □ Forget (about) it! □ How about a lift? □ How about you? □ (I have) nothing to complain about. □ I've heard so much about you. □ Keep quiet about it. □ Keep still about it. □ Keep your mouth shut (about someone or something). □ Let's talk (about it). □ Make no mistake (about it)! □ No doubt about it. □ Nothing to complain about. □ Shut up about it. □ (Someone had) better keep quiet about it. □ (Someone had) better keep still about it. □ That's about the size of it. □ (There is) no doubt about it. □ We need to talk about something. □ We were just talking about you. □ What about it? □ What about you? □ What do you think about that?

ABSOLUTELY

Absolutely! □ Absolutely not!

ACCEPT

I can accept that. □ I can't accept that.

ACQUAINTANCE

Delighted to make your acquaintance. □ (I'm) delighted to make your acquaintance.

AFRAID

Afraid not. □ Afraid so. □ (I'm) afraid not. □ (I'm) afraid so.

AFTER

After while(, crocodile). □ after you.

AFTERNOON

Afternoon. □ (Good) afternoon.

AGAIN

Again(, please). □ Call again. □ Come again. □ Could I see you again? □ Don't make me say it again! □ Don't make me tell you again! □ Do we have to go through all that again? □ Good to see you (again). □ Here we go again. □ Hope to see you again (sometime). ☐ How's that again? ☐ (I) hope to see you again (sometime). ☐ (It's) good to see you (again). ☐ Let's do this again (sometime). ☐ Let's not go through all that again. ☐ Not again! ☐ Run it by (me) again. ☐ Run that by (me) again. ☐ Till we meet again. ☐ Until we meet again ☐ We'll try again some other time. ☐ We must do this again (sometime). ☐ What was the name again? ☐ Will I see you again? ☐ You are something else (again)! ☐ You can say that again!

AGE
Act your age! ☐ Age before beauty. ☐ in this day and age

AHEAD
Go ahead. ☐ (Go ahead,) make my day!

AIM
We aim to please.

ALARM
I don't want to alarm you, but

ALIVE
Look alive!

ALL
all in all ☐ All right. ☐ All right already! ☐ All systems are go. ☐ All the best to someone. ☐ all the more reason for doing something ☐ all things considered ☐ Can't win them all. ☐ Doesn't bother me at all. ☐ Don't spend it all in one place. ☐ Do we have to go through all that again? ☐ Everything's going to be all right. ☐ Everything will work out (all right). ☐ first of all ☐ for all intents and purposes ☐ Haven't got all day. ☐ If that don't beat all! ☐ (I) haven't got all day. ☐ I'm all ears. ☐ (It) doesn't bother me at all. ☐ It's all someone needs. ☐ (It) won't bother me at all. ☐ I was up all night with a sick friend. ☐ Let's not go through all that again. ☐ Not at all. ☐ Of all the nerve! ☐ once and for all ☐ That (all) depends. ☐ That's all someone needs. ☐ The shame of it (all)! ☐ Things will work out (all right). ☐ Where have you been all my life? ☐ Will that be all? ☐ (You) can't win them all.

ALLIGATOR

Later, alligator. □ See you later, alligator.

ALONE

Leave me alone!

ALONG

Have to be moving along. □ Have to move along. □ Have to run along. □ (I) have to be moving along. □ (I) have to move along. □ (I) have to run along. □ (I'm) (just) plugging along. □ (It's) time to move along. □ (It's) time to push along. □ Just plugging along. □ Plugging along. □ Time to move along. □ Time to push along.

ALREADY

All right already!

ALWAYS

Not always. □ You (always) give up too eas(il)y.

ANOTHER

Care for another? □ Don't give it another thought. □ one way or another □ put another way □ Tell me another (one)! □ to put it another way □ (Would you) care for another (one)? □ You've got another think coming.

ANY

Any friend of someone('s) (is a friend of mine). □ Doesn't bother me any. □ in any case □ (It) doesn't bother me any. □ (It) won't bother me any. □ not under any circumstances. □ Won't bother me any.

ANYBODY

Anybody I know?

ANYHOW

anyhow

ANYMORE

Don't see you much around here anymore. □ Not anymore. □ (We) don't see you much around here anymore.

ANYONE
Anyone I know? □ Don't breathe a word of this to anyone.

ANYTHING
Anything else? □ Anything going on? □ Anything new down your way? □ Anything you say. □ Don't do anything I wouldn't do. □ If there's anything you need, don't hesitate to ask. □ (Is) anything going on? □ Is there anything else? □ (Will there be) anything else?

ANYTIME
Anytime. □ Anytime you are ready. □ Come back anytime.

ANYWAY
anyway

ANYWHERE
Put it anywhere.

ARGUE
Can't argue with that. □ (I) can't argue with that.

ARMY
You and what army?

AROUND
Don't see you much around here anymore. □ See you around. □ (We) don't see you much around here anymore. □ What's going on (around here)?

AS
(as) far as I know □ (as) far as I'm concerned □ as I see it □ as it is □ as I was saying □ as such □ as we speak □ as you say □ be that as it may □ Can't say (as) I do. □ Can't say (as) I have. □ far as I know □ far as I'm concerned □ (I) can't say (as) I do. □ may as well □ might as well □ Sure as shooting! □ try as I may □ Your guess is as good as mine.

ASIDE
Step aside.

ASK
(Are you) sorry you asked? □ Couldn't ask for more. □ Doesn't hurt to ask. □ Don't ask. □ Don't ask me. □ (I) couldn't ask for more. □ I couldn't ask you to do that. □ If there's anything you need, don't hesitate to ask. □ If you don't

see what you want, please ask (for it). □ (I'm) sorry you asked (that). □ (It) doesn't hurt to ask. □ (It) never hurts to ask. □ Never hurts to ask. □ Sorry (that) I asked. □ Sorry you asked? □ You asked for it! □ You'll be sorry you asked.

AT

at the present time □ Come in and make yourself at home. □ Doesn't bother me at all. □ Have a go at it. □ Have at it. □ Here's looking at you. □ (It) doesn't bother me at all. □ (It) won't bother me at all. □ Look (at) what the cat dragged in! □ Make yourself at home. □ Not at all.

AWAY

Don't stay away so long. □ Go away! □ Right away. □ You'll never get away with it.

AWFULLY

Thanks awfully.

BACK

Come back and see us. □ Come back anytime. □ Come back when you can stay longer. □ Get back to me (on this). □ Get off my back! □ I'll call back later. □ I'll get back to you (on that). □ Let me get back to you (on that).

BAD

(It's) not half bad. □ Not bad. □ Not half bad. □ (That's) too bad. □ Too bad.

BAG

Bag it! □ Bag your face!

BALANCE

on balance

BALL

Have a ball! □ That's the way the ball bounces.

BARN

Were you born in a barn?

BASTARD

Don't let the bastards wear you down.

BEAT

Beat it! □ Beats me. □ Can't beat that. □ Got me beat. □

(I) can't beat that. □ If that don't beat all! □ (It) beats me. □ (It's) got me beat. □ That beats everything! □ (You) can't beat that. □ You got me beat!

BEAUTY

Age before beauty. □ Got to go home and get my beauty sleep. □ (I've) got to go home and get my beauty sleep.

BEFORE

Age before beauty. □ Haven't I seen you somewhere before? □ Haven't we met before?

BEG

Begging your pardon, but □ Beg pardon. □ Beg your pardon. □ Beg your pardon, but □ (I) beg your pardon. □ (I) beg your pardon, but □ I'll have to beg off.

BELIEVE

believe it or not □ Believe you me! □ Don't believe I've had the pleasure. □ Don't believe so. □ Do you expect me to believe that? □ I believe so. □ I believe we've met. □ I can't believe (that)! □ I don't believe it! □ (I) don't believe I've had the pleasure. □ (I) don't believe so. □ I don't believe this! □ Would you believe! □ You can't expect me to believe that. □ You('d) better believe it! □ You don't expect me to believe that.

BELL

Hell's bells (and buckets of blood)!

BEST

All the best to someone. □ Best of luck (to someone). □ Everything will work out for the best. □ Give my best to someone. □ (The) best of luck (to someone). □ Things will work out for the best. □ to the best of my knowledge

BET

I('ll) bet □ (I) wouldn't bet on it. □ Wouldn't bet on it. □ You bet. □ You bet your boots! □ You bet your life! □ You bet your (sweet) bippy. □ You bet your (sweet) life!

BETCHA

You betcha.

BETTER

Better be going. □ Better be off. □ Better get moving. □

Better get on my horse. ☐ Better hit the road. ☐ Better keep quiet about it. ☐ Better keep still about it. ☐ Better late than never. ☐ better left unsaid ☐ Better luck next time. ☐ Better than nothing. ☐ Better things to do. ☐ Could be better. ☐ Couldn't be better. ☐ Got better things to do. ☐ (I) could be better. ☐ (I) couldn't be better. ☐ (I'd) better be going. ☐ (I'd) better be off. ☐ (I'd) better get moving. ☐ (I'd) better get on my horse. ☐ (I'd) better hit the road. ☐ (It) couldn't be better. ☐ (It's) better than nothing. ☐ (I've) better things to do. ☐ (I've) (got) better things to do. ☐ (I've) never been better. ☐ (I've) never felt better. ☐ (I've) seen better. ☐ Might be better. ☐ Never been better. ☐ Never felt better. ☐ Seen better. ☐ (Someone had) better keep quiet about it. ☐ (Someone had) better keep still about it. ☐ The sooner the better. ☐ (Things) could be better. ☐ (Things) might be better. ☐ You('d) better believe it! ☐ (You'd) better get moving.

BILL
Could I have the bill?

BIPPY
You bet your (sweet) bippy.

BITE
Bite your tongue! ☐ I'll bite.

BLANK
Fill in the blanks.

BLESSING
with my blessing

BLOOD
Hell's bells (and buckets of blood)!

BLOW
It blows my mind!

BOB
No siree(, Bob)! ☐ Yes siree(, Bob)!

BODY
Over my dead body!

BOOK
Not in my book.

BOOT
You bet your boots!

BORN
Were you born in a barn?

BOTHER
Doesn't bother me any. ☐ Doesn't bother me at all. ☐ Don't bother. ☐ Don't bother me! ☐ Don't bother me none. ☐ (It) doesn't bother me any. ☐ (It) doesn't bother me at all. ☐ (It) don't bother me none. ☐ (It) won't bother me any. ☐ (It) won't bother me at all. ☐ Won't bother me any.

BOTTOM
Bottoms up.

BOUNCE
That's the way the ball bounces.

BOWEL
Don't get your bowels in an uproar!

BOY
boy ☐ Boy howdy! ☐ boy oh boy ☐ How's my boy? ☐ How's the boy? ☐ Oh, boy.

BRAVO
Bravo!

BREAK
Break a leg! ☐ Break it up! ☐ Give me a break!

BREATH
Don't hold your breath. ☐ Don't waste your breath. ☐ I don't have time to catch my breath.

BREATHE
Don't breathe a word of this to anyone. ☐ I don't have time to breathe. ☐ (I) won't breathe a word (of it). ☐ Won't breathe a word (of it).

BRING
That brings me to the (main) point. ☐ What brings you here? ☐ which brings me to the (main) point

BUCKET
For crying in a bucket! ☐ Hell's bells (and buckets of blood)!

BULLY

Bully for you!

BURN

That (really) burns me (up)!

BUSINESS

Get your nose out of my business. ☐ How's business? ☐ I'll thank you to mind your own business. ☐ (I'm just) minding my own business. ☐ (It's) none of your business! ☐ (just) taking care of business ☐ Keep your nose out of my business. ☐ Let's get down to business. ☐ Minding my own business. ☐ Mind your own business. ☐ None of your business! ☐ taking care of business

BUSY

been keeping busy ☐ Been keeping myself busy. ☐ (Have you) been keeping busy? ☐ I'm busy. ☐ (I've) been keeping busy. ☐ (I've) been keeping myself busy. ☐ Keeping busy. ☐ Keeping myself busy. ☐ You been keeping busy?

BUSYBODY

I don't want to sound like a busybody, but

BUT

Begging your pardon, but ☐ Beg your pardon, but ☐ (I) beg your pardon, but ☐ I don't want to alarm you, but ☐ I don't want to sound like a busybody, but ☐ I don't want to upset you, but ☐ (I) would if I could(, but I can't). ☐ Thanks, but no thanks. ☐ Would if I could(, but I can't).

BUY

Buy you a drink? ☐ (Could I) buy you a drink?

BY

Been getting by. ☐ by the same token ☐ by the skin of some-one's teeth ☐ by the way ☐ Could I get by, please? ☐ Drop by for a drink (sometime). ☐ Drop by sometime. ☐ Fine by me. ☐ Glad you could drop by. ☐ Glad you could stop by. ☐ How's by you? ☐ (I'm) glad you could drop by. ☐ (I'm) glad you could stop by. ☐ (I'm) just getting by. ☐ (I've) been getting by. □ Just getting by. □ Not by a long shot. □ Okay by me. □ Run it by (me) again. □ Run that by (me) again. □ (That's) fine by me. □ (That's) okay by me. □ (We're) glad you could drop by. □ (We're) glad you could stop by.

BYE

Bye. □ Bye-bye. □ Good-bye. □ good-bye and good riddance □ Good-bye for now. □ (Good-bye) until next time. □ (Good-bye) until then. □ See ya, bye-bye.

CAKE

That takes the cake!

CALL

Call again. □ Could I call you? □ Could I have someone call you? □ Could I tell someone who's calling? □ Don't call us, we'll call you. □ Give me a call. □ I'll call back later. □ Let's call it a day. □ Thank you for calling. □ Time to call it a day. □ Time to call it a night. □ What number are you calling? □ Who's calling(, please)? □ You called?

CAN

Includes *Cannot, Can't.*

□ Can do. □ Can I speak to someone? □ Can it! □ Cannot! □ Can't argue with that. □ Can't beat that. □ Can't be helped. □ Can't complain. □ Can't fight city hall. □ Can't get there from here. □ Can't help it. □ Can too. □ Can't rightly say. □ Can't say (as) I do. □ Can't say as I have. □ Can't say for sure. □ Can't say's I do. □ Can't say that I do. □ Can't say that I have. □ Can't take it with you. □ Can't thank you enough. □ Can't top that. □ Can't win them all. □ Can you excuse us, please? □ Can you handle it? □ Can you hold? □ Come back when you can stay longer. □ How can I help you? □ How can I serve you? □ I can accept that. □ I can live with that. □ I can't accept that. □ (I) can't argue with that. □ (I) can't beat that. □ I can't believe (that)! □ (I) can't complain. □ I can't get over something! □ (I) can't help it. □ (I) can too. □ (I) can't rightly say. □ (I) can't say (as) I do. □ (I) can't say for sure. □ (I) can't say's I do. □ (I) can't say that I do. □ (I) can't say that I have. □ (I) can't thank you enough. □ (I) can't top that. □ I can't understand (it). □ Is there some place I can wash up? □ (It) can't be helped. □ (I) would if I could(, but I can't). □ Neither can I. □ No can do. □ What can I do you for? □ What can I say? □ What can I tell you? □ What else can I do? □ What else can I do for you? □ What more can I do? □ Where can I wash up? □ Would if I could(, but I can't). □ You can say that again! □ (You) can't □ (You) can't beat that. □ You can't expect me to believe that. □ (You) can't fight city hall. □ (You) can't get there from here. □ You can't mean that! □ (You) can't take it with you. □ (You) can't top that. □ (You) can't win them all.

CANDIDLY
speaking (quite) candidly

CARD
Cash or credit (card)?

CARE
Care for another? □ Care if I join you? □ care to? □ Care to dance? □ Care to join us? □ Could(n't) care less. □ (Do you) care if I join you? □ (I) could(n't) care less. □ I don't care. □ (just) taking care of business □ See if I care! □ Take care (of yourself). □ taking care of business □ Who cares? □ (Would you) care for another (one)? □ (would you) care to? □ (Would you) care to dance? □ (Would you) care to join us?

CAREFUL
Be careful.

CASE
in any case

CAT
Look (at) what the cat dragged in! □ Looks like something the cat dragged in. □ (Someone) looks like something the cat dragged in.

CATCH
Catch me later. □ Catch me some other time. □ Catch you

later. ☐ I didn't catch the name. ☐ I didn't catch your name. ☐ I didn't (quite) catch that (last) remark. ☐ I don't have time to catch my breath. ☐ (I'll) catch you later. ☐ (I'll) try to catch you later. ☐ (I'll) try to catch you some other time. ☐ Try to catch you later. ☐ Try to catch you some other time. ☐ What's the catch?

CAUSES
(That causes) no problem.

CEREMONY
Don't stand on ceremony.

CERTAINLY
Certainly! ☐ Certainly not!

CHAIR
Pull up a chair.

CHANCE
Give me a chance! ☐ No chance. ☐ Not a chance! ☐ (There is) no chance. ☐ when you get a chance

CHANGE
Changed my mind. ☐ Change your mind? ☐ (Have you) changed your mind? ☐ (I) changed my mind. ☐ (It's) time for a change. ☐ Time for a change. ☐ Times are changing. ☐ You changed your mind?

CHARMED
Charmed(, I'm sure).

CHASE
Go chase yourself!

CHECK
Check. ☐ Check, please. ☐ Could I have the check?

CHEESE
Say cheese!

CHIN
Keep your chin up.

CIRCUMSTANCES
not under any circumstances. ☐ under no circumstances ☐ under normal circumstances

CITY

Can't fight city hall. □ (You) can't fight city hall.

CLEAR

Clear the way! □ Do I make myself (perfectly) clear? □ (I) read you loud and clear. □ Read you loud and clear.

CLIMB

Go climb a tree!

COLD

Cold enough for you? □ (Is it) cold enough for you?

COME

Come again. □ Come and get it! □ Come back and see us. □ Come back anytime. □ Come back when you can stay longer. □ Come in and make yourself at home. □ Come in and sit a spell. □ Come in and sit down. □ Come in and take a load off your feet. □ Come off it! □ come on □ Come (on) in. □ Come right in. □ Coming through(, please). □ Could I come in? □ Glad you could come. □ How come? □ (I'm) glad you could come. □ They must have seen you coming. □ This is where I came in. □ (We're) glad you could come. □ What's coming off? □ Won't you come in? □ You've got another think coming.

COMEDY

Cut the comedy!

COMPLAIN

Can't complain. □ (I) can't complain. □ (I have) nothing to complain about. □ Nothing to complain about.

CONCERN

(as) far as I'm concerned □ far as I'm concerned

CONSIDER

all things considered

CONTINUE

Could we continue this later?

CONTRARY
on the contrary

COOK
Now you're cooking (with gas)! □ What's cooking?

COOKIE
That's the way the cookie crumbles.

COOL
been keeping cool □ (Have you) been keeping cool? □ I'm cool. □ (I've) been keeping cool. □ Keeping cool. □ You been keeping cool?

COULD
Could be better. □ Could be worse. □ Could have fooled me. □ Could I be excused? □ (Could I) buy you a drink? □ Could I call you? □ Could I come in? □ Could I get by, please? □ (Could I) get you something (to drink)? □ (Could I) give you a lift? □ Could I have a lift? □ Could I have a word with you? □ Could I have someone call you? □ Could I have the bill? □ Could I have the check? □ Could I help you? □ Could I join you? □ Could I leave a message? □ Could I see you again? □ Could I see you in my office? □ Could I speak to someone? □ Could I take a message? □ Could I take your order (now)? □ Could I tell someone who's calling? □ Could I use your powder room? □ Couldn't ask for more. □ Couldn't be better. □ Couldn't be helped. □ Could(n't) care less. □ Couldn't help it. □ Could we continue this later? □ Could you excuse us, please? □ Could you handle it? □ Could you hold? □ Could you keep a secret? □ Glad you could come. □ Glad you could drop by. □ Glad you could stop by. □ How could you (do something)? □ (I) could be better. □ (I) could be worse. □ (I) couldn't ask for more. □ I couldn't ask you to do that. □ (I) couldn't be better. □ (I) could(n't) care less. □ (I) couldn't help it. □ (I'm) glad you could come. □ (I'm) glad you could drop by. □ (I'm) glad you could stop by. □ (It) couldn't be better. □ (It) couldn't be helped. □ (I) would if I could(, but I can't). □ (Things) could be better. □ (Things) could be worse. □ (We're) glad you could come. □ (We're) glad you could drop by. □ (We're) glad

you could stop by. □ who could have thought? □ Would if I could(, but I can't). □ (You) could have fooled me. □ You could have knocked me over with a feather. □ You couldn't (do that)!

COUNT
(I) wouldn't count on it. □ Wouldn't count on it.

COURSE
of course

CREDIT
Cash or credit (card)?

CROCODILE
After while(, crocodile).

CRUMBLE
That's the way the cookie crumbles.

CRY
For crying in a bucket! □ For crying out loud!

CUT
Cut it out! □ Cut the comedy! □ Cut the funny stuff!

DAMAGE
What's the damage?

DANCE
Care to dance? □ (Would you) care to dance?

DARE
You wouldn't dare (to do something)!

DAY
(Go ahead,) make my day! □ Have a good day. □ Have a nice day. □ Haven't got all day. □ (I) haven't got all day. □ in this day and age □ Let's call it a day. □ Make my day! □ That'll be the day! □ Time to call it a day.

DEAD
Over my dead body!

DEAL
What's the deal?

DEATH
You'll be the death of me (yet).

DECLARE
I (do) declare!

DEFINITELY
Definitely! ☐ Definitely not!

DELIGHT
Delighted to have you. ☐ Delighted to make your acquaintance.
☐ (I'm) delighted to have you (here). ☐ (I'm) delighted to
make your acquaintance. ☐ (We're) delighted to have you.

DEPEND
That (all) depends.

DERN
You're dern tootin'!

DEVIL
Speak of the devil.

DIFFERENCE
(It) makes me no difference. ☐ (It) makes no difference to me.
☐ Makes me no difference. ☐ Makes no difference to me.

DIG
Dig in! ☐ Dig up!

DIGGETY
Hot diggety (dog)!

DOCTOR
You're the doctor.

DOG
Hot diggety (dog)! ☐ Hot dog!

DOUBT
I doubt it. ☐ I doubt that. ☐ no doubt ☐ No doubt about
it. ☐ (There is) no doubt about it. ☐ without a doubt

DOWN
Anything new down your way? ☐ (Are) things getting you
down? ☐ Come in and sit down. ☐ Don't let someone or
something get you down. ☐ Don't let the bastards wear you

down. □ Do sit down. □ Down the hatch! □ Let's get down to business. □ Things getting you down? □ What's going down?

DRAG

Look (at) what the cat dragged in! □ Looks like something the cat dragged in. □ (Someone) looks like something the cat dragged in.

DRIFT

(Do you) get my drift? □ Get my drift?

DRILL

What's the drill?

DRINK

Buy you a drink? □ (Could I) buy you a drink? □ (Could I) get you something (to drink)? □ Drop by for a drink (sometime). □ Get you something (to drink)? □ I'll drink to that! □ What are you drinking? □ What would you like to drink?

DRIVE

Drive safely.

DROP

Drop by for a drink (sometime). □ Drop by sometime. □ Drop in sometime. □ Drop it! □ Drop me a line. □ Drop me a note. □ Drop over sometime. □ Drop the subject! □ Glad you could drop by. □ (I'm) glad you could drop by. □ (We're) glad you could drop by.

DUCK

Lovely weather for ducks.

DUE

in due time

DUMB

How dumb do you think I am?

EAR

I'm all ears.

EASILY

Don't give up too eas(il)y! □ You (always) give up too eas(il)y.

EASY

Easy does it. ☐ Hasn't been easy. ☐ I'm easy (to please). ☐ (It) hasn't been easy. ☐ Take it easy. ☐ That's easy for you to say. ☐ Things haven't been easy.

EAT

Hate to eat and run. ☐ (I) hate to eat and run. ☐ Let's eat. ☐ Let's eat something. ☐ What's eating someone? ☐ When do we eat?

EFFECT

or words to that effect

ELSE

Anything else? ☐ Is there anything else? ☐ (So) what else is new? ☐ What else can I do? ☐ What else can I do for you? ☐ What else is new? ☐ (Will there be) anything else? ☐ You and who else? ☐ You are something else (again)!

ENJOY

Enjoy! ☐ Enjoy your meal.

ENOUGH

Can't thank you enough. ☐ Cold enough for you? ☐ Enough is enough! ☐ Enough (of this) foolishness! ☐ Good enough. ☐ Hot enough for you? ☐ (I) can't thank you enough. ☐ (Is it) cold enough for you? ☐ (Is it) hot enough for you? ☐ I've had enough of this! ☐ That's enough! ☐ That's enough for now. ☐ (That's) enough (of this) foolishness!

EVEN

Don't even look like something! ☐ Don't even think about (doing) it. ☐ Don't even think about it (happening).

EVENING

Evening. ☐ (Good) evening. ☐ Thank you for a lovely evening.

EVER

more than you('ll ever) know

EVERY

How's every little thing?

EVERYTHING

Everything okay? ☐ Everything's going to be all right. ☐

Everything will work out (all right). □ Everything will work out for the best. □ Hold everything! □ (Is) everything okay? □ Is that everything? □ That beats everything!

EXCUSE

Can you excuse us, please? □ Could I be excused? □ Could you excuse us, please? □ Excuse me. □ Excuse me? □ Excuse, please. □ Will you excuse us, please? □ Would you excuse me? □ Would you excuse us, please? □ You're excused.

EXPECT

Do you expect me to believe that? □ I expect. □ I expect not. □ I expect (so). □ You can't expect me to believe that. □ You don't expect me to believe that.

EYE

Here's mud in your eye.

FACE

Bag your face! □ Get out of my face! □ Shut your face!

FAIR

Fair to middling. □ No fair!

FAMILY

How's the family? □ How's your family?

FANCY

Fancy meeting you here! □ Fancy that!

FAR

(as) far as I know □ (as) far as I'm concerned □ far as I know □ far as I'm concerned

FEATHER

You could have knocked me over with a feather.

FEED

I'm (really) fed up (with someone or something).

FEEL

(Are you) feeling okay? □ Feeling okay. □ How (are) you feeling? □ How you feeling? □ (I'm) feeling okay. □ (I've) never felt better. □ Never felt better.

FELICITATION

Greetings and felicitations!

FEW

I have to wash a few things out. ☐ Win a few, lose a few.

FIGHT

Can't fight city hall. ☐ Don't give up without a fight. ☐ I won't give up without a fight. ☐ (You) can't fight city hall.

FILL

Fill in the blanks.

FINAL

one final thing ☐ one final word

FIND

Where will I find you?

FINE

Fine by me. ☐ Fine with me. ☐ (It) suits me (fine). ☐ not to put too fine a point on it ☐ Suits me (fine). ☐ (That's) fine by me. ☐ (That's) fine with me.

FINISH

I'm not finished with you.

FIRE

Where's the fire?

FIRST

first of all ☐ in the first place ☐ Ladies first. ☐ Not if I see you first. ☐ You first.

FIVE

Give me five! ☐ Slip me five!

FLIGHT

Have a nice flight.

FLOOR

This is my floor.

FLOP

That's the way the mop flops.

FLY

Go fly a kite! ☐ Got to fly. ☐ How time flies. ☐ (I've) got to fly. ☐ (My,) how time flies.

FOLLOW

Do you follow?

FOOL

Could have fooled me. ☐ (You) could have fooled me.

FOOLISHNESS

Enough (of this) foolishness! ☐ (That's) enough (of this) foolishness!

FOOT

Come in and take a load off your feet.

FOR

all the more reason for doing something ☐ (Are you) ready for this? ☐ Bully for you! ☐ Can't say for sure. ☐ Care for another? ☐ Cold enough for you? ☐ Couldn't ask for more. ☐ Does it work for you? ☐ Do I have to spell it out (for you)? ☐ Drop by for a drink (sometime). ☐ Everything will work out for the best. ☐ for all intents and purposes ☐ For crying in a bucket! ☐ For crying out loud! ☐ For Pete('s) sake(s)! ☐ For pity('s) sake(s)! ☐ For shame! ☐ For sure. ☐ for what it's worth ☐ for your information ☐ Go for it! ☐ Good-bye for now. ☐ Good for you! ☐ Hot enough for you? ☐ (I) can't say for sure. ☐ (I) couldn't ask for more. ☐ I'd like (for) you to meet someone. ☐ If you don't see what you want, please ask (for it). ☐ if you know what's good for you ☐ (Is it) cold enough for you? ☐ (Is it) hot enough for you? ☐ It's for you. ☐ (It's) time for a change. ☐ (It) works for me. ☐ Lovely weather for ducks. ☐ lucky for you ☐ Not for love nor money. ☐ Not for my money. ☐ Nothing for me, thanks. ☐ once and for all ☐ Pardon me for living! ☐ Ready for this? ☐ Say hello to someone (for me). ☐ So much for that. ☐ Take my word for it. ☐ Thanks for having me. ☐ Thanks for the lift. ☐ Thanks for the ride. ☐ Thank you for a lovely evening. ☐ Thank you for a lovely time. ☐ Thank you for calling. ☐ Thank you for inviting me. ☐ Thank you for inviting us. ☐ That's easy for you to say. ☐ That's enough for now. ☐ The same for me. ☐ Things will work out for the best. ☐ Time for a change. ☐ What can I do you for? ☐ What do you know for sure? ☐ What else can I do for you? ☐ What's in it for me? ☐ What's on tap for today? ☐ Works for me. ☐ (Would you) care for another (one)? ☐ You asked for it!

FORBID

God forbid!

FORGET

Don't forget to write. ☐ Forget (about) it!

FRANKLY

frankly ☐ frankly speaking ☐ quite frankly ☐ (speaking) (quite) frankly

FRET

Fret not!

FRIEND

Any friend of someone('s) (is a friend of mine). ☐ I was up all night with a sick friend. ☐ Who's your friend?

FROM

Can't get there from here. ☐ Don't I know you from somewhere? ☐ from my perspective ☐ from my point of view ☐ from where I stand ☐ (You) can't get there from here.

FUN

Have fun.

FUNERAL

It's your funeral.

FUNNY

Cut the funny stuff! ☐ That's funny.

GAS

Now you're cooking (with gas)!

GET

(Are) things getting you down? ☐ Been getting by. ☐ Better get moving. ☐ Better get on my horse. ☐ Can't get there from here. ☐ Come and get it! ☐ Could I get by, please? ☐

(Could I) get you something (to drink)? □ Don't get up. □ Don't get your bowels in an uproar! □ Don't let someone or something get you down. □ (Do you) get my drift? □ (Do you) get the message? □ (Do you) get the picture? □ Get back to me (on this). □ Get lost! □ Get my drift? □ Get off my back! □ Get off my tail! □ Get out of here! □ Get out of my face! □ Get the lead out! □ Get the message? □ Get the picture? □ Get your nose out of my business. □ Get you something (to drink)? □ Got to get moving. □ Got to go home and get my beauty sleep. □ How are you getting on? □ I can't get over something! □ (I'd) better get moving. □ (I'd) better get on my horse. □ I didn't get that. □ I'll get back to you (on that). □ I'll get right on it. □ (I'm) just getting by. □ (I've) been getting by. □ (I've) got to get moving. □ (I've) got to go home and get my beauty sleep. □ Just getting by. □ Let me get back to you (on that). □ Let's get down to business. □ Let's get out of here. □ Let's get together (sometime). □ Things getting you down? □ when you get a chance □ when you get a minute □ (You) can't get there from here. □ (You'd) better get moving. □ You'll get onto it. □ You'll get the hang of it. □ You'll never get away with it.

GIVE

(Could I) give you a lift? □ Don't give it another thought. □ Don't give it a (second) thought. □ Don't give up! □ Don't give up the ship! □ Don't give up too eas(il)y! □ Don't give up without a fight. □ Give it a rest! □ Give it up! □ Give me a break! □ Give me a call. □ Give me a chance! □ Give me a rest! □ Give me a ring. □ Give me five! □ Give me (some) skin! □ Give my best to someone. □ Give you a lift? □ I won't give up without a fight. □ Some people (just) don't know when to give up. □ Something's got to give. □ What gives? □ You (always) give up too eas(il)y.

GLAD

Am I glad to see you! □ Glad to hear it. □ Glad to meet you. □ Glad you could come. □ Glad you could drop by. □ Glad you could stop by. □ (I'm) glad to hear it. □ I'm glad to meet you. □ (I'm) glad you could come. □ (I'm) glad you could drop by. □ (I'm) glad you could stop by. □ (I'm) (very) glad to meet you. □ Very glad to meet you. □ (We're) glad you could come. ☐ (We're) glad you could drop by. ☐ (We're) glad you could stop by.

GO

All systems are go. ☐ Anything going on? ☐ (Are you) going my way? ☐ Better be going. ☐ Don't be gone (too) long. ☐ Do we have to go through all that again? ☐ Everything's going to be all right. ☐ Go ahead. ☐ (Go ahead,) make my day! ☐ Go away! ☐ Go chase yourself! ☐ Go climb a tree! ☐ Go fly a kite! ☐ Go for it! ☐ Going my way? ☐ Go jump in the lake! ☐ Go on. ☐ Got to go. ☐ Got to go home and get my beauty sleep. ☐ Have a go at it. ☐ Have to go now. ☐ Here we go again. ☐ How goes it (with you)? ☐ How're things going? ☐ How's it going? ☐ (I'd) better be going. ☐ (I) have to go now. ☐ I'm gone. ☐ (I) really must go. ☐ (Is) anything going on? ☐ (It) just goes to show (you) (something). ☐ (It's) time to go. ☐ It's time we should be going. ☐ (I've) got to go. ☐ (I've) got to go home and get my beauty sleep. ☐ Just goes to show (you). ☐ Let's go somewhere where it's (more) quiet. ☐ Let's not go through all that again. ☐ Nice going! ☐ Really must go. ☐ That's the way it goes. ☐ (That's the) way to go! ☐ There you go! ☐ Time to go. ☐ Way to go! ☐ What's going down? ☐ What's going on (around here)?

GOD

God forbid! ☐ God only knows! ☐ God willing.

GOOD

Been up to no good. ☐ Be good. ☐ (Good) afternoon. ☐ Good-bye. ☐ good-bye and good riddance ☐ Good-bye for now. ☐ (Good-bye) until next time. ☐ (Good-bye) until then. ☐ Good enough. ☐ (Good) evening. ☐ Good for you! ☐ Good grief! ☐ (Good) heavens! ☐ Good job! ☐ Good luck! ☐ (Good) morning. ☐ (Good) night. ☐ Good talking to you. ☐ Good to be here. ☐ Good to have you here. ☐ Good to hear your voice. ☐ Good to see you (again). ☐ Good to talk to you. ☐ Have a good day. ☐ Have a good one. ☐ Have a good time. ☐ Have a good trip. ☐ if you know what's good for you ☐ I must say good night. ☐ (It's been) good talking to you. ☐ (It's been) good to talk to you. ☐ (It's) good to be here. ☐ (It's) good to have you here. ☐ (It's) good to hear your voice.

☐ (It's) good to see you (again). ☐ (I've) been up to no good. ☐ Keep up the good work. ☐ Very good. ☐ What's the good word? ☐ when I'm good and ready ☐ Your guess is as good as mine.

GOODNESS

Goodness! ☐ (My) goodness (gracious)! ☐ Thank goodness!

GOT

Got better things to do. ☐ Got me beat. ☐ Got me stumped. ☐ Got to be shoving off. ☐ Got to fly. ☐ Got to get moving. ☐ Got to go. ☐ Got to go home and get my beauty sleep. ☐ Got to hit the road. ☐ Got to run. ☐ Got to shove off. ☐ Got to split. ☐ Got to take off. ☐ Haven't got all day. ☐ (I) haven't got all day. ☐ (It's) got me beat. ☐ (I've) (got) better things to do. ☐ (I've) got to be shoving off. ☐ (I've) got to fly. ☐ (I've) got to get moving. ☐ (I've) got to go. ☐ (I've) got to go home and get my beauty sleep. ☐ (I've) got to hit the road. ☐ (I've) got to run. ☐ (I've) got to shove off. ☐ (I've) got to split. ☐ (I've) got to take off. ☐ I've got work to do. ☐ Something's got to give. ☐ You got it! ☐ You got me beat! ☐ You've got another think coming. ☐ (You've) got me stumped. ☐ You've got to be kidding! ☐ You've got to be out of your mind!

GRACIOUS

(My) goodness (gracious)!

GREETING

Greetings. ☐ Greetings and felicitations! ☐ Greetings and salutations!

GRIEF

Good grief!

GUESS

Guess what! ☐ I guess ☐ I guess not. ☐ I guess (so). ☐ Your guess is as good as mine.

GUEST

Be my guest.

HALF
(It's) not half bad. □ Not half bad. □ You don't know the half of it.

HALL
(You) can't fight city hall.

HAND
on the other hand

HANDLE
Can you handle it? □ Could you handle it?

HANG
Hang in there. □ Hang on (a minute). □ Hang on a moment. □ Hang on a second. □ You'll get the hang of it.

HAPPEN
Don't even think about it (happening). □ What happened? □ What's happening?

HAPPY
Be happy to (do something). □ Happy to (do something) □ (I'd be) happy to (do something).

HARD
Don't work too hard.

HAT
talk through one's hat

HATCH
Down the hatch!

HATE
Hate to eat and run. □ (I) hate to eat and run.

HEAD
Heads up! □ off the top of one's head □ (right) off the top of one's head □ Use your head!

HEAR
did you hear? □ (Do) you hear? □ Glad to hear it. □ Good to hear your voice. □ have you heard? □ I didn't hear you. □ I hear what you're saying. □ I hear you. □ (I'm) glad to hear it. □ (I'm) sorry to hear that. □ (I) never heard of such a thing. □ (It's) good to hear your voice. □ I've heard so much

about you. ☐ Never heard of such a thing. ☐ Sorry to hear that. ☐ That ain't the way I heard it. ☐ You hear? ☐ You heard someone.

HEART

Have a heart!

HEAVEN

(Good) heavens! ☐ Heavens! ☐ (My) heavens! ☐ Thank heavens!

HELL

Hell's bells (and buckets of blood)! ☐ Hell with that! ☐ There will be hell to pay. ☐ (To) hell with that!

HELLO

Hello. ☐ Say hello to someone (for me).

HELP

Can't be helped. ☐ Can't help it. ☐ Could I help you? ☐ Couldn't be helped. ☐ Couldn't help it. ☐ Help yourself. ☐ How can I help you? ☐ How may I help you? ☐ (I) can't help it. ☐ (I) couldn't help it. ☐ (It) can't be helped. ☐ (It) couldn't be helped. ☐ May I help you?

HERE

Can't get there from here. ☐ Don't see you much around here anymore. ☐ Fancy meeting you here! ☐ Get out of here! ☐ Good to be here. ☐ Good to have you here. ☐ Having a wonderful time; wish you were here. ☐ Here! ☐ Here's looking at you. ☐ Here's mud in your eye. ☐ Here's to you. ☐ Here we go again. ☐ (I'm) delighted to have you (here). ☐ (I'm) having a wonderful time; wish you were here. ☐ I'm out of here. ☐ (I) never thought I'd see you here! ☐ (It's) good to be here. ☐ (It's) good to have you here. ☐ It's nice to be here. ☐ It's nice to have you here. ☐ I've had it up to here (with someone or something). ☐ Let's get out of here. ☐ look here ☐ Look who's here! ☐ Never thought I'd see you here! ☐ Nice place you have here. ☐ Nice to be here. ☐ Nice to have you here. ☐ (We) don't see you much around here anymore. ☐ What brings you here? ☐ What do you think you are doing here? □ What's going on (around here)? □ Wish you were here. □ (You) can't get there from here.

HESITATE
If there's anything you need, don't hesitate to ask.

HISTORY
The rest is history.

HIT
Better hit the road. □ Got to hit the road. □ (I'd) better hit the road. □ (It's) time to hit the road. □ (I've) got to hit the road. □ Time to hit the road.

HOLD
Can you hold? □ Could you hold? □ Don't hold your breath. □ Hold everything! □ Hold it! □ Hold on (a minute)! □ Hold, please. □ Hold the line(, please). □ Hold the wire(, please). □ Hold your horses! □ Hold your tongue! □ Please hold. □ Will you hold?

HOME
Come in and make yourself at home. □ Got to go home and get my beauty sleep. □ (I've) got to go home and get my beauty sleep. □ Make yourself at home.

HOPE
Hope not. □ Hope so. □ Hope to see you again (sometime). □ (I) hope not. □ (I) hope so. □ (I) hope to see you again (sometime).

HOPEFULLY
hopefully

HORSE
Better get on my horse. □ Hold your horses! □ (I'd) better get on my horse.

HOT
Hot diggety (dog)! □ Hot dog! □ Hot enough for you? □ Hot ziggety! □ (Is it) hot enough for you?

HOUSE

My house is your house. □ Our house is your house. □ Welcome to our house.

HOW

And how! □ How about a lift? □ How about you? □ How (are) you doing? □ How (are) you feeling? □ How are you getting on? □ How can I help you? □ How can I serve you? □ How come? □ How could you (do something)? □ How-de-do. □ How do you do. □ How do you know? □ How do you like school? □ How do you like that? □ How do you like this weather? □ How dumb do you think I am? □ How goes it (with you)? □ How (have) you been? □ How many times do I have to tell you? □ How may I help you? □ How're things going? □ How're things (with you)? □ How's business? □ How's by you? □ How's every little thing? □ How should I know? □ How's it going? □ How's (it) with you? □ How's my boy? □ How's that again? □ How's the boy? □ How's the family? □ How's the wife? □ How's the world (been) treating you? □ How's tricks? □ How's with you? □ How's your family? □ How time flies. □ How will I know you? □ How will I recognize you? □ How you be? □ How you been? □ How you doing? □ How you feeling? □ How you is? □ How you was? □ (My,) how time flies.

HOWDY

Boy howdy! □ Howdy(-do)?

HUMBLE

in my humble opinion

HURRY

Hurry on! □ Hurry up!

HURT

Doesn't hurt to ask. □ (It) doesn't hurt to ask. □ (It) never hurts to ask. □ Never hurts to ask.

IF

Care if I join you? □ Don't mind if I do. □ (Do you) care if I join you? □ (do you) mind if? □ (Do you) mind if I join you?

□ (I) don't mind if I do. □ if I've told you once, I've told you a thousand times □ if I were you □ If that don't beat all! □ If there's anything you need, don't hesitate to ask. □ if you don't mind □ If you don't see what you want, please ask (for it). □ if you know what's good for you □ if you must □ if you please □ if you would(, please) □ (I) wonder if □ (I) would if I could(, but I can't). □ (I) wouldn't if I were you. □ mind if □ Mind if I join you? □ Not if I see you first. □ Not if I see you sooner. □ See if I care! □ What if I do? □ What if I don't? □ what would you say if? □ wonder if □ Would if I could(, but I can't). □ Wouldn't if I were you.

IN

all in all □ Be with you in a minute. □ Come in and make yourself at home. □ Come in and sit a spell. □ Come in and sit down. □ Come in and take a load off your feet. □ Come (on) in. □ Come right in. □ Could I come in? □ Could I see you in my office? □ Dig in! □ Don't get your bowels in an uproar! □ Don't spend it all in one place. □ Drop in sometime. □ Fill in the blanks. □ For crying in a bucket! □ Go jump in the lake! □ Hang in there. □ Haven't seen you in a long time. □ Haven't seen you in a month of Sundays. □ Here's mud in your eye. □ (I) haven't seen you in a long time. □ (I) haven't seen you in a month of Sundays. □ I'll look you up when I'm in town. □ (I'll) see you in a little while. □ in any case □ in due time □ in my humble opinion □ in my opinion □ in my view □ in other words □ in the first place □ in the interest of saving time □ in the main □ in this day and age □ in view of □ keep in mind that □ Keep in there! □ Keep in touch. □ keep (it) in mind that □ Look (at) what the cat dragged in! □ Look me up when you're in town. □ Looks like something the cat dragged in. □ Never in a thousand years! □ never in my life □ Not in a thousand years! □ Not in my book. □ See you in a little while. □ (Someone) looks like something the cat dragged in. □ (Someone will) be with you in a minute. □ (Someone will) be with you in a moment. □ Stuff a sock in it! □ This is where I came in. □ Were you born in a barn? □ What's in it for me? □ With you in a minute. □ Won't you come in?

INFORMATION

for your information

INTENT

for all intents and purposes

INTEREST

in the interest of saving time

INTRODUCE

I would like to introduce you to someone.

INVITE

Thank you for inviting me. □ Thank you for inviting us.

JOB

Good job! □ Nice job!

JOIN

Care if I join you? □ Care to join us? □ Could I join you? □ (Do you) care if I join you? □ (Do you) mind if I join you? □ Mind if I join you? □ (Would you) care to join us?

JOSÉ

No way, José!

JOURNEY

Have a safe journey.

JUMP

Go jump in the lake!

JUST

(I) just want(ed) to □ I know (just) what you mean. □ (I'm) just getting by. □ I'm just looking. □ (I'm just) minding my own business. □ (I'm) (just) plugging along. □ (I'm) (just) thinking out loud. □ (It) just goes to show (you) (something). □ (It's) just what you need. □ (I was) just wondering. □ Just a minute. □ Just a moment. □ Just a second. □ Just getting by. □ Just goes to show (you). □ just let me say □ just like that □ Just plugging along. □ (just) taking care of business □ (just) thinking out loud. □ Just wait! □ just want(ed) to □ Just watch! □ Just what you need. □ Just wondering. □ Just (you) wait (and see)! □ let me (just) say

☐ Some people (just) don't know when to give up. ☐ Some people (just) don't know when to quit. ☐ That's (just) too much! ☐ That's just what you need. ☐ We were just talking about you. ☐ You (just) wait (and see)! ☐ (You) (just) watch! ☐ You're (just) wasting my time.

KEEP

been keeping busy ☐ been keeping cool ☐ Been keeping myself busy. ☐ Been keeping out of trouble. ☐ Better keep quiet about it. ☐ Better keep still about it. ☐ Could you keep a secret? ☐ (Have you) been keeping busy? ☐ (Have you) been keeping cool? ☐ (Have you) been keeping out of trouble? ☐ I'll thank you to keep your opinions to yourself. ☐ (I've) been keeping busy. ☐ (I've) been keeping cool. ☐ (I've) been keeping myself busy. ☐ (I've) been keeping out of trouble. ☐ Keeping busy. ☐ Keeping cool. ☐ Keeping myself busy. ☐ Keeping out of trouble. ☐ keep in mind that ☐ Keep in there! ☐ Keep in touch. ☐ keep (it) in mind that ☐ Keep it up! ☐ Keep (on) trying. ☐ Keep out of my way. ☐ Keep out of this! ☐ Keep quiet. ☐ Keep quiet about it. ☐ Keep smiling. ☐ Keep still. ☐ Keep still about it. ☐ Keep this to yourself. ☐ Keep up the good work. ☐ Keep your chin up. ☐ Keep your mouth shut (about someone or something). ☐ Keep your nose out of my business. ☐ Keep your opinions to yourself! ☐ Keep your shirt on! ☐ (Someone had) better keep quiet about it. ☐ (Someone had) better keep still about it. ☐ What's keeping someone? ☐ Where (have) you been keeping yourself? ☐ You been keeping busy? ☐ You been keeping cool?

KID

I kid you not. ☐ I'm not kidding. ☐ No kidding! ☐ Who do you think you're kidding? ☐ You've got to be kidding! ☐ You wouldn't be trying to kid me, would you?

KITE

Go fly a kite!

KNOCK

Knock it off! ☐ You could have knocked me over with a feather.

KNOW

Anybody I know? ☐ Anyone I know? ☐ (as) far as I know ☐ Don't I know it! ☐ Don't I know you from somewhere? ☐

Don't you know? □ Don't you know it! □ (Do you) know what? □ (Do you) know what I mean? □ (Do you) know what I'm saying? □ (Do you) want to know something? □ far as I know □ God only knows! □ How do you know? □ How should I know? □ How will I know you? □ I don't know. □ if you know what's good for you □ I know (just) what you mean. □ (I) wouldn't know. □ Know something? □ Know what? □ Know what I mean? □ Know what I'm saying? □ Lord knows I've tried. □ more than you('ll ever) know □ Some people (just) don't know when to give up. □ Some people (just) don't know when to quit. □ Want to know something? □ (Well,) what do you know! □ What do you know? □ What do you know for sure? □ What's (there) to know? □ What's to know? □ Who knows? □ Wouldn't know. □ You don't know the half of it. □ You don't know where it's been. □ you know □ You know what? □ You know what I mean? □ You know (what I'm saying)? □ You know what I'm saying? □ You want to know something?

KNOWLEDGE
to the best of my knowledge

LAKE
Go jump in the lake!

LAP
Make a lap.

LAST
I didn't (quite) catch that (last) remark. □ That's the last straw!

LATE
Better late than never. □ Catch me later. □ Catch you later. □ Could we continue this later? □ I'll call back later. □ (I'll) catch you later. □ I'll see you later. □ (I'll) try to catch you later. □ I'll try to see you later. □ Later. □ Later, alligator. □ Perhaps a little later. □ (See you) later. □ See you later, alligator. □ Till later. □ Try to catch you later. □ Until later.

LAUGH
Don't make me laugh! □ You make me laugh!

LEAD

Get the lead out! □ Shake the lead out!

LEAVE

(Are you) leaving so soon? □ Could I leave a message? □ Leave it to me. □ Leave me alone! □ Leaving so soon? □ Take it or leave it. □ You leaving so soon?

LEFT

better left unsaid

LEG

Break a leg!

LESS

Could(n't) care less. □ (I) could(n't) care less. □ more or less

LET

Don't let someone or something get you down. □ Don't let the bastards wear you down. □ just let me say □ Let it be. □ Let me get back to you (on that). □ Let me have it! □ let me (just) say □ Let's call it a day. □ Let's do lunch (sometime). □ Let's do this again (sometime). □ Let's eat. □ Let's eat something. □ Let's get down to business. □ Let's get out of here. □ Let's get together (sometime). □ Let's go somewhere where it's (more) quiet. □ Let's have it! □ Let's not go through all that again. □ Let's shake on it. □ Let's talk (about it).

LIE

No lie?

LIFE

Having the time of my life. □ (I'm) having the time of my life. □ never in my life □ Not on your life! □ Where have you been all my life? □ You bet your life! □ You bet your (sweet) life!

LIFT

(Could I) give you a lift? □ Could I have a lift? □ Give you a lift? □ How about a lift? □ Thanks for the lift.

LIKE

Don't even look like something! ☐ How do you like school? ☐ How do you like that? ☐ How do you like this weather? ☐ I'd like (for) you to meet someone. ☐ I'd like (to have) a word with you. ☐ I'd like to speak to someone, please. ☐ I don't want to sound like a busybody, but ☐ I'm like you ☐ I would like to introduce you to someone. ☐ I would like you to meet someone. ☐ just like that ☐ Like it or lump it! ☐ like I was saying ☐ like you say ☐ Looks like something the cat dragged in. ☐ (Someone) looks like something the cat dragged in. ☐ That's more like it. ☐ What would you like to drink?

LIKELY

Not likely.

LINE

Drop me a line. ☐ Hold the line(, please). ☐ Who's on the line?

LIP

My lips are sealed. ☐ Zip (up) your lip!

LISTEN

I'm listening.

LITTLE

How's every little thing? ☐ (I'll) see you in a little while. ☐ Perhaps a little later. ☐ See you in a little while.

LIVE

I can live with that. ☐ Pardon me for living!

LOAD

Come in and take a load off your feet. ☐ Thanks loads.

LONG

Come back when you can stay longer. ☐ Don't be gone (too) long. ☐ Don't stay away so long. ☐ Haven't seen you in a long time. ☐ (I) haven't seen you in a long time. ☐ Long time no see. ☐ Not by a long shot.

LOOK

Don't even look like something! ☐ Here's looking at you. ☐ I'll look you up when I'm in town. ☐ I'm just looking. ☐ I'm only looking. ☐ look ☐ Look alive! ☐ Look (at) what the cat dragged in! □ look here □ Look me up when you're in town. □ Look out! □ Looks like something the cat dragged in. □ Look who's here! □ Look who's talking! □ (Someone) looks like something the cat dragged in.

LORD
Lord knows I've tried.

LOSE
lose one's train of thought □ Win a few, lose a few.

LOST
Get lost!

LOT
Lots of luck! □ Thanks (a lot). □ Thank you a lot.

LOUD
For crying out loud! □ (I'm) (just) thinking out loud. □ (I) read you loud and clear. □ (just) thinking out loud. □ Read you loud and clear. □ thinking out loud

LOVE
(I) love it! □ Love it! □ Not for love nor money.

LOVELY
I had a lovely time. □ I've had a lovely time. □ Lovely weather for ducks. □ Thank you for a lovely evening. □ Thank you for a lovely time. □ We had a lovely time. □ We've had a lovely time.

LUCK
Best of luck (to someone). □ Better luck next time. □ Good luck! □ Lots of luck! □ (The) best of luck (to someone).

LUCKY
lucky for you

LUMP
Like it or lump it!

LUNCH
Let's do lunch (sometime). □ We('ll) have to do lunch sometime.

MAIN

in the main   ☐   That brings me to the (main) point.   ☐   which brings me to the (main) point

MAKE

Come in and make yourself at home.   ☐   Delighted to make your acquaintance.   ☐   Do I make myself (perfectly) clear?   ☐   Don't make me laugh!   ☐   Don't make me no never mind.   ☐   Don't make me say it again!   ☐   Don't make me tell you again!   ☐   (Do you) want to make something of it?   ☐   (Go ahead,) make my day!   ☐   (I'm) delighted to make your acquaintance.   ☐   (It) don't make me no nevermind.   ☐   (It) makes me no difference.   ☐   (It) makes me no nevermind.   ☐   (It) makes no difference to me.   ☐   Make a lap.   ☐   Make it snappy!   ☐   make it (to something)   ☐   Make it two.   ☐   Make mine something.   ☐   Make my day!   ☐   Make no mistake (about it)!   ☐   Makes me no difference.   ☐   Makes me no nevermind.   ☐   Makes no difference to me.   ☐   Makes no nevermind to me.   ☐   Make up your mind.   ☐   Make your mind up.   ☐   Make yourself at home.   ☐   Want to make something of it?   ☐   What makes you think so?   ☐   You make me laugh!   ☐   You want to make something of it?

MANNER

Mind your manners.   ☐   Remember your manners.

MANY

How many times do I have to tell you?

MATTER

Doesn't matter to me.   ☐   (It) (really) doesn't matter to me.   ☐   Really doesn't matter to me.   ☐   What's the matter (with you)?

MAY

be that as it may   ☐   How may I help you?   ☐   may as well   ☐   May I help you?   ☐   May I speak to someone?   ☐   try as I may

MAYBE

I don't mean maybe!   ☐   Maybe some other time.

MEAL

Enjoy your meal.

MEAN

(Do you) know what I mean? ☐ (Do) you mean to say something? ☐ (Do) you mean to tell me something? ☐ I don't mean maybe! ☐ I know (just) what you mean. ☐ Know what I mean? ☐ You can't mean that! ☐ You know what I mean? ☐ You mean to say? ☐ You mean to tell me something?

MEET

Fancy meeting you here! ☐ Glad to meet you. ☐ Haven't we met before? ☐ Have you met someone? ☐ I believe we've met. ☐ I'd like (for) you to meet someone. ☐ I'm glad to meet you. ☐ (I'm) pleased to meet you. ☐ (I'm) (very) glad to meet you. ☐ (It's) nice to meet you. ☐ I would like you to meet someone. ☐ Nice to meet you. ☐ Pleased to meet you. ☐ Till we meet again. ☐ Until we meet again ☐ Very glad to meet you.

MESSAGE

Could I leave a message? ☐ Could I take a message? ☐ (Do you) get the message? ☐ Get the message?

MIDDLING

Fair to middling.

MIGHT

might as well ☐ Might be better. ☐ (Things) might be better.

MILLION

Thanks a million.

MIND

Changed my mind. ☐ Change your mind? ☐ Don't make me no never mind. ☐ Don't mind if I do. ☐ Don't mind me. ☐ Do you mind? ☐ (do you) mind if? ☐ (Do you) mind if I join you? ☐ (Have you) changed your mind? ☐ (I) changed my mind. ☐ (I) don't mind if I do. ☐ if you don't mind ☐ I'll thank you to mind your own business. ☐ (I'm just) minding my own business. ☐ It blows my mind! ☐ keep in mind that ☐ keep (it) in mind that ☐ Make up your mind. ☐ Make your mind up. ☐ mind if ☐ Mind if I join you? ☐ Minding my own business. ☐ Mind your manners. ☐ Mind your own business. ☐ Never mind! ☐ You changed your mind? ☐ You're out of your mind! ☐ You've got to be out of your mind!

MINUTE

Be with you in a minute. □ Hang on (a minute). □ Hold on (a minute)! □ Just a minute. □ (Someone will) be with you in a minute. □ Wait a minute. □ Wait up (a minute)! □ when you get a minute □ With you in a minute.

MISTAKE

Make no mistake (about it)!

MOMENT

Hang on a moment. □ Just a moment. □ One moment, please. □ (Someone will) be with you in a moment.

MONEY

Not for love nor money. □ Not for my money.

MONTH

Haven't seen you in a month of Sundays. □ (I) haven't seen you in a month of Sundays.

MOP

That's the way the mop flops.

MORE

all the more reason for doing something □ Couldn't ask for more. □ (Do) have some more. □ Have some more. □ (I) couldn't ask for more. □ Let's go somewhere where it's (more) quiet. □ more or less □ More power to you! □ more than you('ll ever) know □ Need I say more? □ No more than I have to. □ once more □ one more thing □ one more time □ Say no more. □ That's more like it. □ What more can I do?

MORNING

(Good) morning. □ Morning.

MOUTH

Keep your mouth shut (about someone or something). □ Took the words right out of my mouth. □ Watch your mouth! □ (You) took the words right out of my mouth.

MOUTHFUL

You (really) said a mouthful. □ You said a mouthful!

MOVE

Better get moving. □ Got to get moving. □ Have to be moving along. □ Have to move along. □ (I'd) better get moving. □ (I) have to be moving along. □ (I) have to move along. □ (It's) time to move along. □ (I've) got to get moving. □ Time to move along. □ (You'd) better get moving.

MUCH

Don't see you much around here anymore. □ I've heard so much about you. □ Nothing much. □ Not much. □ Not (too) much. □ So much for that. □ Thank you so much. □ Thank you very much. □ That's (just) too much! □ (We) don't see you much around here anymore. □ You're too much!

MUD

Here's mud in your eye.

MUM

Mum's the word. □ The word is mum.

MUSIC

Stop the music!

MUST

if you must □ I must be off. □ I must say good night. □ (I) really must go. □ Really must go. □ They must have seen you coming. □ We must do this again (sometime).

NAME

I didn't catch the name. □ I didn't catch your name. □ Name your poison. □ What was the name again?

NEED

If there's anything you need, don't hesitate to ask. □ I need it yesterday. □ It's all someone needs. □ (It's) just what you need. □ Just what you need. □ need I remind you of □ need I remind you that □ Need I say more? □ No need (to). □ That's all someone needs. □ That's just what you need. □ (There is) no need (to). □ We need to talk about something.

NEITHER

Neither can I. □ Neither do I.

NERVE

Of all the nerve! □ What (a) nerve!

NEVER

Better late than never. □ Don't make me no never mind. □ I

never! □ (I) never heard of such a thing. □ (I) never thought I'd see you here! □ (It) never hurts to ask. □ (I've) never been better. □ (I've) never felt better. □ Never been better. □ Never felt better. □ Never heard of such a thing. □ Never hurts to ask. □ Never in a thousand years! □ never in my life □ Never mind! □ Never thought I'd see you here! □ (Well,) I never! □ You'll never get away with it.

NEVERMIND

(It) don't make me no nevermind. □ (It) makes me no nevermind. □ Makes me no nevermind. □ Makes no nevermind to me.

NEW

Anything new down your way? □ (So) what else is new? □ That's a new one on me! □ That's news to me. □ What else is new? □ What's new? □ What's new with you?

NEXT

Better luck next time. □ (Good-bye) until next time. □ (I'll) see you next year. □ Next question. □ See you next year. □ Till next time. □ Until next time.

NICE

Had a nice time. □ Have a nice day. □ Have a nice flight. □ Have a nice trip. □ (I) had a nice time. □ (It's been) nice talking to you. □ It's nice to be here. □ It's nice to have you here. □ (It's) nice to meet you. □ (It's) nice to see you. □ Nice going! □ Nice job! □ Nice place you have here. □ Nice talking to you. □ Nice to be here. □ Nice to have you here. □ Nice to meet you. □ Nice to see you. □ Nice weather we're having.

NIGHT

(Good) night. □ I must say good night. □ I was up all night with a sick friend. □ Nighty-night. □ Time to call it a night.

NO

Been up to no good. □ Don't make me no never mind. □ (I have) no problem with that. □ (It) don't make me no nevermind. □ (It) makes me no difference. □ (It) makes me no nevermind. □ (It) makes no difference to me. □ (It's) no trouble. □ (I've) been up to no good. □ Long time no see. □ Make no mistake (about it)! □ Makes me no difference. □ Makes me no nevermind. □ Makes no difference to me. □ Makes no nevermind to me. □ No can do. □ No chance. □ no doubt □ No doubt about it. □ No fair! □ No kidding! □ No lie? □ No more than I have to. □ No need (to). □ No, no, a thousand times no! □ No problem. □ No problem with that. □ No siree(, Bob)! □ No skin off my nose. □ No skin off my teeth. □ No sweat. □ No, thanks. □ no thanks to you □ No, thank you. □ No trouble. □ No way! □ No way, José! □ No way to tell. □ Say no more. □ Thanks, but no thanks. □ (That causes) no problem. □ (That's) no skin off my nose. □ (There is) no chance. □ (There is) no doubt about it. □ (There is) no need (to). □ (There's) no way to tell. □ under no circumstances

NOGGIN
Use your noggin!

NONE
Don't bother me none. □ (It) don't bother me none. □ (It's) none of your business! □ None of your business!

NOODLE
Use your noodle!

NOR
Not for love nor money.

NORMAL
under normal circumstances

NOSE
Get your nose out of my business. □ Keep your nose out of my business. □ No skin off my nose. □ (That's) no skin off my nose.

NOTE
Drop me a note.

NOTHING
Better than nothing. □ (I have) nothing to complain about. □ (It's) better than nothing. □ Nothing. □ Nothing doing! □ Nothing for me, thanks. □ Nothing much. □ Nothing to

complain about. □ Nothing to it! □ (There's) nothing to it!
□ Think nothing of it. □ You ain't seen nothing yet!

NOW

Could I take your order (now)? □ Good-bye for now. □ Have
to go now. □ (I) have to go now. □ Not right now, thanks. □
now then □ Now what? □ Now you're cooking (with gas)! □
Now you're talking! □ That's enough for now. □ What now?

NUMBER

What number are you calling?

OF

Any friend of someone('s) (is a friend of mine). □ Been keeping
out of trouble. □ Best of luck (to someone). □ by the skin of
someone's teeth □ Don't breathe a word of this to anyone. □
(Do you) want to make something of it? □ Enough (of this) foolishness! □ first of all □ from my point of view □ Get out of
here! □ Get out of my face! □ Get your nose out of my business. □ Haven't seen you in a month of Sundays. □ (Have
you) been keeping out of trouble? □ Having the time of my life.
□ Hell's bells (and buckets of blood)! □ (I) haven't seen you in
a month of Sundays. □ (I'm) having the time of my life. □
I'm out of here. □ (I) never heard of such a thing. □ in the
interest of saving time □ in view of □ I spoke out of turn. □
(It's) none of your business! □ (It's) out of the question. □
(I've) been keeping out of trouble. □ I've had enough of this!
□ (I) won't breathe a word (of it). □ (just) taking care of busi-
ness □ Keeping out of trouble. □ Keep out of my way. □
Keep out of this! □ Keep your nose out of my business. □
Kind of. □ Let's get out of here. □ lose one's train of thought
□ Lots of luck! □ need I remind you of □ Never heard of
such a thing. □ None of your business! □ Of all the nerve!
□ of course □ off the top of one's head □ Out of the ques-
tion. □ (right) off the top of one's head □ Sort of. □ Speak
of the devil. □ Stay out of my way. □ Stay out of this! □
Take care (of yourself). □ taking care of business □ That's
about the size of it. □ (That's) enough (of this) foolishness! □
(The) best of luck (to someone). □ The shame of it (all)! □
Think nothing of it. □ Took the words right out of my mouth.
□ to the best of my knowledge □ Want to make something of

it? □ What do you think of that? □ What do you think of this weather? □ What of it? □ Won't breathe a word (of it). □ You been keeping out of trouble? □ You don't know the half of it. □ You'll be the death of me (yet). □ You'll get the hang of it. □ You're out of your mind! □ (You) took the words right out of my mouth. □ You've got to be out of your mind! □ You want to make something of it?

OFF

Better be off. □ Come in and take a load off your feet. □ Come off it! □ Get off my back! □ Get off my tail! □ Got to be shoving off. □ Got to shove off. □ Got to take off. □ Have to shove off. □ (I'd) better be off. □ (I) have to push off. □ (I) have to shove off. □ I'll have to beg off. □ I'm off. □ I must be off. □ (It's) time to push off. □ (It's) time to shove off. □ (I've) got to be shoving off. □ (I've) got to shove off. □ (I've) got to take off. □ Knock it off! □ No skin off my nose. □ No skin off my teeth. □ off the top of one's head □ (right) off the top of one's head □ (That's) no skin off my nose. □ Time to push off. □ Time to shove off. □ What's coming off?

OFFICE

Could I see you in my office?

OH

boy oh boy □ Oh, boy. □ Oh, sure (someone or something will)! □ Oh, yeah?

OKAY

(Are you) doing okay? □ (Are you) feeling okay? □ been okay □ doing okay □ Everything okay? □ Feeling okay. □ (Have you) been okay? □ (I'm) doing okay. □ (I'm) feeling okay. □ (Is) everything okay? □ (I've) been okay. □ Okay. □ Okay by me. □ Okay with me. □ (That's) okay by me. □ (That's) okay with me. □ You been okay? □ You doing okay?

ON

Anything going on? □ Better get on my horse. □ come on □ Come (on) in. □ Don't stand on ceremony. □ Get back to me (on this). □ Go on. □ Hang on (a minute). □ Hang on a moment. ☐ Hang on a second. ☐ Hold on (a minute)! ☐ How are you getting on? ☐ Hurry on! ☐ (I'd) better get on my horse. ☐ I'll get back to you (on that). ☐ I'll get right on it. ☐ (Is) anything going on? ☐ It's on me. ☐ (I) wouldn't bet on it. ☐ (I) wouldn't count on it. ☐ Keep (on) trying. ☐ Keep your shirt on! ☐ Let me get back to you (on that). ☐ Let's shake on it. ☐ Not on your life! ☐ not to put too fine a point on it ☐ on balance ☐ on the contrary ☐ on the other hand ☐ Shame on you! ☐ Soup's on! ☐ That's a new one on me! ☐ This one's on me. ☐ Whatever turns you on. ☐ What's going on (around here)? ☐ What's on tap for today? ☐ Who's on the line? ☐ Who's on the phone? ☐ Wouldn't bet on it. ☐ Wouldn't count on it.

ONCE

if I've told you once, I've told you a thousand times ☐ once and for all ☐ once more

ONE

Don't spend it all in one place. ☐ Have a good one. ☐ I owe you one. ☐ lose one's train of thought ☐ off the top of one's head ☐ one final thing ☐ one final word ☐ One moment, please. ☐ one more thing ☐ one more time ☐ one way or another ☐ (right) off the top of one's head ☐ talk through one's hat ☐ Tell me another (one)! ☐ That's a new one on me! ☐ This one's on me. ☐ (Would you) care for another (one)?

ONLY

God only knows! ☐ I'm only looking.

ONTO

You'll get onto it.

OPINION

I'll thank you to keep your opinions to yourself. ☐ in my humble opinion ☐ in my opinion ☐ Keep your opinions to yourself!

OR

believe it or not ☐ Cash or credit (card)? ☐ Don't let someone or something get you down. ☐ I'm (really) fed up (with someone or something). ☐ I've had it up to here (with someone or something). ☐ Keep your mouth shut (about someone or something). ☐ Like it or lump it! ☐ more or less ☐ Oh, sure (someone or something will)! ☐ one way or another ☐ or what? ☐ or words to that effect ☐ (Someone or something is) supposed to. ☐ Take it or leave it. ☐ What's with someone or something? ☐ Your place or mine?

ORDER

(Are you) ready to order? ☐ Could I take your order (now)? ☐ Ready to order?

OTHER

Catch me some other time. ☐ (I'll) try to catch you some other time. ☐ in other words ☐ Maybe some other time. ☐ on the other hand ☐ Try to catch you some other time. ☐ We'll try again some other time.

OUT

Been keeping out of trouble. ☐ Butt out! ☐ Cut it out! ☐ Do I have to spell it out (for you)? ☐ Everything will work out (all right). ☐ Everything will work out for the best. ☐ For crying out loud! ☐ Get out of here! ☐ Get out of my face! ☐ Get the lead out! ☐ Get your nose out of my business. ☐ (Have you) been keeping out of trouble? ☐ I don't want to wear out my welcome. ☐ I have to wash a few things out. ☐ (I'm) (just) thinking out loud. ☐ I'm out of here. ☐ I spoke out of turn. ☐ (It's) out of the question. ☐ (I've) been keeping out of trouble. ☐ (just) thinking out loud. ☐ Keeping out of trouble. ☐ Keep out of my way. ☐ Keep out of this! ☐ Keep your nose out of my business. ☐ Let's get out of here. ☐ Look out! ☐ Out of the question. ☐ Out, please. ☐ Shake the lead out! ☐ Stay out of my way. ☐ Stay out of this! ☐ Things will work out (all right). ☐ Things will work out for the best. ☐ thinking out loud ☐ Time (out)! ☐ Took the words right out of my mouth. ☐ Watch out! ☐ You been keeping out of trouble? ☐ You're out of your mind! ☐ (You) took the words right out of my mouth. ☐ You've got to be out of your mind!

OUTSIDE

(Do) you want to step outside? ☐ You want to step outside?

OVER

Drop over sometime. □ I can't get over something! □ Over my dead body! □ You could have knocked me over with a feather.

OWE

I owe you one.

OWN

I'll thank you to mind your own business. □ (I'm just) minding my own business. □ Minding my own business. □ Mind your own business.

PAINT

Do I have to paint (you) a picture?

PARDON

Begging your pardon, but □ Beg pardon. □ Beg your pardon. □ Beg your pardon, but □ (I) beg your pardon. □ (I) beg your pardon, but □ Pardon (me). □ Pardon me for living!

PAY

There will be hell to pay.

PEOPLE

Some people (just) don't know when to give up. □ Some people (just) don't know when to quit.

PERFECTLY

Do I make myself (perfectly) clear?

PERSPECTIVE

from my perspective

PETE

For Pete('s) sake(s)!

PHONE

Who's on the phone?

PICTURE

Do I have to paint (you) a picture? □ (Do you) get the picture? □ Get the picture?

PITY

For pity('s) sake(s)! □ What a pity!

PLACE

Don't spend it all in one place. ☐ in the first place ☐ Is there some place I can wash up? ☐ Nice place you have here. ☐ Your place or mine?

PLEASE

Again(, please). ☐ Can you excuse us, please? ☐ Check, please. ☐ Coming through(, please). ☐ Could I get by, please? ☐ Could you excuse us, please? ☐ Excuse, please. ☐ Hold, please. ☐ Hold the line(, please). ☐ Hold the wire(, please). ☐ I'd like to speak to someone, please. ☐ If you don't see what you want, please ask (for it). ☐ if you please ☐ if you would(, please) ☐ I'm easy (to please). ☐ (I'm) pleased to meet you. ☐ One moment, please. ☐ Out, please. ☐ Please. ☐ Pleased to meet you. ☐ Please hold. ☐ 'Scuse, please. ☐ We aim to please. ☐ Who's calling(, please)? ☐ Will you excuse us, please? ☐ Would you excuse us, please? ☐ Would you please?

PLEASURE

Don't believe I've had the pleasure. ☐ (I) don't believe I've had the pleasure. ☐ My pleasure. ☐ With pleasure.

PLUG

(I'm) (just) plugging along. ☐ Just plugging along. ☐ Plugging along.

POINT

from my point of view ☐ not to put too fine a point on it ☐ That brings me to the (main) point. ☐ which brings me to the (main) point

POISON

Name your poison.

POWDER

Could I use your powder room? ☐ Where is your powder room?

POWER

More power to you!

PRESENT

at the present time

PRESS

Stop the presses!

PROBLEM

(I have) no problem with that. □ No problem. □ No problem with that. □ (That causes) no problem. □ What's the problem?

PROMISE

I promise you!

PROVE

What does that prove?

PURPOSE

for all intents and purposes

PUSH

Don't push (me)! □ (I) have to push off. □ (It's) time to push along. □ (It's) time to push off. □ Time to push along. □ Time to push off.

PUT

I'll put a stop to that. □ not to put too fine a point on it □ put another way □ Put 'er there. □ Put it anywhere. □ Put it there. □ to put it another way

QUESTION

(It's) out of the question. □ Next question. □ Out of the question.

QUIET

Be quiet! □ Better keep quiet about it. □ Keep quiet. □ Keep quiet about it. □ Let's go somewhere where it's (more) quiet. □ (Someone had) better keep quiet about it.

QUIT

Don't quit trying. □ Some people (just) don't know when to quit.

QUITE

Having quite a time. □ I didn't (quite) catch that (last) remark. □ I'm having quite a time □ It doesn't quite suit me. □ quite frankly □ speaking (quite) candidly □ (speaking) (quite) frankly □ This doesn't quite suit me.

READ

Do you read me? □ (I) read you loud and clear. □ Read you loud and clear.

READY

Anytime you are ready. □ (Are you) ready for this? □ (Are you) ready to order? □ Ready for this? □ Ready to order? □ when I'm good and ready

REAL

(I'll) see you (real) soon. □ See you (real) soon.

REALLY

I'm (really) fed up (with someone or something). □ (I) really must go. □ (It) (really) doesn't matter to me. □ Really. □ Really doesn't matter to me. □ Really must go. □ That (really) burns me (up)! □ You (really) said a mouthful.

REASON

all the more reason for doing something

RECOGNIZE

How will I recognize you?

REMARK

I didn't (quite) catch that (last) remark.

REMEMBER

Remember me to someone. □ Remember to write. □ Remember your manners.

REMIND

need I remind you of □ need I remind you that

REST

Give it a rest! □ Give me a rest! □ The rest is history. □ Where is the rest room?

RIDDANCE

good-bye and good riddance

RIDE

Thanks for the ride. □ All right. □ All right already! □ Am I right? □ Be right there. □ Be right with you. □ Come right in. □ Everything's going to be all right. □ Everything will work out (all right). □ (I'll) be right there. □ (I'll) be right with you. □ I'll get right on it. □ Not right now, thanks. □ Right. □ Right away. □ (right) off the top of one's head □ Things will work out (all right). □ Took the words right out of my mouth. □ (You) took the words right out of my mouth.

RIGHTLY

Can't rightly say. □ (I) can't rightly say.

RING

Give me a ring.

ROAD

Better hit the road. □ Got to hit the road. □ (I'd) better hit the road. □ (It's) time to hit the road. □ (I've) got to hit the road. □ Time to hit the road.

ROOM

Could I use your powder room? □ Where is the rest room? □ Where is your powder room?

RUN

Got to run. □ Hate to eat and run. □ Have to run along. □ (I) hate to eat and run. □ (I) have to run along. □ (It's) time to run. □ (I've) got to run. □ Run it by (me) again. □ Run that by (me) again. □ Time to run.

RUSH

Don't rush me!

SAFE

Have a safe journey. □ Have a safe trip.

SAFELY

Drive safely.

SAKE

For Pete('s) sake(s)! □ For pity('s) sake(s)!

SALUTATION

Greetings and salutations!

SAME

by the same token □ I'll have the same. □ Same to you. □ The same for me. □ (The) same to you.

SAVE

in the interest of saving time

SAY

Anything you say. □ as I was saying □ as you say □ better left unsaid □ Can't rightly say. □ Can't say (as) I do. □ Can't say as I have. □ Can't say for sure. □ Can't say's I do. □ Can't say that I do. □ Can't say that I have. □ Don't make me say it again! □ Don't say it! □ (Do you) know what I'm saying? □ (Do) you mean to say something? □ (I) can't rightly say. □ (I) can't say (as) I do. □ (I) can't say for sure. □ (I) can't say's I do. □ (I) can't say that I do. □ (I) can't say that I have. □ I hear what you're saying. □ I must say good night. □ I wish I'd said that. □ just let me say □ Know what I'm saying? □ let me (just) say □ like I was saying □ like you say □ Need I say more? □ say □ Say cheese! □ Say hello to someone (for me). □ Say no more. □ Says me! □ Says who? □ Says you! □ Say what? □ Say when. □ Smile when you say that. □ That's easy for you to say. □ That's what I say. □ Well said. □ What can I say? □ What do you say? □ What do you want me to say? □ What say? □ what would you say if? □ You can say that again! □ You don't say. □ You know (what I'm saying)? □ You know what I'm saying? □ You mean to say? □ You (really) said a mouthful. □ You said a mouthful! □ You said it!

SCAM

What's the scam?

SCHOOL

How do you like school?

SCOOP

What's the scoop?

SCOTT

Great Scott!

SEAL

My lips are sealed.

SEAT

(Is) this (seat) taken?

SECOND

Don't give it a (second) thought. □ Hang on a second. □ Just a second. □ Wait a sec(ond).

SECRET

Could you keep a secret?

SEE

Am I glad to see you! ☐ as I see it ☐ Be seeing you. ☐ Come back and see us. ☐ Could I see you again? ☐ Could I see you in my office? ☐ Don't see you much around here anymore. ☐ (Don't you) see? ☐ Good to see you (again). ☐ Haven't I seen you somewhere before? ☐ Haven't seen you in a long time. ☐ Haven't seen you in a month of Sundays. ☐ Hope to see you again (sometime). ☐ If you don't see what you want, please ask (for it). ☐ (I) haven't seen you in a long time. ☐ (I) haven't seen you in a month of Sundays. ☐ (I) hope to see you again (sometime). ☐ (I'll) be seeing you. ☐ (I'll) see you in a little while. ☐ I'll see you later. ☐ (I'll) see you next year. ☐ (I'll) see you (real) soon. ☐ (I'll) see you then. ☐ (I'll) see you tomorrow. ☐ I'll try to see you later. ☐ (I) never thought I'd see you here! ☐ (It's) good to see you (again). ☐ (It's) nice to see you. ☐ (I've) seen better. ☐ (I've) seen worse. ☐ Just (you) wait (and see)! ☐ Long time no see. ☐ Never thought I'd see you here! ☐ Nice to see you. ☐ Not if I see you first. ☐ Not if I see you sooner. ☐ See? ☐ See if I care! ☐ Seen better. ☐ Seen worse. ☐ See ya! ☐ See ya, bye-bye. ☐ See you. ☐ See you around. ☐ See you in a little while. ☐ (See you) later. ☐ See you later, alligator. ☐ See you next year. ☐ See you (real) soon. ☐ See you soon. ☐ See you then. ☐ See you tomorrow. ☐ the way I see it ☐ They must have seen you coming. ☐ (We) don't see you much around here anymore. ☐ Will I see you again? ☐ You ain't seen nothing yet! ☐ You (just) wait (and see)!

SERVE

Dinner is served. ☐ How can I serve you?

SHAKE

Let's shake on it. ☐ Shake it (up)! ☐ Shake the lead out!

SHAME

For shame! ☐ Shame on you! ☐ The shame of it (all)! ☐ What a shame!

SHIP

Don't give up the ship!

SHIRT
Keep your shirt on!

SHOOT
Sure as shooting!

SHOT
Not by a long shot.

SHOULD
How should I know? □ It's time we should be going.

SHOVE
Got to be shoving off. □ Got to shove off. □ Have to shove off. □ (I) have to shove off. □ (It's) time to shove off. □ (I've) got to be shoving off. □ (I've) got to shove off. □ Time to shove off.

SHOW
(It) just goes to show (you) (something). □ Just goes to show (you).

SHUT
Keep your mouth shut (about someone or something). □ Shut up! □ Shut up about it. □ Shut your face!

SICK
I was up all night with a sick friend.

SIREE
No siree(, Bob)! □ Yes siree(, Bob)!

SIT
Come in and sit a spell. □ Come in and sit down. □ Do sit down.

SIZE
That's about the size of it.

SKIN
by the skin of someone's teeth □ Give me (some) skin! □ No

skin off my nose. □ No skin off my teeth. □ Skin me! □
Slip me some skin! □ (That's) no skin off my nose.

SLEEP

Got to go home and get my beauty sleep. □ (I've) got to go
home and get my beauty sleep.

SLIP

Slip me five! □ Slip me some skin!

SMILE

Keep smiling. □ Smile when you say that.

SNAP

Snap it up! □ Snap to it!

SNAPPY

Make it snappy!

SO

Afraid so. □ (Are you) leaving so soon? □ Don't believe so.
□ Don't stay away so long. □ Don't think so. □ 'Fraid so.
□ Hope so. □ I believe so. □ (I) don't believe so. □ (I)
don't think so. □ I expect (so). □ I guess (so). □ (I) hope so.
□ (I'm) afraid so. □ I 'spose (so) □ Is that so? □ I suppose
(so). □ I suspect (so) □ I think so. □ I've heard so much
about you. □ Leaving so soon? □ so □ So? □ So do I.
□ So much for that. □ So (what)? □ (So) what else is new?
□ 'Spose so. □ Thank you so much. □ What makes you
think so? □ You leaving so soon?

SOCK

Stuff a sock in it!

SOME

Catch me some other time. □ (Do) have some more. □ Give
me (some) skin! □ Have some more. □ (I'll) try to catch you
some other time. □ Is there some place I can wash up? □
Maybe some other time. □ Slip me some skin! □ Some people (just) don't know when to give up. □ Some people (just)
don't know when to quit. □ Try to catch you some other time.
□ We'll try again some other time.

SOMETIME

Drop by for a drink (sometime). □ Drop by sometime. □

Drop in sometime. □ Drop over sometime. □ Hope to see you again (sometime). □ (I) hope to see you again (sometime). □ Let's do lunch (sometime). □ Let's do this again (sometime). □ Let's get together (sometime). □ We('ll) have to do lunch sometime. □ We must do this again (sometime).

SOMEWHERE

Don't I know you from somewhere? □ Haven't I seen you somewhere before? □ Let's go somewhere where it's (more) quiet.

SOON

(Are you) leaving so soon? □ Don't speak too soon. □ (I'll) see you (real) soon. □ (I'll) talk to you soon. □ I spoke too soon. □ Leaving so soon? □ Not if I see you sooner. □ See you (real) soon. □ See you soon. □ Sooner than you think. □ Talk to you soon. □ The sooner the better. □ Yesterday wouldn't be too soon. □ You leaving so soon?

SORRY

(Are you) sorry you asked? □ (I'm) sorry. □ (I'm) sorry to hear that. □ (I'm) sorry you asked (that). □ Sorry. □ Sorry (that) I asked. □ Sorry to hear that. □ Sorry you asked? □ You'll be sorry you asked.

SOUL

Don't tell a soul. □ (I) won't tell a soul. □ Won't tell a soul.

SOUND

I don't want to sound like a busybody, but

SPEAK

as we speak □ Can I speak to someone? □ Could I speak to someone? □ Don't speak too soon. □ frankly speaking □ I'd like to speak to someone, please. □ I spoke out of turn. □ I spoke too soon. □ May I speak to someone? □ Speaking. □ speaking (quite) candidly □ (speaking) (quite) frankly □ Speak of the devil. □ Speak up. □ Who do you want to speak to? □ Who do you wish to speak to? □ With whom do you wish to speak?

SPEECHLESS

I'm speechless.

SPELL

Come in and sit a spell. □ Do I have to spell it out (for you)?

SPEND

Don't spend it all in one place.

SPLIT

Got to split. ☐ (It's) time to split. ☐ (I've) got to split. ☐ Time to split.

STAND

Don't stand on ceremony. ☐ from where I stand

STAY

Come back when you can stay longer. ☐ Don't stay away so long. ☐ Stay out of my way. ☐ Stay out of this!

STEP

(Do) you want to step outside? ☐ Step aside. ☐ You want to step outside?

STICK

Stick with it.

STILL

Better keep still about it. ☐ Keep still. ☐ Keep still about it. ☐ (Someone had) better keep still about it.

STOP

Glad you could stop by. ☐ I'll put a stop to that. ☐ (I'm) glad you could stop by. ☐ Stop the music! ☐ Stop the presses! ☐ (We're) glad you could stop by.

STRAW

That's the last straw!

STRIKE

it strikes me that

STUFF

Cut the funny stuff! ☐ Stuff a sock in it! ☐ That's the stuff!

STUMP

Got me stumped. ☐ (You've) got me stumped.

SUBJECT
Drop the subject!

SUCH
as such ☐ (I) never heard of such a thing. ☐ Never heard of such a thing.

SUIT
It doesn't quite suit me. ☐ (It) suits me (fine). ☐ Suits me (fine). ☐ Suit yourself. ☐ This doesn't quite suit me.

SUNDAY
Haven't seen you in a month of Sundays. ☐ (I) haven't seen you in a month of Sundays.

SUPPOSE
I suppose ☐ I suppose not. ☐ I suppose (so). ☐ (It's) not supposed to. ☐ Not supposed to. ☐ (Someone or something is) supposed to. ☐ (Someone's) not supposed to. ☐ suppose ☐ Supposed to. ☐ Suppose I do? ☐ Suppose I don't? ☐ supposing ☐ Supposing I do? ☐ Supposing I don't?

SURE
Can't say for sure. ☐ Charmed(, I'm sure). ☐ Don't be too sure. ☐ For sure. ☐ (I) can't say for sure. ☐ Likewise(, I'm sure). ☐ Oh, sure (someone or something will)! ☐ Sure. ☐ Sure as shooting! ☐ Sure thing. ☐ What do you know for sure?

SURPRISE
I'm not surprised.

SUSPECT
I suspect ☐ I suspect not ☐ I suspect (so)

SWEAT
Don't sweat it! ☐ No sweat.

SWEET
You bet your (sweet) bippy. ☐ You bet your (sweet) life!

SYSTEM
All systems are go.

TAIL
Get off my tail!

TAKE

Can't take it with you. □ Come in and take a load off your feet. □ Could I take a message? □ Could I take your order (now)? □ Got to take off. □ (Is) this (seat) taken? □ (I've) got to take off. □ (just) taking care of business □ Take care (of yourself). □ Take it easy. □ Take it or leave it. □ Take my word for it. □ taking care of business □ That takes the cake! □ This taken? □ Took the words right out of my mouth. □ (You) can't take it with you. □ (You) took the words right out of my mouth.

TALK

Good talking to you. □ Good to talk to you. □ (I'll) talk to you soon. □ (It's been) good talking to you. □ (It's been) good to talk to you. □ (It's been) nice talking to you. □ Let's talk (about it). □ Look who's talking! □ Nice talking to you. □ Now you're talking! □ talk through one's hat □ Talk to you soon. □ We need to talk about something. □ We were just talking about you. □ Who do you think you're talking to? □ Who do you want (to talk to)? □ Who do you wish to talk to?

TAP

What's on tap for today?

TEACH

That'll teach someone!

TEAR

That tears it!

TELL

Could I tell someone who's calling? □ Don't make me tell you again! □ Don't tell a soul. □ Don't tell me what to do! □ Do tell. □ (Do) you mean to tell me something? □ How many times do I have to tell you? □ if I've told you once, I've told you a thousand times □ (I) won't tell a soul. □ No way to tell. □ Tell me another (one)! □ (There's) no way to tell. □ What can I tell you? □ Won't tell a soul. □ You mean to tell me something? □ You're telling me!

THAN

Better late than never. □ Better than nothing. □ (It's) better than nothing. ☐ more than you('ll ever) know ☐ No more than I have to. ☐ Sooner than you think.

THANK

Can't thank you enough. ☐ (I) can't thank you enough. ☐ I'll thank you to keep your opinions to yourself. ☐ I'll thank you to mind your own business. ☐ No, thanks. ☐ no thanks to you ☐ No, thank you. ☐ Nothing for me, thanks. ☐ Not right now, thanks. ☐ Thank goodness! ☐ Thank heavens! ☐ Thanks. ☐ Thanks (a lot). ☐ Thanks a million. ☐ Thanks awfully. ☐ Thanks, but no thanks. ☐ Thanks for having me. ☐ Thanks for the lift. ☐ Thanks for the ride. ☐ Thanks loads. ☐ Thank you. ☐ Thank you a lot. ☐ Thank you for a lovely evening. ☐ Thank you for a lovely time. ☐ Thank you for calling. ☐ Thank you for inviting me. ☐ Thank you for inviting us. ☐ Thank you so much. ☐ Thank you very much.

THEN

(Good-bye) until then. ☐ (I'll) see you then. ☐ now then ☐ See you then. ☐ then ☐ Till then. ☐ Until then.

THERE

Be right there. ☐ Can't get there from here. ☐ Hang in there. ☐ If there's anything you need, don't hesitate to ask. ☐ (I'll) be right there. ☐ Is someone there? ☐ Is there anything else? ☐ Is there some place I can wash up? ☐ I've been there. ☐ Keep in there! ☐ Put 'er there. ☐ Put it there. ☐ (There is) no chance. ☐ (There is) no doubt about it. ☐ (There is) no need (to). ☐ (There's) nothing to it! ☐ (There's) no way to tell. ☐ There will be hell to pay. ☐ There you are. ☐ There you go! ☐ What's (there) to know? ☐ Who's there? ☐ (Will there be) anything else? ☐ (You) can't get there from here.

THING

all things considered ☐ (Are) things getting you down? ☐ Better things to do. ☐ Don't worry about a thing. ☐ Got better things to do. ☐ How're things going? ☐ How're things (with you)? ☐ How's every little thing? ☐ I have to wash a few things out. ☐ (I) never heard of such a thing. ☐ (I've) better things to do. ☐ (I've) (got) better things to do. ☐ Never heard of such a thing. ☐ one final thing ☐ one more thing ☐ Sure thing. □ (Things) could be better. □ (Things) could be worse. □ Things getting you down? □ Things haven't been easy. □ (Things) might be better. □ Things will work out (all right). □ Things will work out for the best.

THINK

See also *THOUGHT.*

Don't even think about (doing) it. □ Don't even think about it (happening). □ Don't think so. □ How dumb do you think I am? □ (I) don't think so. □ (I'm) (just) thinking out loud. □ I think not. □ I think so. □ (just) thinking out loud. □ Sooner than you think. □ thinking out loud □ Think nothing of it. □ What do you think? □ What do you think about that? □ What do you think of that? □ What do you think of this weather? □ What do you think you are doing here? □ What makes you think so? □ Who do you think you are? □ Who do you think you're kidding? □ Who do you think you're talking to? □ You've got another think coming.

THOUGHT

Don't give it another thought. □ Don't give it a (second) thought. □ (I) never thought I'd see you here! □ lose one's train of thought □ Never thought I'd see you here! □ who could have thought? □ who would have thought?

THOUSAND

if I've told you once, I've told you a thousand times □ Never in a thousand years! □ No, no, a thousand times no! □ Not in a thousand years!

THROUGH

Coming through(, please). □ Do we have to go through all that again? □ Let's not go through all that again. □ talk through one's hat

TICKET

That's the ticket!

TILL

Till later. □ Till next time. □ Till then. □ Till we meet again.

TIME

at the present time □ Better luck next time. □ Catch me some other time. □ Don't waste my time. □ Don't waste your time. □ (Good-bye) until next time. □ Had a nice time. □ Have a good time. □ Haven't seen you in a long time. □ Having a wonderful time; wish you were here. □ Having quite a time. □ Having the time of my life. □ How many times do I have to tell you? □ How time flies. □ I don't have time to breathe. □ I don't have time to catch my breath. □ if I've told you once, I've told you a thousand times □ I had a lovely time. □ (I) had a nice time. □ (I) haven't seen you in a long time. □ (I'll) try to catch you some other time. □ (I'm) having a wonderful time; wish you were here. □ I'm having quite a time □ (I'm) having the time of my life. □ in due time □ in the interest of saving time □ (It's) time for a change. □ (It's) time to go. □ (It's) time to hit the road. □ (It's) time to move along. □ (It's) time to push along. □ (It's) time to push off. □ (It's) time to run. □ (It's) time to shove off. □ (It's) time to split. □ It's time we should be going. □ I've had a lovely time. □ Long time no see. □ Maybe some other time. □ (My,) how time flies. □ No, no, a thousand times no! □ one more time □ Thank you for a lovely time. □ Till next time. □ Time for a change. □ Time (out)! □ Times are changing. □ Time to call it a day. □ Time to call it a night. □ Time to go. □ Time to hit the road. □ Time to move along. □ Time to push along. □ Time to push off. □ Time to run. □ Time to shove off. □ Time to split. □ Try to catch you some other time. □ Until next time. □ We had a lovely time. □ We'll try again some other time. □ We've had a lovely time. □ You're (just) wasting my time.

TODAY

What's on tap for today?

TOGETHER

Let's get together (sometime).

TOKEN

by the same token

TOMORROW

(I'll) see you tomorrow. □ See you tomorrow.

TONGUE

Bite your tongue! ☐ Hold your tongue! ☐ Watch your tongue!

TOO

Can too. ☐ Don't be gone (too) long. ☐ Don't be too sure. ☐ Don't give up too eas(il)y! ☐ Don't speak too soon. ☐ Don't work too hard. ☐ (I) can too. ☐ I spoke too soon. ☐ Not (too) much. ☐ not to put too fine a point on it ☐ That's (just) too much! ☐ (That's) too bad. ☐ Too bad. ☐ Yesterday wouldn't be too soon. ☐ You (always) give up too eas(il)y. ☐ You're too much! ☐ You, too.

TOOT

You're dern tootin'!

TOOTH

by the skin of someone's teeth ☐ No skin off my teeth.

TOP

Can't top that. ☐ (I) can't top that. ☐ off the top of one's head ☐ (right) off the top of one's head ☐ (You) can't top that.

TOUCH

Keep in touch.

TOWN

I'll look you up when I'm in town. ☐ Look me up when you're in town.

TRAIN

lose one's train of thought

TREAT

How's the world (been) treating you?

TREE

Go climb a tree!

TRICK

How's tricks?

TRIP

Have a good trip. ☐ Have a nice trip. ☐ Have a safe trip.

TROUBLE

Been keeping out of trouble. ☐ (Have you) been keeping out of trouble? ☐ It isn't worth the trouble. ☐ (It's) no trouble. ☐ (I've) been keeping out of trouble. ☐ Keeping out of trouble. ☐ No trouble. ☐ You been keeping out of trouble?

TRY

Don't quit trying. ☐ (I'll) try to catch you later. ☐ (I'll) try to catch you some other time. ☐ I'll try to see you later. ☐ Keep (on) trying. ☐ Lord knows I've tried. ☐ try as I may ☐ Try to catch you later. ☐ Try to catch you some other time. ☐ We'll try again some other time. ☐ You wouldn't be trying to kid me, would you?

TURN

I spoke out of turn. ☐ Whatever turns you on.

TWO

Make it two.

UNDER

Been under the weather. ☐ (I've) been under the weather. ☐ not under any circumstances ☐ under no circumstances ☐ under normal circumstances

UNDERSTAND

I can't understand (it). ☐ I don't understand (it).

UNTIL

(Good-bye) until next time. ☐ (Good-bye) until then. ☐ Until later. ☐ Until next time. ☐ Until then. ☐ Until we meet again.

UP

Been up to no good. ☐ Bottoms up. ☐ Break it up! ☐ Cheer up! ☐ Dig up! ☐ Don't get up. ☐ Don't give up! ☐ Don't give up the ship! ☐ Don't give up too eas(il)y! ☐ Don't give up without a fight. ☐ Give it up! ☐ Heads up! ☐ Hurry up!

☐ I'll look you up when I'm in town. ☐ I'm (really) fed up (with someone or something). ☐ Is there some place I can wash up? ☐ (I've) been up to no good. ☐ I've had it up to here (with someone or something). ☐ I was up all night with a sick friend. ☐ I won't give up without a fight. ☐ Keep it up! ☐ Keep up the good work. ☐ Keep your chin up. ☐ Look me up when you're in town. ☐ Make up your mind. ☐ Make your mind up. ☐ Pull up a chair. ☐ Shake it (up)! ☐ Shut up! ☐ Shut up about it. ☐ Snap it up! ☐ Some people (just) don't know when to give up. ☐ Speak up. ☐ That (really) burns me (up)! ☐ Wait up (a minute)! ☐ What (have) you been up to? ☐ What's up? ☐ What you been up to? ☐ Where can I wash up? ☐ You (always) give up too eas(il)y. ☐ Zip it up! ☐ Zip (up) your lip!

UPROAR
Don't get your bowels in an uproar!

UPSET
I don't want to upset you, but

USE
Could I use your powder room? ☐ Use your head! ☐ Use your noggin! ☐ Use your noodle!

VERY
(I'm) (very) glad to meet you. ☐ Thank you very much. ☐ Very glad to meet you. ☐ Very good.

VIEW
from my point of view ☐ in my view ☐ in view of

VOICE
Good to hear your voice. ☐ (It's) good to hear your voice.

WAIT
Just wait! ☐ Just (you) wait (and see)! ☐ Wait a minute. ☐ Wait a sec(ond). ☐ Wait up (a minute)! ☐ You (just) wait (and see)! ☐ You wait!

WANT
(Do you) want to know something? ☐ (Do you) want to make something of it? ☐ (Do) you want to step outside? ☐ I don't want to alarm you, but ☐ I don't want to sound like a busybody, but ☐ I don't want to upset you, but ☐ I don't want to wear

out my welcome. ☐ If you don't see what you want, please ask (for it). ☐ (I) just want(ed) to ☐ just want(ed) to ☐ Want to know something? ☐ Want to make something of it? ☐ What do you want me to say? ☐ Who do you want to speak to? ☐ Who do you want (to talk to)? ☐ You want to know something? ☐ You want to make something of it? ☐ You want to step outside?

WASH

I have to wash a few things out. ☐ Is there some place I can wash up? ☐ Where can I wash up?

WASTE

Don't waste my time. ☐ Don't waste your breath. ☐ Don't waste your time. ☐ You're (just) wasting my time.

WATCH

Just watch! ☐ Watch! ☐ Watch it! ☐ Watch out! ☐ Watch your mouth! ☐ Watch your tongue! ☐ (You) (just) watch! ☐ You watch!

WAY

Anything new down your way? ☐ (Are you) going my way? ☐ by the way ☐ Clear the way! ☐ Going my way? ☐ Have it your way. ☐ Keep out of my way. ☐ No way! ☐ No way, José! ☐ No way to tell. ☐ one way or another ☐ put another way ☐ Stay out of my way. ☐ That ain't the way I heard it. ☐ That's the way it goes. ☐ That's the way the ball bounces. ☐ That's the way the cookie crumbles. ☐ That's the way the mop flops. ☐ (That's the) way to go! ☐ (There's) no way to tell. ☐ the way I see it ☐ to put it another way ☐ Way to go!

WEAR

Don't let the bastards wear you down. ☐ I don't want to wear out my welcome.

WEATHER

Been under the weather. ☐ How do you like this weather? ☐ (I've) been under the weather. ☐ Lovely weather for ducks. ☐ Nice weather we're having. ☐ What do you think of this weather?

WELCOME

I don't want to wear out my welcome. □ Welcome. □ Welcome to our house. □ You're welcome.

WELL

may as well □ might as well □ well □ Well done! □ (Well,) I never! □ Well said. □ (Well,) what do you know!

WHEN

I'll look you up when I'm in town. □ Look me up when you're in town. □ Say when. □ Since when? □ Smile when you say that. □ Some people (just) don't know when to give up. □ Some people (just) don't know when to quit. □ When. □ When do we eat? □ when I'm good and ready □ when you get a chance □ when you get a minute

WHERE

from where I stand □ Let's go somewhere where it's (more) quiet. □ This is where I came in. □ Where can I wash up? □ Where have you been all my life? □ Where (have) you been keeping yourself? □ Where is the rest room? □ Where is your powder room? □ Where's the fire? □ Where will I find you? □ You don't know where it's been.

WHILE

After while(, crocodile). □ (I'll) see you in a little while. □ See you in a little while.

WHO

Could I tell someone who's calling? □ Look who's here! □ Look who's talking! □ Says who? □ Who cares? □ who could have thought? □ Who do you think you are? □ Who do you think you're kidding? □ Who do you think you're talking to? □ Who do you want to speak to? □ Who do you want (to talk to)? □ Who do you wish to speak to? □ Who do you wish to talk to? □ Who is it? □ Who is this? □ Who knows? □ Who's calling(, please)? □ Who's on the line? □ Who's on the phone? □ Who's there? □ Who's your friend? □ Who was it? □ who would have thought? □ You and who else?

WHOM

With whom do you wish to speak?

WHY
that's why! ☐ why ☐ why don't you? ☐ Why not?

WIFE
How's the wife?

WILCO
Roger (wilco).

WILLING
God willing.

WIN
Can't win them all. ☐ Win a few, lose a few. ☐ (You) can't win them all.

WIRE
Hold the wire(, please).

WISH
(Don't) you wish! ☐ Having a wonderful time; wish you were here. ☐ (I'm) having a wonderful time; wish you were here. ☐ I wish I'd said that. ☐ Who do you wish to speak to? ☐ Who do you wish to talk to? ☐ Wish you were here. ☐ With whom do you wish to speak? ☐ You wish!

WITH
Be right with you. ☐ Be with you in a minute. ☐ Can't argue with that. ☐ Can't take it with you. ☐ Could I have a word with you? ☐ Fine with me. ☐ Hell with that! ☐ How goes it (with you)? ☐ How're things (with you)? ☐ How's (it) with you? ☐ How's with you? ☐ I can live with that. ☐ (I) can't argue with that. ☐ I'd like (to have) a word with you. ☐ (I have) no problem with that. ☐ (I'll) be right with you. ☐ I'm not finished with you. ☐ I'm (really) fed up (with someone or something). ☐ I'm with you. ☐ I've had it up to here (with someone or something). ☐ I was up all night with a sick friend. ☐ No problem with that. ☐ Now you're cooking (with gas)! ☐ Okay with me. ☐ (Someone will) be with you in a minute. ☐ (Someone will) be with you in a moment. ☐ Stick with it. ☐ (That's) fine with me. ☐ (That's) okay with me. ☐ (To)

hell with that! □ What's new with you? □ What's the matter (with you)? □ What's with someone or something? □ with my blessing □ With pleasure. □ With whom do you wish to speak? □ With you in a minute. □ (You) can't take it with you. □ You could have knocked me over with a feather. □ You'll never get away with it.

WITHOUT
Don't give up without a fight. □ I won't give up without a fight. □ without a doubt

WONDER
I don't wonder. □ (I was) just wondering. □ (I) wonder if □ Just wondering. □ wonder if

WONDERFUL
Having a wonderful time; wish you were here. □ (I'm) having a wonderful time; wish you were here.

WORD
Could I have a word with you? □ Don't breathe a word of this to anyone. □ I'd like (to have) a word with you. □ in other words □ (I) won't breathe a word (of it). □ Mum's the word. □ one final word □ or words to that effect □ Take my word for it. □ The word is mum. □ Took the words right out of my mouth. □ What's the good word? □ Won't breathe a word (of it). □ (You) took the words right out of my mouth.

WORK
Does it work for you? □ Don't work too hard. □ Everything will work out (all right). □ Everything will work out for the best. □ (It) works for me. □ I've got work to do. □ Keep up the good work. □ Things will work out (all right). □ Things will work out for the best. □ Works for me.

WORLD
How's the world (been) treating you?

WORRY
Don't worry. □ Don't worry about a thing. □ Not to worry.

WORSE
Could be worse. □ (I) could be worse. □ (I've) seen worse. □ Seen worse. □ (Things) could be worse.

WORTH

for what it's worth ☐ It isn't worth it. ☐ It isn't worth the trouble.

WOULD

Don't do anything I wouldn't do. ☐ if you would(, please) ☐ (I) would if I could(, but I can't). ☐ I would like to introduce you to someone. ☐ I would like you to meet someone. ☐ (I) wouldn't bet on it. ☐ (I) wouldn't count on it. ☐ (I) wouldn't if I were you. ☐ (I) wouldn't know. ☐ What would you like to drink? ☐ what would you say if? ☐ who would have thought? ☐ Would if I could(, but I can't). ☐ Wouldn't bet on it. ☐ Wouldn't count on it. ☐ Wouldn't if I were you. ☐ Wouldn't know. ☐ Would you believe! ☐ (Would you) care for another (one)? ☐ (would you) care to? ☐ (Would you) care to dance? ☐ (Would you) care to join us? ☐ Would you excuse me? ☐ Would you excuse us, please? ☐ Would you please? ☐ Yesterday wouldn't be too soon. ☐ You wouldn't be trying to kid me, would you? ☐ You wouldn't dare (to do something)! ☐ You wouldn't (do that)!

WRITE

Don't forget to write. ☐ Remember to write.

WRONG

What's wrong?

YEAH

Oh, yeah?

YEAR

(I'll) see you next year. ☐ Never in a thousand years! ☐ Not in a thousand years! ☐ See you next year.

YESTERDAY

I need it yesterday. ☐ Yesterday wouldn't be too soon.

YET

You ain't seen nothing yet! ☐ You'll be the death of me (yet).

ZIGGETY

Hot ziggety!

ZIP

Zip it up! ☐ Zip (up) your lip!

NTC'S ENGLISH LANGUAGE DICTIONARIES
The Best, By Definition

English Language References

Beginner's Dictionary of American English Usage
British/American Language Dictionary
Common American Phrases
Contemporary American Slang
Essential American Idioms
Everyday American English Dictionary
Forbidden American English
NTC's American Idioms Dictionary
NTC's Dictionary of Acronyms & Abbreviations
NTC's Dictionary of American English Pronunciation
NTC's Dictionary of American Idioms, Slang &Colloquial Expressions (Electronic Book)
NTC's Dictionary of American Slang & Colloquial Expressions
NTC's Dictionary of American Spelling
NTC's Dictionary of English Idioms

NTC's Dictionary of Everyday American English Expressions
NTC's Dictionary of Grammar Terminology
NTC's Dictionary of Literary Terms
NTC's Dictionary of Phrasal Verbs & Other Idiomatic Verbal Phrases
NTC's Dictionary of Proverbs & Clichés
NTC's Dictionary of Quotations
NTC's Dictionary of Shakespeare
NTC's Dictionary of Theatre & Drama
NTC's Dictionary of Word Origins
NTC's Dictionary of Easily Confused Words
NTC's Thesaurus of Everyday American English
NTC's Dictionary of American English Phrases

For Juveniles

English Picture Dictionary
Let's Learn English Picture Dictionary

For further information or a current catalog, write:
NTC Publishing Group
4255 West Touhy Avenue
Lincolnwood, Illinois 60646-1975 U.S.A.